CHILDREN'S LEARNING DIFFICULTIES

*For Kirsten
and for
Robert, Sarah and Brian*

CHILDREN'S LEARNING DIFFICULTIES

A Cognitive Approach

Julie Dockrell and
John McShane

BLACKWELL
Oxford UK & Cambridge USA

First published 1993

Blackwell Publishers
108 Cowley Road
Oxford   OX4 1JF
UK

238 Main Street, Suite 501
Cambridge, Massachusetts 02142
USA

British Library Cataloguing in Publication Data
A CIP catalogue record for this book is available from the British Library.

Library of Congress Cataloging-in-Publication Data
Dockrell, Julie.
    Children's learning difficulties : a cognitive approach / Julie
Dockrell and John McShane.
        p.   cm.
    Includes bibliographical references (p.   ) and index.
    ISBN 0–631–17016–2. — ISBN 0–631–17017–0 (pbk.)
    1. Learning disabilities.   2. Cognition in children.   I. McShane,
John, 1949– .   II. Title.
LC4704.D63 1992
371.9—dc20   92–19116
                                                            CIP

Typeset in 11 on 13pt Plantin
by Graphicraft Typesetters Ltd., Hong Kong
Printed in Great Britain by T.J. Press Ltd., Padstow, Cornwall.

This book is printed on acid-free paper

Contents

Acknowledgements

This book is the result of many long discussions with children, practitioners and especially each other. We became interested in learning difficulties as a result of contact with children who experienced problems. As we attempted to analyze these problems we became increasingly frustrated by the fact that theories of cognitive development were not easily applied to cases of learning difficulties. This problem became more prominent when one of us (J. D.) was carrying out clinical work with children and devising intervention programmes in schools and clinics.

The practical experience gained by working with the children has been invaluable in our understanding of the problems and our realization of the difficulties experienced by practitioners and parents. To this end the advice provided in the field by more experienced practitioners is gratefully acknowledged. In particular Mike Gibson and Stephen Cogill helped challenge many assumptions and asked decisive questions when supervising case work. Judith Zur and Shona Munro always played an invaluable role when analysing problems and formulating intervention plans. Special thanks go to the Nuffield Hearing and Speech Centre, in particular Veronica Connery and Tony Martin and all the staff at the Nuffield Preschool Speech and Language Unit. Their clinical insight and probing questions forced us to think more deeply about the relation between theory and practice.

We are grateful to Neville Austin, Pat Hasan, David Messer, Hamid Rehman, Christa Schreiber Kounine, Chris Sterling, and Dan Wright who read chapters. W. B. Dockrell read drafts of several of the chapters and provided us with many helpful comments and suggestions. Vanessa Cragoe very kindly typed the references.

Our respective families have been very tolerant and supportive and we thank them for that. The cover of this book is a detail from a painting called 'The Conqueror'. Learning difficulties do not have an inevitable course. We believe that if one understands the cognitive problems experienced by children with learning difficulties practitioners will be in a better position to alleviate the problems that arise.

John McShane died tragically two weeks after we had completed checking the proofs of this book. John had a strong wish to improve our understanding of children's cognitive processes and a desire to help children with learning difficulties. He believed that it was only when we understand the basic processes of development that we would have effective applications of developmental theory. He made a significant contribution to this aim.

John was a much respected developmental psychologist and an exceptional colleague. He will be remembered with love and affection and will be greatly missed.

J.D. September 1992

1

Understanding Learning Difficulties: A Cognitive Frame of Reference

Overview

This chapter considers a number of general issues relating to learning difficulties. Our concern is to provide a framework within which the practical issues of assessment and intervention can be related to theoretically-driven research on the cognitive basis of learning difficulties. We begin by considering the prevalence and variety of learning difficulties. We then review methods of classification and raise a number of critical issues about classification. The subsequent section of the chapter discusses the task, the child, and the environment as three elements of a framework within which to understand learning difficulties. Most research and much practice is concerned with the task by child interaction. This can be addressed by considering the information processing requirements of a task and the child's current cognitive abilities. The child's cognitive system is discussed at the levels of a cognitive architecture, knowledge representation, task processes, and executive processes. Learning difficulties require assessment and intervention. The basis of these should be the child's current performance on cognitive tasks.

Children's Learning Difficulties

Many children experience difficulties in learning. The difficulty can either be specific, as occurs when a child experiences problems with some particular task such as reading, or it can be general, as occurs when learning is slower than normal across a range of tasks. In this book we shall consider both specific and general learning difficulties.

To identify a learning difficulty an assessment must be carried out. Based on the results of this a programme of intervention may be implemented. Any assessment or intervention with a child experiencing problems makes, of necessity, assumptions about the basis of those problems. For assessments to be reliable and valid the practitioner must be aware of the range of variables that can influence a child's performance on particular tasks. To transform these assessments into effective interventions the practitioner must design a programme that takes account of the task requirements, the child's behaviour and cognitive skills, and the environmental context in which intervention will occur. Both assessment and intervention require an understanding of the demands that a task places on a child's cognitive system and the abilities of that system to deal with these demands. Our major concern is to consider what is currently known about the cognitive demands of tasks such as language, reading, and number and the problems that children with learning difficulties experience with these tasks.

How prevalent are learning difficulties? Rutter et al. (1970), in a detailed study of over 2,000 children on the Isle of Wight, found that overall 16 per cent of children aged between 9 and 11 years had some handicap that hindered their educational progress. Summarizing these and other data (Kellmer-Pringle et al., 1966; Rutter et al., 1975a; Webb, 1967) the Report of the Committee of Enquiry into the Education of Handicapped Children and Young People (Warnock, 1978) concluded that in Britain at any one time about one child in six is likely to require some form of special educational provision. This figure includes both those children who are experiencing some temporary difficulty in learning and those who have more persistent long-term learning difficulties. A similar figure has been reported by Chazan et al. (1980) from a survey of all the 4-year-olds who had been born in a six-month period in 1972 in two counties of England. Chazan et al. found that 21 per cent of their sample were judged to have special needs of a mild, moderate, or severe nature that required further investigation. The highest proportions of problems in Chazan et al.'s survey were in the areas of speech and language development and behavioural adjustment.

In the United States, the US Department of Education statistics indicate that approximately 12 per cent of children between the ages of 3 and 21 years received special education services in 1987 (Meisels and Wasik, 1989). The major types of difficulty in order of prevalence were 'speech impairment, mental retardation, learning disabilities, emotional disturbance, crippling conditions and other health impairments, hearing impairment, visual impairment, deafness, and multihandicapped problems'. Although the figures for the US are lower than the figures for Britain, the basis of calculation is different: the US figures record the proportion of children receiving special education services; the British figures record the proportion of children believed to be in need of special education services.

It is evident that there is a sizeable group of children that can be regarded as having a learning difficulty on either a temporary or permanent basis. But what are learning difficulties, and how does one determine whether or not a child has a learning difficulty? These are questions to which there are no simple answers. Despite considerable research effort and many attempts at definition, there is still no generally accepted operational definition of what constitutes a learning difficulty. As Hooper and Willis (1989) point out, this is because learning difficulties are a heterogeneous group of difficulties.

The most obvious distinction is between children who have general learning difficulties and thus experience problems with most types of subject matter, and those who have a specific difficulty – with reading or mathematics, for example. The latter groups are sometimes said to have a specific learning difficulty because their major problem is with one type of material and not with all forms of learning. However, the distinction between general learning difficulties and specific learning difficulties is not as straightforward as it might seem: children said to have a specific learning difficulty often experience difficulties with more than one type of subject matter, without necessarily experiencing difficulties with all subject matter. Given the variety of types of learning difficulty, it is necessary to consider in what ways they can be classified.

Classification of Learning Difficulties

Classification systems can have a variety of purposes. Aetiological systems of classification are concerned with classifying learning difficulties in terms of the originating cause. Functional systems are concerned with classifying on the basis of the current level of functioning, which may be measured in a variety of ways.

Aetiological classification systems group difficulties together as a function of their cause. This is of considerable benefit when the aim is to examine the range of difficulties to which a particular aetiology can give rise. It can also be of benefit in predicting the long-term outcome of a difficulty, provided that many similar difficulties have been encountered in the past. It is worth distinguishing between two different types of aetiological classification systems: those in which there is an identifiable cause of a difficulty and those in which there is an hypothesized cause. In cases of identifiable damage, such as to the peripheral sense organs, it is often possible to intervene at the organic level. Many cases of hearing or visual impairment, or motor abnormalities such as cleft palate, can be improved either by surgical intervention or the provision of sensory aids. Organic diagnosis is useful because there is the possibility of organic intervention. In cases of a suspected learning difficulty it is of vital importance to ensure that thorough tests of the relevant sensory systems are conducted. This applies especially to the auditory system, where defects often go undetected.

However, aetiological classification systems have two disadvantages for those concerned with dealing with learning difficulties. First, a large number of difficulties have an unknown aetiology. Thus they can be assigned only to a default category of 'difficulties with an unknown origin' in an aetiological classification system. Since these difficulties may have no homogeneity, either in terms of cause or outcome, this is an unsatisfactory category. The second disadvantage of an aetiological classification system is that difficulties that have a similar origin may, nevertheless, have different manifestations, and may require different intervention strategies. It would be better, from the point of view of those required to intervene, to be able to classify learning difficulties in terms of the child's performance on specific tasks and to be able to relate this to possible strategies of intervention.

If we turn from aetiological to functional classification, the basis of the classification shifts from the cause of the difficulty to some measure of the child's current level of performance. In functional classification systems two groups of children are often distinguished on the basis of measures of intelligence. The first group consists of those children whose level of intellectual development is significantly below average (as assessed by an intelligence test) and who are therefore likely to perform less well than age matched peers on a range of intellectual tasks. These children are often called 'slow learners', and in more severe cases 'mentally handicapped'.

The second group consists of those children whose overall level of intellectual development is normal but who nevertheless have specific difficulty with some particular task, such as reading. On assessment, children with specific difficulties usually have a performance profile in which there is a marked difference between their level of achievement in their area of specific difficulty and their levels of achievement in other areas of cognitive functioning. Because of this, such children are often said to show a discrepancy between their achievement and their aptitude in the area of difficulty. Such children are said to have a 'specific learning difficulty' in Great Britain, or a 'learning disability' in the United States.

The method of distinguishing between general and specific difficulties in terms of discrepancies in cognitive profiles is problematic. In the first place, there are many methodological limitations in the way in which discrepancy scores are computed (Reynolds, 1984–5; Shepard, 1980). Second, the concept of discrepancy between achievement and aptitude, while intuitively plausible, has never been operationalized in a satisfactory manner

(Epps et al., 1983). Third, children who initially experience a specific learning difficulty sometimes then experience other difficulties as a result: language difficulties can lead to difficulties with reading because reading draws upon the language system (see chapter 4); while reading difficulties can lead to difficulties with arithmetic because arithmetic requires reading abilities (see chapter 5). Finally, children who experience general learning difficulties often show considerable competence in a specific area of cognitive functioning. This observation is particularly striking when different aetiological groups of general learning difficulties are considered separately (Burack et al., 1988).

Until recently in Britain, children with learning difficulties were classified into eleven categories, which had been introduced following the Education Act of 1944. These categories included blind, partially-sighted, deaf, partially-deaf, delicate, diabetic, educationally subnormal, epileptic, maladjusted, physically handicapped, and those with speech defects (Pritchard, 1963). The Warnock Report argued that this system of classification had a number of faults:

• It pinned a single label on each child, many of whom suffered from more than one disability
• It unnecessarily stigmatized children and schools
• It promoted confusion between a child's disability and the form of special education required
• It focused attention on only a small proportion of children who were likely to require some form of special educational provision
• It suggested that a child categorized as, for example, 'educationally sub-normal' suffers from an intrinsic deficiency whereas often the deficiency has been in the social and cultural environment
• It perpetuated a sharp distinction between two groups of children – the handicapped and the non-handicapped

The report therefore recommended 'that the statutory categorization of handicapped pupils should be abolished'. In its place, the report recommended that children in need of special educational provision should be identified on the basis of a detailed profile of their needs following assessment. However, the report recognized that some specialist terminology was required for children who require special educational provision. Accordingly it recommended 'that the term "children with learning difficulties" should be used in future to describe both those children who are currently categorized as educationally sub-normal and those with educational difficulties who are often at present the concern of remedial services'. The report also suggested that learning difficulties might be described as *mild, moderate,* or *severe,* and children with particular difficulties only, such as a reading difficulty, should be described as having a *specific learning difficulty*.

The move from categorical labels to statements of educational needs has much to recommend it because it recognizes that assessment should be related to intervention. But removing the seeming comfort of categorical labels turns the emphasis onto the behavioural and cognitive profiles of children with special educational needs. What, for example, is a specific reading difficulty? Are all specific reading difficulties the same? How does one identify and assess reading difficulties? And the same questions can obviously be posed for other specific difficulties and also for general learning difficulties. Needs can only be identified if the child's current difficulties can be identified. In fact Warnock's proposal is not the abandonment of classification but a call for a new system of classification. This new system will not necessarily be categorical; it is much more likely to be dimensional, reflecting a profile of the relevant strengths and needs that the child currently possesses on dimensions that are relevant to the execution of an educational skill. As Doris (1986: 39) has remarked: 'The diagnosis of an entity in either medicine or education is an academic exercise unless it is related to prognosis, therapeutic intervention, and/or prevention.' At present, there is very little direct relation between classification of learning difficulties and effective forms of intervention (Forness, 1988).

In this book we shall be concerned with the cognitive basis of specific learning difficulties in the areas of language, reading, and mathematics; and with general learning difficulties. The central question that we shall address is this: In what ways are the cognitive systems of children with learning difficulties less well able to deal with task demands than are the cognitive systems of children developing normally?

A Framework for Understanding Learning Difficulties

There are three parts to our framework for understanding learning difficulties: the task, the child, and the environment. The analysis of each has a contribution to make to the understanding and treatment of learning difficulties. The task or tasks with which a child has difficulty must be analysed so that the component skills necessary for successful performance are understood. The child is the person currently experiencing difficulty with the task, so obviously it is important to have methods to assess the child's current cognitive abilities, together with any other relevant psychological attributes. Once these have been assessed, the cognitive demands that are made on the child's current abilities can be determined. The environment is the external context in which the child's difficulty is manifested; and aspects of the environment may be contributory factors to the child's difficulty. Understanding the role of the environment may be especially important in relation to learning difficulties. Children with learning difficulties may be more dependent on their environment than normal children, while children without learning difficulties may be robust and buffered against environmental factors or situations that may have a serious effect on children with learning difficulties.

In order to understand the reasons why a child performs a cognitive task less well than the norm it is necessary to get a clear picture of what is involved in successfully performing the task in question, and then use this understanding to analyse where the problems lie for the child with learning difficulties. Thus, cognitive models of learning difficulties must include analysis of the demands of the task, how it is performed by children developing normally, and the current performance capabilities of the child with a learning difficulty.

The types of difficulties with which we are particularly concerned are those that impede educational achievement, such as difficulties with language, reading, or mathematics. We shall call these areas *domains*. We might expect to find that general learning difficulties involve processes that are shared by many domains (but domain-specific processes may additionally be involved). Specific learning difficulties are likely to involve only domain-specific processes. Thus, for example, if a child is experiencing a specific difficulty with reading, then we might expect to find that the nature of this difficulty lies within the cognitive processes that are dedicated to reading. If, on the other hand, reading difficulties are only one of a range of learning difficulties experienced by the child, then we might expect to find that general cognitive processes are implicated, and possibly domain-specific processes also. However, these are empirical matters, which can only be addressed by research.

Learning difficulties occur for a variety of reasons. One reason is that the child has some inherent cognitive difficulty that makes learning some skill or skills more difficult than normal. However, some difficulties – perhaps the majority – are the result of educational or environmental problems that are unrelated to the child's cognitive abilities. Ineffective teaching strategies can seriously affect a child's level of achievement (Brennan, 1979). Early school failure can lead to a lack of self-confidence with subsequent detrimental effects on learning (see chapter 7). A variety of variables associated with home background can also contribute to learning difficulties (Rutter et al., 1975b). Sometimes all of the different factors are intertwined. But, whatever the primary cause, children with learning difficulties have fallen behind their peers in mastering some important aspect of learning. The practical tasks are to find out why this is so, and then to try to do something about it.

As an example of this analytical framework let us consider a child (Susan) who has difficulty learning how to write her own name. By the time children reach school age they bring with them a repertoire of skills which should be sufficient to cope with the demands of the school environment, one of which is to write one's own name. If a child is having difficulties with this task the contributory factors may come from the child, the environment, or both. Let us consider how Susan's problem might have arisen and how it might be dealt with.

First, the problem might have an environmental cause. If Susan, for some reason, had not had a range of experiences with fine-motor coordination in her preschool years she would not be in a position to profit from the instruction provided in the classroom. Tasks that are too difficult for her might lead to re-peated failures and this would exacerbate rather than ameliorate her difficulty. In this case her early environment failed to provide appropriate experiences and later the school was insensitive to her needs.

Alternatively, Susan might be lacking in the movement skills necessary to function in the school environment. Some children arrive at school lacking in movement skills despite having had a range of appropriate preschool experiences. Sugden and Keogh (1990) point out that children with such fine motor skill problems do not constitute a homogeneous group. Problems may occur in the planning of motor movements, and in unsteady or unco-ordinated movements, or there may be an inability to interpret sensory inputs. A range of explanations has been offered for these problems (Sugden and Sugden, 1991). For some children these problems will result in writing difficulties and intervention will be required for the child to cope with the demands of the curriculum. The critical factor for designing an intervention pro-gramme for Susan, irrespective of the origins of the problem, would be an analysis of the task demands.

We must now ask what are the requisite skills for writing one's name so that an intervention programme can be designed. To do this we must break the task down into its basic components (see below). This analysis of the task needs to be grounded in an understanding of the skill acquisition of the developing child. The task requires a certain degree of fine motor skill, which the child will usually be presumed to have on entering school, and a knowledge of how to form the letters of the alphabet, which will usually be taught in school. Once the basic components of the task have been accurately identified, the child's performance on each component can be gauged. The assessment will need to evaluate the child's performance in context and not on a single test. An accurate description of the precise problems that the child shows should lead to appropriately matched interventions. That is, assessment should result in a prescription for inter-vention and a means by which the consequences of the inter-vention may be evaluated and measured (see chapter 2). The intervention will need to be designed so that the environment can adequately support it. There is no point designing a programme that requires one-to-one support in the classroom if there is no one to carry out this programme.

Thus, while the child's problem may occur for a range of different reasons, a comprehensive understanding of the task demands is necessary for both assessment and intervention, regardless of the origin of the problem.

The Task

In order to understand the demands that a task places on the child, it is necessary to carry out a *task analysis*. The aim of a task analysis is to decompose a larger task into a series of smaller tasks. Once we know what this series of smaller tasks is, we can determine to what extent a child with a difficulty can carry out each of the subtasks. In this way we attempt to identify as precisely as possible the exact nature of the difficulty. Identification allows intervention to be focused more precisely. Figure 1.1 shows a task analysis for writing letters of the alphabet.

How can we identify the subtasks? This is a matter of both analysis and experimentation. If the task is well understood, then it is often possible to proceed by analysis. Let us take the analysis presented in figure 1.1 further and consider a child who has difficulty in writing letters. We can decompose any letter into the individual lines that make it up, and the way in which they are connected together. We could now determine whether or not a child can draw the individual lines, irrespective of forming letters. If the child cannot draw the lines, then we could decide to work on improving the child's skill at this. Some further task analysis of what is required in order to draw lines might be required. If the child can draw lines reasonably well, then we might concentrate intervention on the skill of joining these lines together at appropriate orientations in order to form letters.

Not all tasks are as easy as this to analyse. What if the task with which the child is having difficulty is spoken language? Before we can decompose this task, we must have some knowledge of how the language system operates. We cannot just rely on our intuitions here; we must study the system in order to determine how it operates. This is where data from the normal process of development is relevant. Examining how children normally

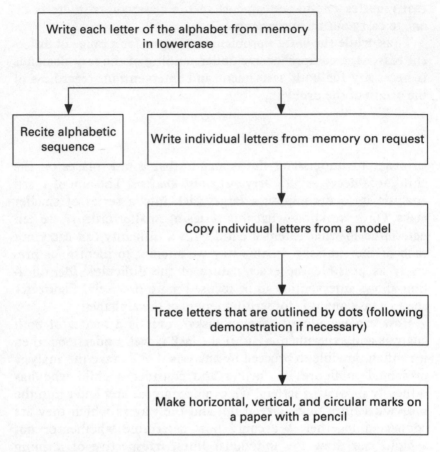

Figure 1.1 *Task analysis of writing letters. The task is represented in the top box. If the child cannot perform the task at this level proceed to establish prerequisite skills in a systematic fashion.*

master a task will provide guidelines on where the problem lies for a child with learning difficulties. Thus, models of the normal process of acquisition will be a crucial prerequisite to the study of learning difficulties and the attempt to specify the precise source of the difficulty. However, it is also the case that data on task performance from populations who experience learning difficulties can itself inform theories of normal development (Campione and Brown, 1978; Hodapp and Burack, 1990).

In comparing the performance of children with learning

difficulties with normally developing children on some task, it is often necessary to make comparisons with more than one group. The issue of choosing the relevant comparison groups for children with learning difficulties is extremely important. If we simply wish to know what the extent of the difference is between a group of children with learning difficulties and their peers, then we can compare groups matched on age. However, suppose that we wish to test a hypothesis about the cause of the learning difficulty. We cannot, in most cases, test this hypothesis by a direct comparison of a group of children with learning difficulties and a group of age matched peers. Let us illustrate this with a specific example.

When children are learning to read they often have to sound out new or unfamiliar words. To do this they must match individual sounds of the language with individual letters of a word. Knowledge of the sound structure of language is often referred to as phonological awareness. Suppose that we are interested in testing the hypothesis that a cause of reading difficulties is poor phonological awareness of the structure of words. Now, suppose that we test a group of children who have reading difficulties and compare their performance on a task of phonological awareness with a group of the same age who have made normal progress in learning to read. Further, suppose that we find that the children with reading difficulties perform more poorly on the task of phonological awareness than the normal children. Does this mean that the differences in phonological awareness are causing reading difficulties? Not necessarily. The superior reading ability of the normal group could well account for their superior phonological awareness rather than being the result of it. The normal group will have had more experience with translating words into sounds *because they are learning to read more quickly*. Thus, it is quite possible that the difference in reading skill is the cause of the difference in phonological awareness rather than the other way round. In general, we cannot determine the cause of a learning difficulty by comparing children experiencing that difficulty with age matched peers.

There are other comparisons that we can make in order to clarify the issue. We could compare the group with reading difficulties with a younger group who have the same reading ability. We do not know from the comparison of the age matched groups how the normal group would have performed on the phonological awareness task when they only had the same reading skills as the children who are having reading difficulties. We can discover this by using a younger group of children learning to read at the normal rate who have reached the same level of skill at reading as the group with reading difficulties. If we find that, in spite of their younger age, the children matched for reading ability have superior phonological awareness, then there are grounds for strongly suspecting that poor phonological awareness may be the cause of the reading difficulty. If, on the other hand, there is no difference between the groups, or the group with reading difficulties have a phonological awareness that is superior to the younger normal readers, then we have failed to support the hypothesis (although neither of these findings disprove the hypothesis).

However, even finding that children with reading difficulties had poorer phonological awareness than younger children with the same reading skills would not prove conclusively that poor phonological awareness is a cause of reading difficulties. It is possible that the development of both reading and phonological awareness are under the control of some third component of the cognitive system, which is the real cause of the difficulty. In general, we can never completely eliminate such an alternative. In spite of this, if we were to find that children matched for reading ability had superior phonological awareness to an older group of children experiencing a difficulty with reading, then we would have good reasons to conduct intervention studies to determine whether there are methods of improving phonological awareness that would also improve reading performance.

A third method that we could use would be to study the longitudinal relation between the skill in which we are interested and the abilities that are presumed to be causally related to it. This is more time-consuming than the other methods but, as we shall see in later chapters, it is a very valuable method of studying causal relations.

The Child

Our approach throughout this book is one in which the child's cognitive system is discussed in terms of its ability to process the information that is critical to the successful performance of a task. The study of the normal process of cognitive development provides useful guidelines as to what should be studied in children with learning difficulties. Once we understand how development normally proceeds, we can ask in what ways the development of children with learning difficulties differs. Do children with learning difficulties use the same cognitive processes as normal children, or do they differ in the way in which they process information? If they use the same processes, in what ways is processing less effective than in normal children? If not, in what ways do the processes differ? The more detailed our models of normal development, the more detailed the comparisons we can make and thus the more precisely can intervention be targeted.

We consider these issues at two levels. The first level is the general structures and processes of the system, which apply to any cognitive domain. A difficulty at this level is likely to manifest itself in impaired functioning across a variety of domains. The second level is the particular structures and processes relevant to a given domain. A difficulty at this level is likely to have direct effects on a particular domain, but it may have an indirect effect on other domains.

In addition to the cognitive processes that are central to a task, there is a variety of other mental processes that affect a child's performance. These include executive and motivational processes, which can be regarded as control mechanisms that play a central role in the regulation of the cognitive system. Children with learning difficulties often have poor executive strategies and reduced motivation to attempt a task because of a history of failure. These factors, therefore, constitute additional child variables that must be taken into account in the analysis of learning difficulties. The environment will also play a role in the manifestation of learning difficulties.

The Environment

The environment is the context in which the child and the task interact. Understanding the environment is important in two respects. First, the environment can, in some cases, be a major contributory factor to a child's problems. If this is the case, then intervention should seek to change as much as possible the factors in the environment that are contributing to the child's difficulty. Second, even if the environment is not a contributory factor to a learning difficulty, it is sometimes possible to modify it in such a way that it facilitates the acquisition of the skill that the child lacks. We shall illustrate the role of the environment primarily in relation to intervention.

The environment consists of the external physical and social world of the child. There are different levels at which the environment can be discussed. Bronfenbrenner (1979) has proposed a four-part model that is useful in considering the different levels, which is shown in figure 1.2. The first and most local level is called the microsystem. Bronfenbrenner defines the microsystem as: 'a pattern of activities, roles, and interpersonal relations experienced over time by the developing person in a given setting with particular physical and material characteristics' (p. 22). The microsystem for children includes the places they inhabit, the people who live there with them, and the things they do together.

An important part of Bronfenbrenner's definition is that he emphasizes both the physical setting and the relationships between the individuals in that setting. The social relations in a microsystem can determine the success or failure of the activities that occur in that setting. For example, intervention programmes that are technically well-defined can fail if the relationship between the child and the teacher is not one that facilitates co-operation and participation.

Direct intervention with learning difficulties usually takes place in a particular setting, such as a classroom, for a limited period of time. This constitutes one microsystem that the child inhabits. However it is only one of several. Children encounter different microsystems in the course of their daily activities. For intervention to be maximally effective, it is desirable that as many as possible of the skills being trained in one microsystem also are practised in other microsystems. The development of reading provides a good example of this. Reading is primarily taught in schools, but the amount and kind of support that is provided

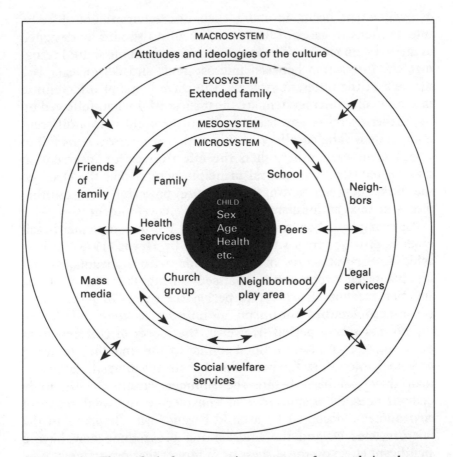

Figure 1.2   *The ecological system:* microsystem *refers to relations between the child and the immediate environment;* mesosystem *refers to the network of interrelationships of settings in the child's immediate environment;* exosystem *refers to social settings that affect the child but do not directly impinge upon him or her; and* macrosystem *refers to the attitudes, mores, beliefs, and ideologies of the culture.*
(Source: Garbarino, 1982)

in the home also has a significant effect on the child's progress (Topping and Wolfendale, 1985).

The success of intervention thus depends on processes occurring in more than one environment. Bronfenbrenner uses the term *mesosystem* to describe situations in which behaviour is a function of events that occur in more than one environment. Ideally, interventions in cases of learning difficulties should be designed as mesosystem models. The intervention programme should recognize the interaction between microsystems and design exercises for each of the different systems. Intensive bouts of intervention in a particular microsystem are most successful when followed up by further exercises and training when the child is in a different microsystem. The corollary of this is that if microsystems fail to complement each other, then the effectiveness of intervention may be reduced. The central principle here is that the stronger the links between settings, the more powerful the resulting mesosystem as an influence on the child's development.

An example of how microsystems can fail to complement each other is provided by a study conducted by Heyns (1978) on how achievement test scores of schoolchildren from advantaged and disadvantaged backgrounds changed during the period of the summer vacation. During this period the scores of pupils from advantaged families continued to improve as they did during the normal school period. However, the scores of children from disadvantaged families declined so that by the time they returned to school, they were further behind their advantaged classmates than they had been before the summer vacation. This study demonstrates the importance of considering the total range of environments occupied by a child because what happens in the microsystems beyond the intervention programme may have a significant effect on the success or failure of that programme.

The design of an intervention programme itself can be tailored to the individual child, or it can be part of a larger attempt to intervene with a group of children. The way in which a programme is designed is affected by a further aspect of the environment that must be considered in relation to intervention: the *exosystem*. The exosystem is concerned with social settings that do not necessarily contain children but may nevertheless indirectly affect them, such as the workplace of the child's parents and local community services. Bronfenbrenner emphasizes the importance of exosystem support on a child's development. For example, flexible work schedules, paid maternity and paternity leave, and sick leave for parents whose children are ill are ways in which exosystem factors can affect a child.

The last level of Bronfenbrenner's model is the *macrosystem*. It is not a specific environmental context but refers to the ideology and values of a culture, which affect decisions made at other levels of the model. One example to which we wish to draw attention here is the values that affect decisions about the educational provision for children with learning difficulties. For example, the issue of whether children with learning difficulties should be educated in normal schools following, at relevant points, an individual programme designed to overcome their particular difficulties, or whether these children should be educated in special schools, is determined by a complex set of educational and economic factors, which reflect the values of a particular culture at a particular time (see Wolfendale, 1987, for a recent analysis).

Interaction of Task, Child, and Environment

The task, the child, and the environment constitute the elements of a framework that can be brought to bear on the conceptualization of learning diffiiculties. However, in dealing with practical aspects of difficulties the practitioner is faced with a child who has a difficulty on some task in a particular environment. The practitioner must deal with this situation as it presents itself and conduct assessment and intervention within the constraints of available resources. In effect, this will mean considering the task by child interaction in order to determine the nature of the child's difficulty and effecting what intervention is possible. The research literature on learning difficulties also reflects this viewpoint, being concerned with elucidating the cognitive basis of difficulties, and, to a lesser extent, with evaluating the effects of strategies of intervention within a particular setting. Much less frequently, there is consideration of the effects of intervention across settings or of the combined effects of intervention in more than one setting. We shall consider this literature in succeeding chapters. Inevitably our emphasis will follow the available research and will be mostly concerned with the task by child interaction in learning difficulties. In order to consider this interaction we shall require a more detailed model of how the cognitive system functions.

The Cognitive System

In this section we shall consider the structure of the cognitive system at four levels: the cognitive architecture, mental representations, task processes, and executive processes. The architecture is the basic structure of the cognitive system, which provides the necessary components that make learning possible. Learning must occur by processing input from the environment. Mental representations are the codes used by the cognitive system during the processing of input. Task processes are the methods used to manipulate representations, some of which occur automatically and some of which require the use of conscious strategies. Executive processes control and manage the cognitive system's use of task strategies.

The Cognitive Architecture

One of the most obvious things about children is that they learn a great deal during the course of childhood. In order for this learning to occur at all, the child must be equipped at birth with a cognitive system that is capable of learning. It used to be thought that the infant's cognitive system contained just a few simple innate principles of learning at birth and that everything else was the result of these principles operating on the input received. In the last thirty years or so, the study of infant behaviour has revealed that the infant is born with a rich organizational structure for processing information. Considerable progress has been made in understanding the structure of the major sensory systems of vision (Banks and Salapatek, 1983) and hearing (Aslin et al., 1983). These are the systems that deliver information to the central processes of the cognitive system. The innate structure of the cognitive system is called its *architecture*. The cognitive architecture provides the foundations that make learning possible.

One of the major differences between contemporary theories of the cognitive system and earlier theories is the extent of both the general and domain-specific *central processes* that are postulated to be innate. Studies of infants have shown that they can distinguish between different simple stimuli, form simple categories, recognize a stimulus over a period of time, and learn associations between stimuli. These findings tell us that the infant must have a well-organized system for processing information at birth. The mechanisms of association, discrimination, categorization, and the processes of recognition memory must all be present in order for the infant to be able to do these things (see McShane, 1991).

A major architectural feature of cognition is the organization of the memory system. Traditionally, the memory system has been thought of as involving two types of memory: short-term and long-term. Atkinson and Shiffrin (1968) proposed that these were separate stores; short-term memory being a limited capacity temporary store that could hold about seven items of information at a time; long-term memory being a permanent store of unlimited capacity.

The model of short-term memory has been refined considerably since this initial proposal, notably by Baddeley and Hitch (1974), but the central idea of the initial proposal – that there is a system of limited capacity that stores information temporarily – remains an essential part of later models. Atkinson and Shiffrin thought of the short-term store as a passive structure. Baddeley and Hitch saw it as a much more active set of subsystems that were involved in the processing of incoming information. They called this set of subsystems *working memory*. The working memory system contains a central executive, whose main purpose is to regulate attention and thereby control the input to the system. Working memory stores incoming information in either an auditory or visual store, depending on the modality of the input. The auditory store consists of two components: a phonological store (this being the form in which verbal material is represented in working memory) and an articulatory rehearsal process. Material will only remain in the phonological store for a relatively brief time unless it is refreshed by rehearsal. Figure 1.3 shows a model of the memory system.

In order to be used at a later time, knowledge must be stored in some way by the cognitive system. Long-term memory is where information is stored on a permanent basis. From the beginning of life, children are able to store associative information in long-term memory. Creating associations between events is part of the

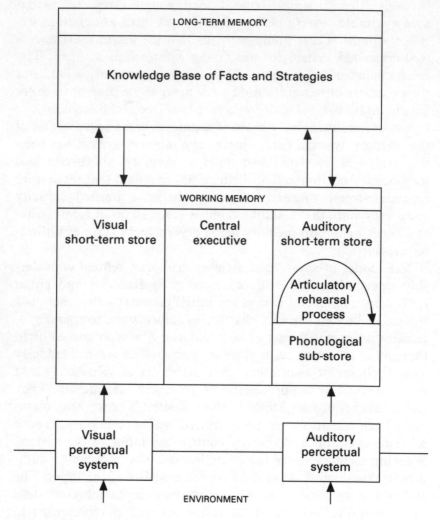

Figure 1.3 *A model of the memory system showing short-term memory as a working memory system.*

innate capabilities of the cognitive system. Long-term memory is not purely an associative system, however; association is simply part of the organizational foundation on which more complex types of information structures are built. It is to the organization of knowledge that we now turn.

Mental Representations

The knowledge that is stored in long-term memory derives from the external environment, but the input received will be acted upon and transformed several times by the cognitive system before it is stored. The general term for the structure of information is *mental representation*. Some mental representations serve only to create intermediate structures between the input and the stored form of knowledge. As an example of this consider that we do not recall exactly what has been said in conversation, except for a moment, but we do recall the gist of what has been said. Clearly, in this case, the information processing system only represents the literal form of the input for a moment or so, and then transforms this and stores something different from the exact verbal input. We shall use the term *knowledge base* for the information that is stored on a permanent basis by the cognitive system.

The knowledge base in any domain is the facts that are known about that domain. As children develop, their knowledge base increases, and this allows them to retrieve information about the domain directly from memory. This can greatly aid task performance. As an example, consider the difference it makes to the time taken to add numbers if the solution can be retrieved directly from the knowledge base rather than obtained by using a counting strategy to add the numbers (see chapter 5). The gains are not only in solution time. The cognitive system can only engage in a limited amount of conscious processing at any one time. Being able to retrieve knowledge directly means that processing resources can be devoted to other activities.

Understanding the way in which information is represented in the knowledge base of any domain is an important part of understanding how tasks are performed within that domain. If we understand the normal representation of knowledge, then we can enquire, in cases of learning difficulties, to what extent the child's knowledge base is adequate for the tasks on which the child is experiencing difficulty (see chapter 7).

Task Processes

In order to transform external input to an internal representation, it is necessary to process the input. The cognitive system contains a variety of automatic methods of processing (such as the creation of associations) but these are supplemented to a considerable extent by learned strategies for manipulating information. In infancy, most of the processes that operate on input are not under conscious control; rather, they operate automatically. Thus the processing of sensory input, or attending to one aspect of the environment rather than another, are not the result of conscious decisions by the child.

As development proceeds, the use of conscious strategies becomes increasingly important. Instead of simply responding to the environment, the child is now attempting to solve problems about the environment. This requires the use of conscious strategies. Thus, in order to be able to recall unfamiliar material, it is usually necessary to rehearse it; in order to be able to subtract multi-digit numbers, it is necessary to be able to borrow across columns. These strategies are learned during childhood. Often, in cases of learning difficulties, the relevant strategies are learned or deployed less effectively than is usual.

As an example consider reading and pronouncing a novel word, a task with which children are continually faced. Most people can make a reasonable attempt at pronouncing novel words by breaking the word down into recognizable syllables. Even though the word itself may never have been encountered before, its component syllables will have been, and the knowledge of how to pronounce these enables an attempted pronunciation to be made. This may seem easy enough but the strategy has to be acquired as part of the process of learning to read. Some children have considerable difficulty in using such strategies. Teaching children how to use strategies appropriately is one method of intervention commonly used in cases of learning difficulties.

Executive Processes and Metacognitive Knowledge

Executive processes are those processes concerned with planning and regulating activities. Some executive processes are, at least partially, under automatic rather than conscious control. The process of attention is an example of this. Attention functions in part automatically in orientating the sensory systems to sources of information in the environment. Attention also is partially under conscious control, in that we can often decide how our attention is going to be focused.

In the main, we shall be concerned with executive processes that control conscious strategies. The control of strategies depends upon the child's understanding of how the strategy relates to a particular goal. This understanding is part of what is called *metacognitive knowledge*. Metacognitive knowledge is knowledge about one's own cognitive system and how it functions. In relation to learning difficulties it is useful again to consider the task by child interaction and to distinguish between knowledge about the task and beliefs about the person. Knowledge about the task is the child's understanding of the relation between the application of particular strategies and performance on the task. The absence of a specific piece of metacognitive knowledge is often a reason why a child fails to apply a strategy to a task. Thus, a child who does not know that rehearsal improves recall of material being studied is unlikely to use rehearsal as a strategy. In this case the child lacks knowledge about the relation between a specific strategy and task performance. Often, imparting this knowledge in conjunction with training in the execution of the strategy can lead to considerable improvements in performance (see chapter 7). But this type of task-based training can be hindered if the child has acquired negative beliefs about his own cognitive system. Many children who have learning difficulties become convinced that they will not succeed on a task because they lack the ability to do so. This metacognitive belief can hinder task-based training because it affects the amount of effort that the child is willing to allocate to the task. A child who has had a history of failure to learn some skill may come to believe that there is no relation between the amount of effort employed in applying a strategy and success with the strategy, and may therefore be unwilling to try very hard with new strategies.

Assessment and Intervention

There are different stages in dealing with any learning difficulty, as shown in table 1.1. First an assessment must be sought by someone, such as a parent or teacher, with whom the child has

Table 1.1 *Stages in assessment and intervention of a learning difficulty.*

Stage 1	Decide to seek assessment
Stage 2	Assess to provide profile of strengths and needs
Stage 3	Set aims and objectives
Stage 4	Design and implement intervention programme
Stage 5	Assess effects of intervention programme
Stage 6	Discontinue intervention or set further aims and objectives

regular contact. Part of the assessment will involve obtaining a profile of the child's cognitive strengths and needs, especially of the cognitive skills relevant to the suspected difficulty (see chapter 2). Assessments are performed in order to determine whether the initial suspicion of a learning difficulty was accurate or mistaken. Not all suspicions that a child has a learning difficulty are well-founded; some are the result of excessive expectations being placed on a child; some occur because of behavioural or emotional problems. The aim of assessment is to identify the processing problems relevant to a child's learning difficulty. Once this has been done, it is possible to consider how best to rectify the situation. The first step here is to set the aims of intervention and then set objectives that will constitute the targets to be achieved in intervention. The next step is to design the intervention programme itself. Ainscow and Tweddle (1979) emphasize the importance of ensuring that the first two or three objectives are ones that have been at least partially mastered by the child. The success of intervention is measured by the extent to which it meets the aims and objectives that have been set. This measurement is a repeated assessment following intervention. This is necessary in order to ensure that the objectives specified are actually moving the child in the right direction.

The model that we have proposed is an iterative one, which follows a test–teach–test philosophy. We should stress that the process we have outlined is a framework for assessment and intervention rather than a formula for rigid application. There are many additional considerations that must be taken into account by those who confront the practical task of dealing with learning difficulties. Not the least of these is the resources available for assessment and intervention and whether individual or group treatment should (and can) be provided. However, within this larger framework, the task of determining and dealing with the cognitive basis of learning difficulties remains.

Summary

Learning difficulties affect a substantial number of children in our society. These difficulties are heterogeneous. They may be mild, moderate, or severe, may be general or specific, and may be of short or long duration. To the practitioner these difficulties require assessment and intervention. To the theorist they require explanation in terms of models of cognitive functioning.

Learning difficulties can be classified in a variety of different ways. The most relevant classification is in terms of the underlying cognitive basis of the difficulty because it is cognitive functioning that intervention seeks to affect. Assessment should therefore present a profile of the child's current strengths and needs within relevant domains of cognitive functioning.

In developing a framework for understanding learning difficulties, it is necessary to consider the processing demands of the task and the role of the environment in relation to the skills that the child possesses. The major contribution of a cognitive analysis of learning difficulties is to the understanding of the task by child interaction. The normal pattern of development in acquiring a cognitive skill provides the essential background against which to analyse the processing demands of a task and the way in which processing skills develop. The development of these skills can be considered in more detail in terms of the cognitive architecture, mental representations, task processes, and executive processes.

2
Assessing Learning
Difficulties

Overview

This chapter considers the process of identifying and analysing learning difficulties. We begin by discussing the problems in identifying a learning difficulty and specifying the origins of the presenting difficulty. An initial suspicion of a learning difficulty needs to be followed by a comprehensive evaluation and diagnosis. We contrast norm-referenced and criterion-referenced methods of assessment. The process of assessment is intimately linked to models of learning; we consider the range of approaches that can be used to identify the problems that a child experiences. The strengths and limitations of assessing intelligence, abilities, and developing approaches based on task analysis are discussed. The importance of making assessment a continuous process is emphasized and the link to intervention highlighted.

The Assessment Process

In chapter 1 we identified three central issues in our analysis of learning difficulties – the task, the child, and the environment. Assessment is a process by which information is collected for a specific purpose. It is a process which should guide decision making about a child by identifying a profile of strengths and needs. Assessment should be hypothesis driven and these hypotheses should be based on an understanding of the child and the cognitive components of learning difficulties as well as an analysis of the child's current learning environment. Assessment is not a synonym for testing, although appropriate testing may well form an integral part of the process. In fact a single isolated test score is of little or no value. 'For a score to have meaning and to be of social or scientific utility some sort of frame of reference is needed' (Gardner, 1962).

Traditionally the assessment process has focused on the child. The process involved in child-centred assessment involves three steps which are not always explicitly differentiated:

- identifying the existence of a problem
- evaluating the nature of that problem
- making a diagnosis

Once the problem has been assessed appropriate interventions can be planned and implemented.

Identification

Identifying the existence of a problem is not always straightforward. Generally it entails making a judgement about the child's development in comparison to his peers. In identifying the problem most would agree that current difficulties in learning should serve as the criteria for locating a problem. Previous developmental problems may inform the analysis but present performance should be the critical factor for identification.

Problems with learning may present in different ways. Some children will be identified because they are falling behind their peers on particular tasks. Yet others will bring themselves to the attention of professionals because of misbehaviour. Informal observations which highlight a child's 'inability to attend', 'immaturity', or 'failure to listen to instructions' may well be indicators that a child is experiencing problems with learning. It is, of course, essential to consider the particular behaviour in relation to the context in which it occurs. Let us consider a child who is falling

Table 2.1 *Possible factors contributing to reading problems and potential levels of investigation.*

Locus of Problem	Level of investigation
Inappropriate reading material	Teacher and class
Inadequate staffing	School organization
Difficulties with translating letters to sounds	Child (see chapter 4)
Lack of experience with reading	Home school liaison (see chapter 1)

behind his peers in reading attainment. The child's behaviour may have arisen for a range of reasons. Table 2.1 lists a range of possible causes of reading delay and potential levels of investigation.

Parents and teachers are often the first to notice problems. Parents have a wealth of developmental experience with the child. They see the child functioning in a wide range of situations and are in a privileged position to notice problems. Teachers can compare a child's performance in group situations and are aware of the special demands a child may place on teaching resources. A teacher might note that a child may require considerably more time to learn a task than other children. Alternatively the focus of the teacher's concern might lie in the detailed instruction required by a specific child in contrast to the rest of the class. Once a learning difficulty is suspected, referrals can then be made to a multi-disciplinary child development team, a psychologist, or a remedial specialist who can perform a detailed assessment to establish what the nature of the problem is.

Screening

It is not always possible to identify a problem in the home or in the classroom. Moreover, there is variability in both the sensitivity of parents and teachers to problems and the extent to which parents and teachers will tolerate problems. Both of these factors could lead either to a child's special educational needs not being identified or to a child erroneously being labelled as having a learning difficulty. In an attempt to circumvent differences among individuals in recognizing learning difficulties screening procedures have been introduced in many areas.

Screening is a widely used procedure in medicine. Large populations are surveyed to identify individuals who are showing specific health problems or who may in the future experience difficulties. For example, all new-born infants in Great Britain are tested for phenylketonuria. This is a genetic condition of the digestive tract which if left untreated can lead to general learning difficulties. However, problems can be avoided if a child is given a special diet early on.

In the field of special education, screening aims to identify children who are 'at risk' of learning problems. Since screening involves surveying a large group of children it is not a personalized process. In educational settings screening is a process in which test scores or teacher ratings are used to identify individual children who need further evaluation and possible recommendation for remedial intervention. Screening must, therefore, by its very nature focus on particular issues rather than seeing the child as a whole. Screening to identify areas in which a child is making slow progress at the time of the investigation allows for immediate intervention, if required.

Screening can be a very effective means of identifying children who lack a particular skill or set of skills at a particular point in time. However, there are two important considerations in interpreting the results of such assessments. First, simply because a child lacks a particular skill at the point of screening does not mean that we can predict performance at a later date. Second, educational screening may fail to identify children who later show problems. In fact, the use of screening for *predicting* later difficulties has been called into question for a number of reasons (see Lindsay and Wedell, 1982, for a detailed review). For this reason information arising from the screening process should be linked to the curriculum or particular task which the child needs to master. Unfortunately, although educational screening should lead to follow-up, this rarely occurs (Gipps et al., 1983).

Evaluation

The process of evaluation usually involves formal testing of a child's cognitive skills and academic attainments. Such assessments are used to confirm that a child's development is disordered or delayed. In clinical or educational settings evaluation fulfils two additional functions: it provides an empirical basis for differential diagnosis and it highlights areas for intervention. In essence the evaluation process is trying to detect *whether* a learning difficulty actually exists, *what* the learning difficulty is, *why* the learning difficulty exists and *how similar* this difficulty is to problems experienced by other children. The existence of similar patterns of problems across children, in theory, allows for classification and differential diagnosis. Goldstein et al. (1975) argue that assessment and classification schemes encourage overgeneralizations about individual children. There is a tendency for educators to perceive similarly labelled children as alike in strengths and weaknesses when, in fact, they are often quite different. Assessment and intervention should be linked, though this has tended not to be the case (Locke, 1978; Ysseldyke, 1987). Few of the existing evaluation procedures have been designed to lead directly to remediation (Muller et al., 1981).

We consider evaluation to be an activity the objective of which is to collect accurate and reliable information about a particular individual's competence. The evaluation is begun with the aim of testing out hypotheses and as it proceeds, further hypotheses will need to be considered. For example, it is commonplace to begin an evaluation by searching for gross differences in expected behaviour patterns. As the process continues, specific and possibly explanatory mechanisms are considered. Given this, evaluation can never follow one simple pattern.

Investigating the child alone is inadequate (Mischel, 1977; Clarke, 1978). We need to consider the wider context within which the child is located. Problems do not always arise from the individual child. Children may be responding to an educational system or family environment that does not meet their needs. It is important to consider the interactive nature of the problems and the context in which they occur (Burden, 1981). In this chapter we are concerned with the ways in which the cognitive skills of the child can be assessed. Appropriate instructional practices and school organization can reduce and in some cases prevent the manifestation of learning difficulties. However, when they occur it is important that an accurate assessment of the child's current cognitive status is provided.

Once a problem has been recognized, evaluation will need to be ongoing to monitor progress and reassess special educational needs. To address a child's special educational needs an assessment should be diagnostic and prescriptive. The goal of diagnostic and prescriptive assessment is one of analysing over time the particular interactions between child, task, and setting. Such an assessment is less likely to fall prey to labelling since the child is *not* viewed as solely responsible for the problem, rather the problem is seen to result from the dynamic interplay of the child, the task, and the environment. Labelling has the dangers of lessening chances for individual instruction.

Three sets of tools may be used either alone or in combination to assist in identifying some of the factors involved:

- standardized norm-referenced tests
- criterion-referenced tests, developmental profiles, or checklists
- observational procedures or teaching experiments

A wide variety of assessment devices can be used for the evaluation and diagnosis of school-age children (Sattler, 1988). The situation with younger children is different as there are few valid instruments available from birth to 3 years (Cicchetti and Wagner, 1990).

Norm-Referenced tests   Norm-referenced tests provide information about where an individual lies on a particular ability (for example, naming vocabulary) or attainment (for example, reading) in comparison to peers of the same age. The measurements produced are of varying degrees of sophistication: ranks, centiles, standardized scores. Rank and centile scores are highly susceptible to over-interpretation (Tindal and Marston, 1986). Whatever the measure, the basic principle of norm-referenced tests is to define a continuum of performance from lowest to highest, and the measure assigned to a particular individual locates his position on that continuum. The test results measure the product of the learning difficulty and serve as indicators of the differences that exist between a child and his peers on a particular task or set of tasks. Some of these tests have a value as a first line method in identifying the existence of a problem. However, they do not provide a direct link to intervention since the scores do not provide details of what the child knows or does not know, nor do they elucidate the processes that are involved in the child's difficulty. Norm-referenced tests focus exclusively on the child's contribution to the learning difficulty. Currently norm-referenced methodology characterizes most of special education assessment (Ysseldyke and Thurlow, 1984).

An important consideration with norm-referenced tests is their retest reliability and validity. Retest reliability is the extent to which the test will produce the same results when the same child is measured at another point in time. For example, for intelligence tests, retest reliability over a one month period is high. The basic definition of validity is the extent to which a test measures what it is supposed to measure. There are a number of different kinds of test validity. Validity can be assessed by comparing a test with a similar test designed to measure the same functions (concurrent validity); thus, one reading test might be compared with another. Alternatively, the results of the test can be compared with another measure of the attribute (construct validity). In this case a test designed to assess reading might be validated against children's abilities to read text. Reliability and validity are not always considered by clinicians when they use tests. For example, in a survey of learning disabilities programmes, Thurlow and Ysseldyke (1979) found that, on average, 11 different assessment devices were used to collect data about school-aged children but the number ranged from 3 to 39. Of the devices used by three or more programmes only 25 per cent were considered to be technically adequate in terms of reliability, validity, and standardization sample. Clearly the use of unreliable measures renders the identification of a learning difficulty problematic.

Criterion-Referenced Tests Criterion-referenced tests are concerned with the skills required to complete a task or set of tasks. A previously specified set of criteria are used to assess children.

Table 2.2 *Suitable items for criterion-referenced assessment of arithmetic achievement.*

Specified Task	Skill Achieved	Date
Adds single-digit numbers without carrying		
Adds single-digit numbers with carrying		
Adds two digit numbers without carrying		
Adds two digit numbers with carrying		
Subtracts single digit numbers without borrowing		
Subtracts single digit numbers with borrowing		
Subtracts two digit numbers without borrowing		
Subtracts two digit numbers with borrowing		

The criteria are used to identify problems in relation to task specific skills. Such tests help identify whether or not an individual possesses some particular skill or competence and may allow for the analysis of error patterns. For example, a criterion-referenced assessment of aspects of the arithmetic curriculum might include the items listed in table 2.2. These tests are not designed to discriminate among individuals in the same way that norm-referenced tests do. Rather, they are designed to provide a clear indication of what a child can and cannot do and thereby are a guide to what skills should be taught next. A test can be constructed so that it is both norm-referenced and criterion-referenced. Figure 2.1 illustrates the relation between the two types of measures in a single instrument.

Criterion-referenced tests are characterized by the deliberate attempt to yield measurements that are directly interpretable in terms of specified performance standards. Despite this emphasis,

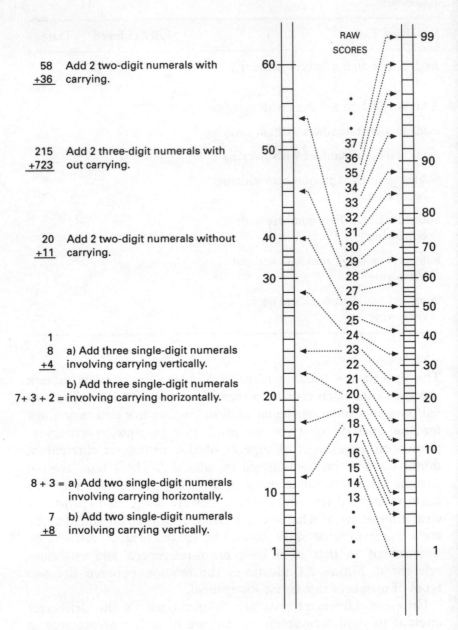

Figure 2.1 *Hypothetical example of two ways to reference test scores: criterion referencing and norm referencing.*
(Source: Nitko, 1980)

there is no single type of test that can be identified as the proto-type criterion-referenced test (Nitko, 1980). The assessment tool will depend on the nature of the domain and the focus of the scale. A well-defined domain is necessary to identify potential test items. Thus, to develop a criterion-referenced tool for reading we must know what the constituent skills are for reading. However, the tool might focus on different dimensions and this would result in the construction of quite different scales. We could, for example, consider level of competence (what items can be read), or proficiency (how fluently reading proceeds), or the develop-mental prerequisites to reading.

One of the strengths of criterion-referenced approaches is that they allow for a conceptual analysis of the types of errors that the child makes. Analysis of the errors made in performing a task can play an important part in understanding children's difficulties. Errors can be viewed as a mismatch between strategies and task demands. Errors can reflect the kind of information processing that a particular child uses and, by corollary, where intervention should be targeted. Thus, the nature of the task becomes a critical component in criterion-referenced approaches. This has impli-cations for how the task should be presented and organized for the child. By contrast, norm-referenced tests focus on correct answers rather than incorrect ones. Moreover, they do not allow for an assessment of response quality.

However, identification of what needs to be measured in a criterion-referenced test is not a simple matter. Each test must serve to distinguish among those individuals who have and those who have not achieved sufficient mastery of a particular skill, and mastery must be a valid and reliable predictor of the next devel-opmental step. This requires a psychological understanding of the particular domain. Moreover, the particular steps must be specified in a clear and objective fashion. This is more easily achieved for highly structured areas such as self-help skills, and less easily achieved for complex skills such as language. Much effort has been directed towards establishing or enhancing the content validity of criterion-referenced tests. As Pilliner (1979) has stated: 'The quality of a criterion-referenced test depends on the extent to which item content reflects the domain from which the items were derived.' The detailed nature of these tests allows more specific and appropriate treatment decisions to be made than norm-referenced tests do, because they focus on the nature of the task and the manner in which the constituent parts may support or impede learning.

Teaching Experiments   When a criterion-referenced test does not exist or does not give detailed enough information, or when the child will be affected by the constraints of standardized testing, teaching experiments can be designed. Teaching experiments focus on the individual child and the interplay of information processing skills in a particular situation. Using learning as an assessment technique one can use a test–teach–test model as a means of gauging an individual's ability to retain the content of the material and to transfer the principles learned to new tasks. If a criterion-referenced test exists it can serve as an indicator of where to pitch initial teaching. This approach forces the practitioner to be precise about the task components and can make the assessment both relevant and meaningful. Moreover, such an approach allows the practitioner to incorporate task, child, and environment into the conceptualization of the learning difficulty. However, since there is no external standard the practitioner will not be able to generalize the conclusions to other tasks and other contexts.

The following example, based on a real case will serve to illustrate the potential role of teaching experiments. Katy is a 5-year-old child with severe speech and language problems and a mild hearing loss. Her teachers are concerned that Katy has 'no memory' and therefore cannot learn. Her teachers feel there is no evidence that Katy remembers what she has been doing from one teaching session to the next, even when these are only minutes apart. When Katy is asked about previous activities she either answers irrelevantly or attempts to distract the teacher. She cannot complete norm-referenced verbal memory tests because of her language problems and the results of non-verbal memory tasks are suspect because of her visual problems. The teaching staff need to know what Katy can remember. In this instance Katy was provided with a series of pictures depicting various aspects of her activities. In response to the teacher's question Katy could point to a picture rather than respond verbally or by signing.

Once Katy had been taught how to use the system she performed well. Katy was 100 per cent correct over a 10 day test period. Clearly Katy retained the relevant information. Further investigations were carried out to determine the precise nature of Katy's problems.

Where is the problem?

The various methods that exist for evaluation of learning difficulties can be unreliable. Ysseldyke et al. (1983) raise a number of serious problems about the way in which learning difficulties are assessed. Children can be *falsely* identified as having a problem. Epps et al. (1983) found considerable variability in the number of pupils identified as having learning difficulties depending on the formula applied. This is supported by Ysseldyke et al. (1983) who applied several popular definitions of learning difficulties to the test scores of 'normal children'. They found that 85 per cent of children with no objective learning difficulty were identified as having such a difficulty by at least one definition. When the same criteria were applied to children already defined as having a learning difficulty, 4 per cent of these children were not identified by any definition. Moreover, in a previous study when educators were provided with test data from normal children, in a simulated decision making task, more than half of the participants identified average children as eligible for education (Algozzine and Ysseldyke, 1981). This is particularly problematic because once children are assessed and labelled it is difficult to reverse the process. Clearly, the methods of identifying learning difficulties should be carefully scrutinized. The results of a national survey in the United States suggested that students who are referred for special education enter 'a one way street leading to placement in special education' (Algozzine et al., 1983).

Many children with difficulties go undetected and some children are referred for special assessments for reasons that are unrelated to their particular cognitive skills. A number of analyses of learning difficulties programmes in the US (Christianson et al., 1982; Mehan et al., 1981) have suggested that referral, identification, and placement of pupils were influenced, even determined in part, by institutional constraints. Mehan et al.

(1981) identified powerful institutional constraints that affected the referral and placement process and thus the nature of educational decisions about individual pupils. A similar point has been made by Gregory (1980) in Britain. He has highlighted how some individual referrals may be the formulation of a problem that is largely the result of organizational inadequacies rather than within-child variables. Children can be brought to the attention of an educational psychologist because a school cannot cope with the child's behaviour. The same children might have their needs dealt with quite adequately in a different environment. By contrast, there may well be certain schools that are able to cater for a wide range of special educational needs.

Children who do not learn need not necessarily be unintelligent, they may simply be responding to a home environment or educational establishment that leaves them with little option. Consistency in performance may sometimes be legitimately re-interpreted in the light of the consistency of the environment. In fact a major deficiency of traditional assessment systems is the tendency to ignore the interactive nature of teaching and learning and to place sole responsibility on the child (White and Haring, 1980). A referral or a test result alone may lead to the assumption that a problem exists solely within the child, whereas a number of factors influence identification.

Diagnosis

Identification of a learning difficulty should be followed by a detailed analysis of the problem. Thus, the next stage of the assessment process involves diagnosing the particular type of learning difficulty a child is experiencing and the processes that are responsible for the difficulty. These may be within the child, external to the child, or a combination of the two. How a particular difficulty has been described may influence this second stage of the assessment process. Practitioners will be alert to the dangers of becoming trapped by the initial descriptions which would predetermine further assessment. In the following example the clinician would need to investigate a range of options in the assessment process:

Tom is a 4-year-old experiencing problems with communicating in the nursery school. He does not speak to either staff or his peers and communicates his needs by means of gestures. He is an amenable young boy who seems a bit young for his years.

Diagnosis of Tom's special educational needs might focus on a general problem or a specific language difficulty, or an emotional difficulty. Alternatively, a detailed account of the prerequisite skills for communication which are presently absent in Tom might be listed. Flexibility must be maintained in the procedure, irrespective of the initial hypothesis tested by the practitioner.

Children may have quite specific difficulties which initially only affect one area of cognitive performance. These problems may be conceived of as domain specific. In the case of Tom this might be in the area of language. A more detailed assessment will then be required which identifies exactly what it is about the language system that causes the child problems (see chapter 3). By contrast, there will be other children who appear to have problems in all or most areas of development. Difficulties may exist with language, problem solving, adapting to the environment and so on. In such situations the assessor should be looking for both general and specific processing difficulties (see chapter 6). There exists a wide range of permutations between these two examples and it is the assessor's task to delineate the range and extent of a particular child's difficulties in context over time.

This process is not simple. There are no uncomplicated solutions and there are many pitfalls in planning an adequate assessment. For example, finding one aspect of cognitive functioning in which a child is performing below expectation does not necessarily mean that this is an explanation of why a child is not progressing in the expected fashion. If a child is having problems learning and a memory difficulty is identified, the memory problem does not necessarily explain the learning difficulty. Two factors that correlate need not be causally related. While it is possible that memory difficulties cause learning difficulties it is equally possible that learning difficulties lead to reduced performance on certain memory tasks. For example, the extent of the child's knowledge base influences the types of processing that can be carried out (see chapter 7). It is important to understand why and how the problem can influence learning. Many mistakes of assessment have been made because of ill-formulated conceptions of the learning process. A theoretical framework that guides our understanding of learning difficulties and their assessment is an important prerequisite for intervention.

Approaches to Assessment

How an assessment is carried out is determined by what are considered to be central factors in the cognitive system, although a practitioner's use of a framework is rarely explicit. Norm-referenced approaches, particularly those based on IQ testing, are widely used in Britain. Quicke (1980) asked nearly 300 British Educational Psychologists which tests they regularly used in their work and found that the most popular was the WISC-R (82 per cent). For some psychologists such approaches provide a ready-made procedure when confronted with a child experiencing problems. It is necessary to consider the status of such approaches to arrive at a satisfactory understanding of the issues at hand. We therefore need to consider models of learning and the ways in which these models have been translated into assessment procedures.

There are many different types of assessment and the focus of a particular assessment will be dictated by our understanding and conceptualization of the cognitive system and the learning process (Siegler and Richards, 1982). There have been three major approaches to assessment based on different conceptualizations of the cognitive factors underlying learning difficulties:

- assessment of intelligence
- assessment of specific abilities
- assessment of information processing components

Approaches which emphasize intelligence or specific abilities translate directly into tools for assessing problems. By contrast, the information processing approach serves to highlight the knowledge and processes required to solve particular tasks and does not, in and of itself, identify the appropriate tools for assessment.

Approaches that focus on the identification of a general factor which distinguishes performance among children emphasize the use of psychometric tests for assessing intelligence. In such cases the importance of quantifiable dimensions along which individuals can be ordered is being highlighted. This results in a gross classification of groups of children as having either mild, moderate, or severe learning difficulties.

By contrast, there are approaches that focus on discrepancies in abilities within a single child. The abilities approach has led, over the last 30 years, to a mushrooming of variables that are thought to explain the specific problems experienced by children in learning. There is no generally accepted specific learning difficulty classification. Attempts have been made to explain such differences from both neurological and psychological perspectives.

Hooper and Willis (1989) provide an insightful review of the status of neurological assessment and classification. Neurological dysfunction is given a central role in some American definitions of 'learning disabilities'. However, soft neurological signs fare poorly in predicting learning difficulties in preschoolers (Horn and Packard, 1985). Moreover, the present evidence suggests it is unjustified to distinguish a particular syndrome of learning disabilities or a specific learning difficulty from other problems on the basis of neurological impairment (Franklin, 1987). While it is the case that some children with specific learning difficulties have neurological impairments, it is the child's abilities and skills that should be the crucial variables for diagnostic assessment and programme development.

Initially the search for psychological variables that might explain children's specific learning difficulties attempted to identify a single process variable. More recently there has been an awareness that specific learning difficulties are a heterogeneous set of problems and no single variable is likely to explain all learning problems. For example, Kavale and Nye (1985–6) carried out a meta-analysis of a number of studies and concluded that specific learning difficulties are a complex and multivariate set of problems that are not easily explained by impairments in one area of cognitive functioning. This is hardly surprising since the term *specific learning difficulties* denotes children with reading, spelling, writing, language, and mathematical difficulties. These processes, though related, are dissociable. Smead and Schwartz (1987) have pointed out that until a clear research base explains the relations among such variables, intervention strategies, and successful learning outcomes, the practitioner is left with a host of potential causes and cures. Let us now consider the impact of these various approaches in terms of assessment mechanisms.

Testing for Intelligence

Galton (1883) initiated the statistical study of intelligence and defined intelligence as 'that faculty which the genius has and the idiot has not'. Since the time of Galton, psychometricians have attempted to explain differences in intellectual performance among children as being due to differences in the quantity of 'intelligence'. There has never been general agreement about the meaning of 'intelligence'. In a symposium published in 1921 in the Journal of Educational Psychology, 13 psychologists gave 13 different views about the nature of intelligence, although there was much in common in their definitions. There are still many different definitions and conceptions of intelligence (Sternberg and Detterman, 1986).

The measurement of intelligence has been dominated by psychometric tests (for example, Stanford–Binet, WISC-R, WHIPPSI-R, and the British Ability Scales). The first psychological testing program began with Alfred Binet's development of the intelligence test designed to meet the needs of educational selection. The aim was to identify those children who might not benefit from public education; the hope was that an unbiased evaluation of scholastic aptitude could be developed. Such tools are still in demand. The British Ability Scales are designed to assess general mental capacity or educability (Warburton, 1970). The psychometric model explains intelligence in terms of a hierarchical and correlational structure of various intellectual abilities. However, the subtests that make up these measures were not developed from a coherent theory of the intellectual skills for school learning. Rather, they were merely a sample of the kinds of knowledge and skill that are empirically related to performance on school tasks (Torgesen, 1989). As a result, it is not clear what responses to

IQ tests tell us about the nature of a child's learning difficulties, although they may be useful in establishing that there is a difficulty. Some authors have suggested that intelligence ought to be regarded as a descriptive rather than an explanatory term (Olson, 1986). Most definitions explicitly affirm that by introducing the term one is to some extent explaining performance, not describing it. However, critics of this approach question the value of measuring intelligence. Howe (1988: 358) argues that:

> there are no strong grounds for believing that identification of someone's measured intelligence justifies any kind of meaningful statement about the individual's achievements, abilities or attributes, or even detailed predictions except in narrowly circumscribed circumstances .... A report of a person's level of tested intelligence provides rather little information about that individual and considerably less than many writers ... appear to believe.

In considering IQ scores it is necessary to bear in mind a number of issues that are relevant to the interpretation of these scores. These include confidence intervals, stability, and predictive utility. Intelligence tests are norm-referenced tools designed to assess an individual's cognitive functioning. Like all norm-referenced measures they will always contain some margin of error (Harris, 1983). This means that whenever an intelligence test result is reported, confidence intervals (95 per cent confidence levels) should be identified. This allows a range of scores to be reported within which will lie an individual's true score 95 per cent of the time.

In the past the measurement of IQ has been interpreted as an unchangeable estimate of an individual's cognitive ability. The prevailing assumption of the stability of IQ scores has been challenged in a number of ways. It has been known for quite some time that IQ is not a very stable measure in childhood, especially among younger children (Brooks-Gunn and Weintraub, 1983; Hindley and Owen, 1978; Honzik et al., 1948; Honzik, 1983; Kopp and McCall, 1982; Sontag et al., 1958).

There is a critical difference between stability on a test measure and using it as a means of predicting potential. It is quite unjustifiable to make a statement about an individual child's potential on the basis of a single test score (Gillham, 1974). In fact texts in educational measurement and assessment routinely warn against interpreting IQ scores as measures of intellectual potential (Anastasi, 1988; Cronbach, 1984).

There are two more recent approaches to the predictive basis of IQs. The first approach derives from the work of Fagan (1982) and attempts to identify alternative measures of cognitive functioning in infancy. Fagan and his colleagues have developed a screening device for the early detection of intellectual deficits – The Fagan Test of Infant Intelligence. The test assesses the infant's ability to discriminate familiar from novel stimuli. The display of competence in early visual information processing is argued to provide an index to future cognitive functioning (Fagan et al., 1986).

The second approach focuses on whether IQ is more stable for some groups of children than others (Largo et al., 1990). Siegel (1979) argues that low scores on the Bayley test in infancy predict low scores on language, cognitive, perceptual, and visual motor tests in later childhood. However, it is necessary to distinguish between aggregate and individual data. While Siegel's conclusions apply to the group of children with low Bayley scores, *as a group*, they do not necessarily apply to every individual case. Prediction is hampered in individual children by dissociations in development, organic impairment and major life events (Largo et al., 1990). Thus, a low Bayley score for an individual child should alert those involved with the child to the possibility of later learning difficulties but it is by no means a definite predictor of these difficulties.

Intelligence test scores are indicators of how well an individual has performed on a particular test. Intelligence tests do not provide data concerning the processes and strategies that are responsible for learning. Since the 1970s a large number of investigators have focused on the information processing requirements of intelligent behaviour. Information processing theories permit the decomposition of intelligent behaviour into components, each of which can serve as a locus for training and intervention (Sternberg, 1978). According to Willson (1989), rather than using psychometric criteria for item selection, intelligence tests should be developed with deliberate attention to the memory and the processing demands required to process each item. Test developers should specify carefully the demands required for each process intended for an item.

Unless the necessary components of successful performance on test items are known it is difficult to identify steps for remediating learning problems. Binet himself was keen to focus on the educability of intelligence, but his successors have tended not to follow this route. Intelligence tests are not geared to intervention. In fact, it is implicit in the analysis that little can be done except match task demands and the curriculum to the child's 'level of functioning'.

In an attempt to address this issue it has been suggested that the key to remediation lies in the subtest scores. Wechsler introduced a major innovation into the testing of intelligence by incorporating a distinction between verbal and performance scales. This distinction is frequently used by clinicians (Lezak, 1988). However, many studies have shown that not all verbal subtests measure verbal functions and at least one performance test on the WISC has a considerable verbal loading. Many educational psychologists and neurologists choose not to use the global IQ and focus on profiles of subtest scores instead.

Hallahan and Bryan (1981) argue that it is inappropriate to use discrepancy scores between subtests *alone* as the criterion for diagnosing specific learning difficulties (see also Kavale, 1988). There are many psychometric difficulties inherent in discrepancy formulas and it is not at all clear when a discrepancy becomes clinically meaningful. For example, Kaufman (1976) has noted that large differences in subtest scores are common. Lynch et al. (1982) show that there is significant variability in profiles for normal preschool children and that the use of differences in subtest levels to interpret abnormality is fraught with uncertainty. Even if reliable and significant differences are identified it is not obvious what interventions would be required.

Identifying profiles of skills is an important step. The critical issue is to identify exactly what should be measured. The best that can be said of IQ and IQ-related tests is that they produce a moderate probability statement about whether a child is likely to have learning difficulties or not. Accurate and detailed diagnosis will require additional procedures.

Testing for Abilities

The term *specific learning difficulty* is sometimes used to describe those children who, in spite of having average, near-average, or above-average IQ, still experience difficulty with some basic aspect of learning (Coles, 1978). Children with lower-than-average IQs who have learning difficulties have been called 'mentally handicapped' rather than described as having a specific learning difficulty (see chapter 6). However, there are problems with such an approach. There have been attempts in the United States to change the definition of specific learning difficulties to include children who have below average intellectual functioning (Hammill et al., 1981).

Performance on an IQ test often depends critically upon those skills with which the child is experiencing difficulty. Thus, it is not surprising to find that children regarded *by schools* as 'learning disabled' but not as 'retarded' have IQ scores below the mean of the general population (Hallahan and Kauffman, 1977). There is considerable debate surrounding the nature of differential diagnosis using IQ tests. An alternative is available through the use of ability tests, which attempt to identify specific processing deficits.

A wide range of tests of specific abilities exist. The choice of a particular test will vary according to the problems a child is suspected of having. Nevertheless, the general principles remain the same. Ability tests are designed to focus on specific processes thought to be essential for the child to be successful in his academic efforts. The measurement of specific and discrete areas of development was designed as a diagnostic procedure to pinpoint the deficient areas needing remediation.

Throughout the 1960s and early 1970s specific learning difficulties assessments were dominated by the abilities model. The theories of Cruickshank (Hallahan and Cruickshank, 1973), Frostig (Frostig and Horne, 1964), Kirk (Kirk et al., 1961) and Kephart (1960) directed educators to assess children's strengths and weaknesses with a variety of tests. Primary emphasis was given to perceptual–motor skills and psycholinguistic abilities. Children were tested in these specific areas and exercises were designed to improve their performance on the designated skills. From this perspective the source of the problem was seen to be exclusively within the child.

The educational relevance of abilities tests and the consequent prescriptive teaching based on these tests has been called into question. For example, the Frostig Developmental Test of Visual Perception is designed to assess five areas of perception that are postulated to underlie the ability to read. Low scores in any of the areas are presumed to be diagnostic of a perceptual deficiency or developmental lag which may require one of five types of remedial training or instruction. However, Smith and Marx (1972: 117) concluded that there are serious limitations with the test and that whatever the Frostig test measures 'it is not reading ability and caution should be exercised in using it as a screening instrument to predict future reading achievement or as a device to diagnose specific perceptual variables underlying reading deficiency'.

Use of the accompanying training procedures is equally questionable in relation to reading. When children trained on the Frostig visual perceptual training programme are compared with children working solely with regular reading materials their scores on standardized reading tests do not differ significantly (Hammill, 1972). However, they do perform better on the Frostig materials; that is, training is specific to types of materials on the test and does not improve reading skills.

The Illinois Test of Psycholinguistic Ability (ITPA) is a widely used test which purports to measure input, processing, and output abilities that underlie language development. This test is comprised of 12 subtests. Hammill and Larsen (1974) found that 9 of the 12 subtests lack predictive validity for any aspect of academic achievement and two of the remaining three, as well as the composite score, dropped below practical significance when intelligence was partialled out. Thus, only one subtest (grammatical closure) was significantly correlated with reading and its theoretical significance has been called into question. There is controversy over the effectiveness of ITPA training (Hammill and Larsen, 1974).

Many other tests exist that are designed to measure specific abilities. Their reliability and validity is discussed by Salvia and Ysseldyke (1985) and also by Coles (1978), who concluded that the results of the reliability studies are equivocal at best. A major concern with such tests is their construct validity. It is not clear that the models underlying such tests are sound. Moreover, simply extending the number of tests used does not improve the situation. A test battery is only as good as the tests that make it up. However, the main problem with the abilities model is the lack of adequate descriptions of the processing skills that are important for effective learning, and the lack of techniques for measuring processing deficiencies (Torgesen, 1979). The particular relevance of information processing lies in clarifying goals that were not conceptually sound in abilities training.

Critics of the specific abilities approach argue that its impact on instructional programmes was simply to divert time and effort from instruction in the academic skills with which the children are having difficulty. The preponderance of present evidence suggests that the direct teaching of academic skills leads to better results (Reid and Hresko, 1981).

The identification of process variables is central to our understanding of learning difficulties. The specific abilities model is suspect on theoretical grounds. It appears that the abilities model has generally identified the wrong processes. Both the perceptual–motor and psycholinguistic models treat psychological processes as if they were separate and unitary entities. Our present understanding of cognitive processes has provided a more detailed and complex account of the cognitive system. Some researchers have argued that fewer modality-specific measures should be used and more measures evaluating the interactive components of learning should be developed. Moreover, the need to consider the tasks to which these processes are applied has been acknowledged. Thus, there is considerably more attention paid to the interaction between particular domains of knowledge and the strategies that can be applied to manipulate the representations in these domains (see chapter 7).

Task Analysis

Rather than look to specialized curricula to remediate learning problems attempts have been made to identify the skills necessary to solve a particular task. Information processing theories guide the practitioner in identifying the cognitive prerequisites required to complete a task.

Task analysis involves breaking a task down into its component subtasks and in turn breaking each subtask into its components. Task analysis identifies what to teach and effectively these components become the teaching objectives. Task analysis forms part of a behavioural approach to teaching. It is curriculum based and is concerned with analysing the content of what a child has learned and what needs to be learned. Assessment and remediation strategies are directed towards specifying and teaching learning hierarchies of skill prerequisites for *actual* tasks the child has been unable to accomplish and thus the strategies are criterion-referenced. Criterion-referenced testing cannot easily be separated out as a testing activity, rather it should be integrated in the day to day running of the classroom (Hofmeister, 1975). This has led to the curriculum being made up of objectives, particularly in some special schools. Such approaches are usually not concerned with the evaluation of any other generalized cognitive difficulties that the child may have.

However, criterion-referenced tests and task analysis suffer from the same sources of unreliability as norm-referenced tests. For most criterion-referenced devices and systems there are no data regarding reliability and validity (Salvia and Ysseldyke, 1985). Moreover, decisions need to be made about whether a learning hierarchy is correct or incorrect. The learning hierarchy must be based on our current understanding of cognitive processes. Even strong supporters of this approach (Ainscow and Tweddle, 1979) acknowledge that objectives are hard to write in some subject or skill areas (see chapter 7).

One of the major criticisms of task analysis and learning objectives is the conceptualization of the learning process. There may be a number of routes by which a child can acquire mastery, rather than a single instructional hierarchy that is common to all children. When a task analysis is being performed, it is assumed that each child will learn the task components in the same order, because the task is analysed and not the learning processes or the learning context. An over-reliance on task components can lead to a rigid application of prescriptive teaching, which takes no account of the knowledge a child brings to any given task or the specific strategies that a child utilizes.

The task analysis framework has had a number of positive

impacts on the field of learning difficulties. Focus on a particular task and its subcomponents has highlighted the deficiencies of some of the norm-referenced tests and resulted in a precise analysis of performance on specific, relevant tasks. Moreover, the emphasis on continuous monitoring of specific sets of behaviours linked to specific instructional objectives makes assessment a continuous process and emphasizes the tasks that the child is performing.

General Issues in Assessment

The goal of diagnostic and prescriptive teaching becomes one of analysing and then restructuring the particular interactions between child, task, and setting that are producing learning difficulties. In the past, process models and task analysis models of assessment have been treated separately, though they are both examples of a diagnostic/prescriptive approach. However, diagnostic/prescriptive assessment can only really be achieved if all elements in the equation are included. Such an approach to assessment involves both an understanding of the task and the processes involved. The process model should specify sets of strategies that are domain specific and sets that are general. For example, in the domain of number there will be certain processes that are specific to arithmetic and arithmetic alone (task-based); there may also be some domain independent processes or skills that the child must master in order to be competent at arithmetic. By focusing on the task or domain, on what has to be learned, and on how it might be learned, it is possible to move away from a solely child-based deficit model.

Further assessment should be directed at those functional skills and behaviours essential to the academic and social life of children. This approach does not imply that there will be one single processing deficit that will account for all learning difficulties, nor that one specific deficit will necessarily account for all the problems in one domain. It is essential to view diagnostic and prescriptive teaching in the light of what we already know about learning difficulties. Attempts to present single explanatory mechanisms will be misleading and will detract from the strength of this approach.

Assessments of children with learning difficulties often result in a profile of test results which is fed back to teachers and schools. On the whole, such profiles are viewed as unhelpful by the receiver of this information. In Britain, O'Hagan and Swanson's (1983) data indicate that teachers strongly support the view that assessments are helpful but are less positive in valuing the content of the assessment, or the advice on treatment given. The value merely resides in rubber-stamping the teacher's own opinion. Similar results have been found in the United States. Ysseldyke and Algozzine (1983) report data that indicate that test results are often viewed as useless by the teacher – other than as serving to confirm the obvious, that the child has learning problems – and do not indicate the specific curriculum and be-havioural changes that would lead to a more successful educa-tional experience for the child. If assessment is intimately linked with intervention this should go some way to addressing the real needs of the teachers, schools, and parents.

As we argued in chapter 1 current developments in our under-standing of cognitive development have created a significant shift in the orientation to learning difficulties (see also Bauer, 1982; Reid and Hresko, 1981). Information processing provides a frame-work to understand the range of requirements for successful task completion and identification of the possible processes which produce problems when learning a task. Difficulties have been postulated within the cognitive architecture in speed of infor-mation processing (Anderson, 1986, 1992; Eysenck, 1987), knowl-edge representation (Alexander and Judy, 1988), strategy use (Borkowski et al., 1987), and metacognitive skills (Brown, 1978). The mechanisms which are postulated to explain learning difficulties vary across types of problems and within problem groups. Thus, for example, different explanations have been invoked to explain arithmetic problems and problems with read-ing. Such domain specific models fit well with our current under-standing of cognitive development. The following chapters will use this framework to help our understanding of the difficulties which arise within particular domains. Further, such an approach allows for a specification of the range of skills necessary to solve a particular task and thus provides an explanatory mechanism for the types of difficulties which may arise within a domain. In the following chapters we will outline the difficulties that children experience within specific domains and with general learning. Our analysis will be in terms of both the task and the processing requirements necessary to achieve mastery of the task.

Summary

In this chapter we have argued that the child's difficulties should be addressed in terms of the present level of performance. Assessment should include an evaluation of the environment in which the problem is occurring, an analysis of the task, and a diagnosis of the difficulties experienced by the child. To assess the child's skills a combination of norm-referenced and criterion-referenced tests will be required. While the former may serve to validate initial suspicions of a problem they will not provide any detailed information on the nature of the child's difficulty. Criterion-referenced tests will help target appropriate intervention. The criterion-referenced test will need to be based on an understanding of the information processing requirements of the task, which will allow for the identification of the basic task subcomponents. Attention will need to be paid to the interaction between particular domains of knowledge and the strategies that can be applied to manipulate representations.

3
Specific Difficulties with Language

Overview

In this chapter we shall consider specific difficulties in processing language. We first consider the distinction between language delays and language disorders, and then discuss the prevalence of language difficulties and issues in their classification. We then briefly outline the different components that constitute the language system: phonology, the lexicon, syntax, semantics, and pragmatics. Explanations of language difficulties have focused on factors both within and beyond the language system – we consider the factors within the system, and discuss each component of the system in turn, first with respect to normal development and then with respect to the types of difficulties that may be encountered with the component. Next we consider the role of factors beyond the language system under three headings: auditory processing, working memory, and cognitive processes. In the final sections of the chapter we consider the implications of the types of processes we have discussed for the issues of classification and delay and disorder. The last section of the chapter considers issues of assessment and intervention.

The Identification and Description of
Language Difficulties

Language difficulties are problems or disorders in comprehending or producing speech. The American Speech-Language-Hearing Association (ASHA) provides a comprehensive definition of language disorders:

> A language disorder is the abnormal acquisition, comprehension or expression of spoken or written language. The disorder may involve all or some of the phonologic, morphologic, semantic, syntactic or pragmatic components of the linguistic system. Individuals with language disorders frequently have problems in sentence processing or in abstracting information meaningfully for storage or retrieval in short-term and long-term memory. (ASHA, 1980: 317–18)

Noting that a child experiences a language difficulty simply indicates that something has gone wrong with the language system. It does not provide an explanation of why the problem has occurred nor what maintains the problem. Language difficulties may occur for a variety of reasons. Sometimes there is a precipitating organic cause such as hearing loss, which affects language comprehension, or a defect in the neuromotor control of the vocal tract, which affects language production. Sometimes a child has inadequate early language experiences and this prevents the normal process of language acquisition from occurring (see Skuse, 1984). Sometimes language difficulties are one manifestation of a general overall impairment in learning and cognitive functioning (see chapter 6). There also is a large group of children who experience language difficulties in the absence of any of these causes.

The identification of language difficulties is problematic. Language difficulties obviously represent a difference from the norm of language development. Identification of early language difficulties will often depend on the sensitivity of the child's caretakers in recognising a child who is at the extreme end of the normal distribution for passing language milestones. However, this norm itself is not easy to characterize; there is considerable diversity in the rate at which children acquire language. Thus, there is no exact point that divides normal development from that which should cause concern.

Delay

A delay in language development is often the first indicator of a language difficulty. A number of behaviours have been suggested as indicators of delay. Ingram (1972) suggests that no speech at 18 months should serve as a marker while Stackhouse and Campbell (1983) use unintelligible speech at school age as their criterion. In addition, receptive or expressive language one to two standard deviations below non-verbal IQ is frequently used as indicating a specific language delay. Difficulties, however, are subtle and are not always tapped by the measurement devices that exist. The population of children with language difficulties is likely to be quite heterogeneous. As Aram and Nation (1982: 37) point out:

> With the diversity seen in child language disorders it is most likely that this population includes a range of distinctions: children who represent the lower end of the normal distribution, children who are clearly delayed but are developing along an expected pattern, and children whose pattern of language behaviour is clearly deviant for their age or stage of development.

Disorder

Aram and Nation here raise the issue of language delays and language disabilities or disorders. Distinguishing these requires a further criterion than delay. Stark et al. (1983) and Bishop and Rosenbloom (1987) draw a logical distinction between language delay and language disorder. In the latter case children's language acquisition is thought to follow a *different* pattern from the norm, with, for example, a child experiencing difficulties with a particular syntactic structure or producing speech in a dysfluent fashion.

However, atypical development is not an easy distinction to operationalize. Atypical patterns are defined differently by different researchers. Suggested signs include use of abnormal structures and/or processes and discrepancies between abilities in different language components (Byers Brown, 1976; Ingram,

Table 3.1   *Prevalence of communication problems among 4-year-olds reported by Chazan et al. (1980).*

Problem area	Mild problem	Severe problem	Total	% of full sample (7,320)
Speech articulation	455 (6%)	219 (3%)	674	9.2
Expressive language	397 (5%)	159 (2%)	556	7.6
Listening to stories	340 (4%)	126 (2%)	466	6.4
Receptive language	219 (3%)	83 (1%)	302	4.1

Source: Chazan and Laing, 1982.

1972). To establish that a disorder exists as opposed to a delay in development a child's language must be compared with children of an equivalent language age. For example, if a 6-year-old has a language age of 3 years his profile of skills and competencies needs to be contrasted with other children with an equivalent language age. It is only recently that studies have begun to include language age controls, thus allowing the issue of delay versus disorder to be addressed by empirical evidence.

Prevalence

Establishing the prevalence of language difficulties is a complex enterprise. Reliable prevalence figures depend on clear-cut criteria for identifying difficulties. However, there is no general agreement on the criteria that define a language difficulty and thus estimates vary according to the criteria used. Most prevalence studies have focused on preschool as opposed to school-aged children.

Recent studies have produced preschool prevalence rates ranging from 3 to 15 per cent. As an indication, in a survey of over 7,000 children, Chazan et al. (1980) reported that over 8 per cent of the sample had a severe language problem and 18 per cent had a mild problem. Table 3.1 shows a breakdown of the problems.

One of the major difficulties in interpreting prevalence data about language difficulties is knowing the extent to which the data reflect underlying problems in processing language and the extent to which they reflect delays in acquiring the language system. The initial identification of a language difficulty often occurs as a result of the failure to acquire or combine words. However, the age at which children begin to use or combine words varies widely. Thus it is not clear to what extent delays represent problems and to what extent they represent natural variability in acquiring language. Morley (1972), for example, found that 10 per cent of children at 2 years manifested language problems, 6 per cent did so at 3 years 9 months, and between 3 and 5 per cent did so at 4 years 9 months. These data suggest that some children overcome an initial delay. This was borne out by Bishop and Edmundson (1987b), who found that approximately 40 per cent of children who had language problems at 4 years had resolved these problems by the middle of the fifth year. Those who did not, however, continued to manifest difficulties later on (Bishop and Adams, 1990). Similar findings were reported in Weiner's (1985) review of studies of long-term outcome, which show that 60 per cent of children who had language difficulties during preschool years continue to exhibit language problems at the age of 10 years. Further, there is no indication that language problems decline appreciably above the age of 10 years. Many of the children with specific language difficulties experience additional problems. Several longitudinal studies of children with language difficulties have reported a high rate of linguistic, educational, and social impairment persisting many years after the language difficulty was first diagnosed (Aram et al., 1984; Aram and Nation, 1980; Bishop and Adams, 1990; Fundudis et al., 1979; Hall and Tomblin, 1978; Stevenson, 1984).

Classifying Language Difficulties

There is no agreed-upon system for classifying language difficulties. As we have discussed in chapter 1, classification can be aetiological or functional. The traditional classification of language difficulties has followed a medical framework, which uses a mixture of aetiological and functional criteria (Bishop and Rosenbloom, 1987). When there is a known aetiology, this provides information about characteristics of the child and about expectations for language performance. Webster (1986), for example, discusses the implications of various types of hearing impairment for language development and the designing of an appropriate school curriculum. When there is an evident physiological cause, aetiological classification systems are quite refined. However, they tend to be undifferentiated for the large class of language difficulties that do not have an identifiable physiological cause.

Some children have slow or faulty development of language in the absence of any obvious aetiological criteria. These children cause a special problem for an aetiological classification system since there is no evidence of such factors as deafness, motor deficits, or socio-emotional disorders to explain their language difficulty. For example, relatively few children with *specific language difficulties* show direct evidence of brain damage or have a history of neurological disease, and there is little evidence of an unusually high frequency of perinatal problems in this population (Bishop, 1987). In an aetiological system, classification of these children must be done by applying the negative criterion that language difficulties occur in the absence of any obvious explanatory factors. It is with the group of children who have no obvious aetiological basis for their language problems that we are concerned in this chapter.

The terms *developmental dysphasia, specific developmental language disorders,* or *specific language impairment* have been used to refer to children with language problems when other explanatory factors are excluded. A problem with these categories is that they do not lead directly to an understanding of those aspects of language behaviour that are in need of modification. A wide range of language difficulties is subsumed under these terms. Difficulties with a variety of components of the language system have been described (Byers Brown and Edwards, 1989). Many of these descriptions arise from clinical studies where researchers attempt to identify specific subgroups of the disorder (Rapin and Allen, 1983). However, deriving classifications from clinical data may impose an artificial homogeneity on the spectrum of language difficulties. In a review of classification systems, Bishop and Rosenbloom

(1987: 36) comment: 'No sooner does one identify a set of categories than one encounters children who seem to belong to no category, or whose characteristics fall between two categories.' There are many different types of difficulty and it is unclear how the proliferation of a labelling system enhances our understanding unless it is constrained by a framework. A theoretical framework that is sensitive to the unique aspects of difficulties experienced within the language system is required.

The Basis of a Classification System

In the first instance it is necessary to establish what would be the basis of a comprehensible and acceptable classification system for language difficulties. Otherwise, it is possible to generate as many subgroups as there are children. There are two basic prerequisites for structuring an approach to language problems:

- an understanding of the pattern of normal language development
- a detailed description of how the language system represents and processes linguistic information

The first of these prerequisites provides the developmental perspective on the acquisition of language and draws attention to the changes that should occur. A model that provides information about the normal acquisition of language also provides the basis of norm-referenced criteria. Further, it provides information about the course of development and a set of standards that can be used for judging the appropriateness of intervention targets. The second prerequisite is concerned with the nature of the processing that occurs within the component parts of the language system. It provides the explanatory base underlying linguistic behaviour and the patterns of change that occur in its development.

An analysis of language difficulties in these terms would both describe the child's language with reference to normal language development and classify the difficulty with reference to the processing mechanisms involved. Such an approach not only describes the child's language behaviour but in addition attempts to identify the linguistic and cognitive basis for the behaviour.

A distinction should be drawn between the understanding and the production of language. In normal development children generally understand utterances before they produce them. In understanding a particular word or utterance children generally are provided with a range of non-linguistic cues which guide and constrain the inferences they will make about the meaning of the utterance. Thus they do not have to rely completely on the language itself. By contrast, when required to produce a word or an utterance the child must rely on the language system – he must both access the appropriate word or grammatical construction and transform this into an acceptable linguistic output. Thus, production places more demands on the language system than does comprehension. Difficulties in comprehension usually lead also to difficulties in production (Bishop and Edmundson, 1987a). However, production difficulties can occur in the absence of any comprehension difficulty.

The Language System

The major purpose of language is communication. But communication relies on the structure of the language system, hence we must look both to the components that constitute language and to the communicative use of the system as a whole. The language system consists of a series of components that include the lexicon, phonology, and syntax.

In considering the structure of language we have to consider several different levels of detail. Language is built around words. The store of words possessed by an individual is called *the lexicon*. Words also have an internal sound structure, which is the phonological level of analysis; and they can be combined together to make sentences, which is the syntactic level of analysis. We can consider the structure of language at three levels then: lexical, phonological, and syntactic.

We also have to consider the way in which words and sentences have meaning. This is generally considered under the topics of semantics and pragmatics. The meaning of a word is acquired by learning to pair a particular sound pattern with a particular concept. The meaning of a sentence is a more complex affair. It is not enough simply to string the meanings of the individual words together; the relation between these meanings is governed by the way in which the syntactic structure of a sentence constrains semantic interpretation (see Pinker, 1989, for a recent discussion).

Pragmatics is concerned with how the listener interprets the speaker's intentions. This process often requires the listener to make inferences because intentions are not usually explicitly stated. Thus, the listener must draw upon his knowledge of human motives and of how other minds work in interpreting language at this level.

The lexicon, phonology, syntax, semantics, and pragmatics constitute the various representations available for deployment during speaking and understanding. Each can be studied and assessed independently of the others. However, this does not mean that the components operate independently; they interact in the overall process of comprehending and producing speech as figure 3.1 shows.

Language problems present in different forms. The distinctions among the lexicon, phonology, syntax, semantics, and pragmatics help focus initial assessments and subsequent interventions. The first step in considering language difficulties is to identify with which particular components of the language system the child is experiencing difficulties. In order to do this it is necessary to assess the child's competence with each of the components.

Explanations of Language Difficulties

What causes language difficulties? Given the complexity of the language system, and the extent to which it interacts with the rest of the cognitive system, it is unlikely that language difficulties will have a single cause. This is particularly so because there is a range of difficulties. Some children appear to have difficulties confined to a particular component, while others have more generalized difficulties across different components; so in discussing explanations of language difficulties it is necessary to be precise about the type of difficulty for which an explanation is supposed to hold.

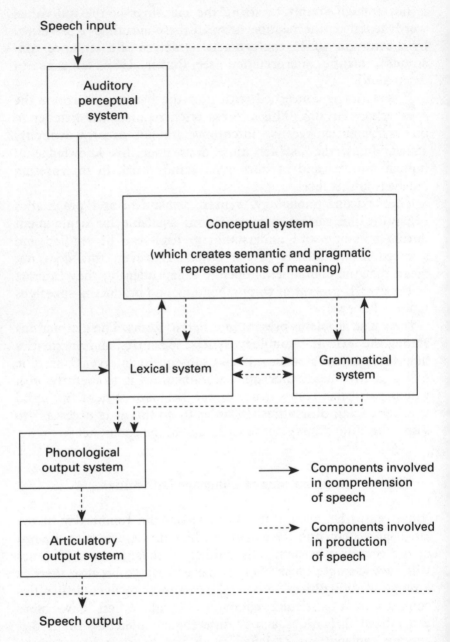

Figure 3.1 *The major components involved in the comprehension and production of speech.*

Two sorts of processes have been widely considered as causes of language difficulties: structural processes of the language system itself and cognitive processes on which the language system depends. The latter have been quite widely researched. In fact, until recently the dominant research paradigm has been one in which language difficulties were investigated by correlating a measure of language with a measure of some nonlinguistic cognitive factor that was hypothesized to be the cause of the language difficulty. A variety of cognitive factors have been considered including auditory perceptual processing (Leonard, 1989), sequencing and temporal processing (Tallal and Piercy, 1978), and processes of working memory (Gathercole and Baddeley, 1990).

However, much recent research has been influenced by arguments that the language system may be an autonomous cognitive domain that relies very little on general cognition for the analysis of the phonology and the syntax of the input (Fodor, 1983). Apart from the status of the relation between language and other aspects of cognition, it makes sense to discuss first the linguistic aspects that may be involved in cases of language difficulties and then to ask what general cognitive resources may be implicated in these difficulties.

Problems Within the Language System

To describe and understand the problems experienced by children with language learning we need to map the types of problems experienced by children onto a model of language processing. Figure 3.1 will help us to understand the problems that are encountered with language and the way in which certain difficulties are related. Children can have isolated difficulties within a component, but it is more common for difficulties to be experienced across a range of components, with varying degrees of severity, in both comprehension and production (Haynes and Naidoo, 1991).

The Phonological Structure of Words

Words have an internal sound structure, which can be analysed at several different levels, such as stress pattern, syllable structure, and phonological structure. Phonemes are the individual sound units that make up a word and, more importantly, distinguish one word from another. Thus, /b/ and /p/ are phonemes of English because they distinguish words such as *bin* and *pin* and *bit* and *pit*. In general, the letters of a language are closely, but not perfectly, related to the phonemes of the language.

Although phonemes are the basic sound units that carry meaning, they are not the ultimate elements of language. This can easily be seen by considering the way in which /s/ is pronounced in *sing* and *lose*. Phonological theory explains differences such as this by postulating that phonemes are composed of bundles of phonetic features, which are subject to rules of pronunciation. Thus, /s/ is pronounced differently in the words above because of specifiable features of the other phonemes in the words.

There is a limited set of such features, which are innate to human beings. That is to say, the phonological features themselves are not learned; what children have to learn is which features are used by their particular language because any given language does not use all the features. Children discover the relevant features of their language from the linguistic input they receive. The identification and organization of these features is a prerequisite for acquiring other aspects of language.

Phonemes are combined together to make up syllables. In considering syllable structure it is useful to divide phonemes into two large classes: consonants and vowels. Syllables usually have either a CV or a CVC pattern. In language acquisition, the initial words are usually single syllable words with a CV pattern or reduplication of this pattern in CVCV as in *mama* and *dada*. Words that have a CVC pattern in the adult language are often reduced to a CV pattern in children's speech. Thus, the /g/ in *dog* might be dropped initially to give a pronunciation resembling *duh* (where the *uh* is an informal representation of a vowel). These examples illustrate that lexical expression may be limited by the developmental state of the phonological system.

Comprehension generally precedes production throughout phonological acquisition (Ingram, 1989). Phonological organization, however, begins after the child's acquisition of the first words. There is considerable development and refinement of the phonological system throughout the preschool period. Processes of simplification (as illustrated above) gradually drop out as the system matures.

Phonological Problems

Children with disordered phonological development may present with a set of persisting processes which are similar to those observed in normal development. This means they often continue to use simplifying processes long after these have been dropped by normal children. The result of this persistence is a phonological system in which very early processes coexist with later ones. Other patterns may present: chronological mismatch, unusual/idiosyncratic processes, variable use of processes, systematic sound preferences (Grunwell, 1985). Ingram (1989) describes the phonological disorders as substitutions, omissions, and additions and the aim of analysis as identifying the rules that lie behind them. It is possible to identify at least two types of functional articulation disorders, that is cases where there is no noticeable organic reason for a child's speech to be abnormal. There are those cases in which the child's problem is solely located in the production side – in planning and executing articulatory movements. Ingram (1989) calls these *phonetic difficulties*. There are also children who have an inadequate or deviant phonological system: these organizational difficulties are referred to as *phonemic difficulties*. As one example, children in this latter group may not produce a sound correctly when it is required yet may use that sound as a substitute for another.

If the child's difficulty is only on the output side (that is, in phonology-motor translation) then there are no direct syntactic implications. However, there may be problems with the articulation of particular sounds which have implications for syntax (for instance, inflections may be absent), or words may be combined in an unusual fashion as in *outsidein*. However, central representational problems present in cases of phonemic difficulties are likely to create syntactic difficulties because the input received by the syntactic representation system is likely to be impoverished. For example, many words can have a suffix added to form a new word of a different grammatical class as when *collide* becomes *collision*. In such cases complex phonological changes often occur, which are likely to be impeded among children with phonemic difficulties. We therefore expect phonological and syntactic difficulties will often co-exist.

The Lexicon and Semantics

Words are the basic units of language. They convey meaning in their own right and they can be combined together to create sentences. The store of words that a child acquires makes up the child's vocabulary or lexicon. During childhood the rate of vocabulary acquisition is astonishing. It has been estimated that from the end of the child's first year until 5 or 6 years of age some ten new words a day are acquired on average (Miller, 1986; Miller and Gildea, 1986).

There are two quite distinct aspects of lexical acquisition. The first concerns the relation between the word and the world, which is the child's acquisition of word meanings. The second concerns the way in which the internal structure of a word can be modified, which is the child's acquisition of morphology.

Acquiring the meaning of a new word can be an extended process lasting many months and in some cases years. No one teaches the child ten new words a day. Nor are words learned in a one-off fashion. Children's early word meanings are sometimes not the same as adult meanings (Clark, 1983). For example, children sometimes overextend the range of objects or actions to which a new word can refer. One child used the word *strangle* to refer to a hand tightening action around any part of her body, such as arm and leg, as well as the conventional action around the neck.

Acquiring the meaning of a new word involves realizing what objects in the world the new word refers to and developing a representation of the ways in which various words are connected or distinguished within the language system. The task of learning the meanings of new words is supported by the experience and knowledge that children bring to the task at hand (Dockrell and Campbell, 1986). The breadth of the child's experience will influence the size of the lexicon.

Learning a new word is the process of associating the word with an existing concept. Concepts are the mental categories by which we organize experience. Human cognition makes use of a wide range of concepts of different types and levels of generality. Many of these concepts are learned independently of language. Concepts of everyday objects, properties, and actions are the most basic for language because it is with these concepts that individual words are associated. There is a level of generality, called the basic level (Rosch et al., 1976), at which humans prefer to form concepts. Most common names refer to objects at this level. Unless the child is presented with strong evidence to the contrary, new words will be associated with basic level objects.

Morphology is the study of the internal structure of words and the ways in which this structure is affected by other words. Some aspects of morphology are controlled by syntactic considerations, such as adding -s to nouns to express the plural or -ed to verbs to express the past tense. This is called *inflectional morphology*. Other aspects are regarded as purely lexical, such as the way in which the noun *imagination* is a derivative of the verb *imagine*. This is called *derivational morphology*. Once a word has been derived, it functions in its own right. However, with inflectional morphology, the decision whether or not to add the inflection must be made each time that a sentence is generated. Thus, children must master inflectional morphology in order to carry on the day-to-day task of communication. Children's early utterances are free of inflectional morphemes, which gives two-word speech its telegraphic appearance. Inflections such as the plural morpheme -s on nouns and the progressive morpheme -ing and the past tense morpheme -ed on verbs are acquired during the preschool years (R. Brown, 1973; McShane and Whittaker, 1988; McShane et al., 1986). Once acquired, inflections themselves can be the basis of learning the syntactic category of a novel word (Dockrell and McShane, 1990). Thus, the occurrence of -ing as a suffix is sufficient to allow the child to categorize a novel word as a verb.

Lexical and Semantic Problems

One of the hallmarks of language difficulties is the late emergence of words. Children with language difficulties are slower at learning new words than children of a similar language age (Rice et al., 1990). It is not clear at present what processes are responsible for this but one possibility, which we shall discuss below, is that learning is slower because new words are not retained for a sufficient amount of time in working memory.

Speech-language pathologists and special educators often encounter children who experience 'word-finding' difficulties. These difficulties are readily apparent in conversation. Such difficulties are often first suspected on the basis of behaviours such as frequent and pronounced hesitations, circumlocution, use of filler items such as *uh*, and the overuse of indefinite terms. Byers Brown and Edwards (1989) suggest that children manifest these problems in two different ways: some children who have difficulty in retrieving lexical items appear quiet and non-communicative because of the sparseness of spoken language, while others who have similar word finding difficulties appear almost garrulous because they use a variety of conversation fillers in their efforts to retrieve words.

Word-finding difficulties are often measured using structured naming tasks. For example Wiig et al. (1982) found that 8-year-old language 'impaired' children made more errors than age matched controls despite being able both to select the correct picture when given a name and to produce the correct names in a delayed imitation task. Generally children with word finding difficulties have good comprehension.

What processing problems might account for such difficulties? The most common explanation postulates that such children have difficulties accessing the word from memory. Since children with word finding difficulties are able to perform recognition tasks correctly the word must be stored in memory. However, recognition tasks require less processing than recalling an item. A recognition task requires a simple matching response. By contrast, recall requires the child to identify the object or action to be named, access the appropriate semantic domain and choose the correct item. Kail and Leonard (1986) suggest that there are other factors than the process of accessing the word that cause problems for these children. They focus on the types of representations that these children have within semantic domains. They suggest that children with word-finding difficulties have less elaborate representations of the word than normal children, which would make it harder for the child to find the relevant word for a given concept. This has direct implications for intervention.

Rather than requiring training on retrieval strategies they suggest that children require training that provides a more detailed representation of the meaning of the word.

Words often need to be inflected to indicate such things as number or tense. Children with language difficulties frequently have problems with these aspects of language. As we have pointed out, these problems may often accompany phonological difficulties, but they can also occur in the absence of phonological difficulties. We shall discuss these below in relation to syntactic problems.

Syntactic Structure

Syntax is the set of principles that determine how words can be combined together in a grammatical fashion. For syntactic purposes words are classified into parts of speech such as nouns and verbs, and there are rules that determine how these parts can be combined together to form phrases and sentences. Syntax governs such things as the order of words in a sentence, the role of functional words, such as articles, and the ways in which content words are inflected. The major tasks for the child in acquiring a grammar are to learn to treat words as members of a grammatical category and to learn the legitimate ways of combining grammatical categories.

Children begin to combine words together towards the end of the second year (McShane, 1980). This development marks the beginning of the use of words to qualify each other; the child has now begun to build relations between words. Thus a dog is no longer just *dog* but *more dog* or *black dog* and so on. These early word combinations seem to be lexical combinations – that is to say the words are combined on the basis of the meaning of the individual words rather than on the basis of grammatical principles (Braine, 1976). At this point the child's language lacks all grammatical inflections – *two duck* will be said instead of *two ducks* – and grammatical function words – *book table* will be said instead of *the book is on the table*. The addition of these grammatical elements begins between the ages of two and three years. This marks the true beginnings of the acquisition of syntax.

Average sentence length increases throughout the preschool

years, from just above one word at 2 years to four words at 3.5 years and eight words by 6 years. Of more importance than the length is the gradual mastery of syntactic structure. There are many aspects to this, of which we shall mention a few: the use of articles before nouns; the use of prepositions to indicate direction and location; the way in which verbs can be modified to indicate different tenses; and the control of the ordering of words in a sentence by the phrase-structure rules of syntax.

Syntactic Problems

Recently, Clahsen (1989; 1991) and Leonard (1989) have described the linguistic characteristics of children with grammatical problems. In general the language of these children has normal ordering of the phrases in a sentence. However, within a phrase the non-content words are often missing. Thus, in the sentence *the dog chased the cat*, the definite article *the* may be omitted. Inflections on content words may also be omitted. Thus, the -*ed* on *chased* might be omitted by a child with syntactic problems. The sentence above might then be produced as *dog chase cat*. In addition, these children frequently have difficulty with auxiliary verbs such as *be, have*, and *do* in constructions such as *he is working, he has worked*, and *he did not work*.

Leonard (1989) suggests that the difficulty that these children experience in the acquisition of the grammatical morphemes such as determiners, inflections, and auxiliary verbs may possibly be traced back to problems in phonological processing. He argues that the morphemes that the children fail to produce all have 'low phonetic-substance' in that they are unstressed syllables of shorter duration than adjacent morphemes. If children with syntactic difficulties have difficulty in perceiving low phonetic-substance morphemes in the input that they receive, then this will hinder their acquisition of selective aspects of grammar, although other aspects will be unaffected.

This finding is consistent with some well-established experimental findings reported by Tallal and Piercy (1978). They found that perception of speech sounds such as consonants and vowels was poorer for children with language difficulties than for normal children. Of particular relevance was the fact that a major difficulty was caused by sounds of brief duration. Tallal and Piercy argued that the source of the difficulty was an impairment in auditory processing. This locates the difficulty at an earlier stage than Leonard (1989) suggests. However, the effect will be the same: children will have syntactic difficulties because they have problems in processing sounds that are brief and unstressed in a neighbourhood of longer more highly stressed sounds.

However, not all syntactic problems originate from earlier stages of processing. Some children seem to have a very poor knowledge of syntactic structure. This was demonstrated by Van der Lely (1990), who compared on two tasks the ability of a group of children with language difficulties with younger children who had similar language abilities. One task required the child to infer the meaning of a new verb when the action was demonstrated. Thus, the children were shown an action and told 'this is mooking' and were then asked to explain what mooking was. The groups did not differ in their abilities to do this. However, when the new word was introduced within the context of a sentence without the benefit of a demonstration of the action to which it referred, as in 'the dog voozes the cat', the children with language difficulties were poorer than the control subjects at making up some meaning for the word and acting out an interpretation. Van der Lely argued that her results showed that the children with language difficulties had a specific difficulty in using syntactic information as a guide to meaning, which normal children can do without difficulty (Dockrell and McShane, 1990).

Pragmatics

Words and sentences have to be used in the right way to be communicatively effective. It is perfectly possible for a sentence to be syntactically well-formed but for it to fail to make sense in context. This is a pragmatic failure.

Pragmatics concerns the interface between language as a system and the goals and intentions of human communication. On the production side, pragmatics concerns our abilities to make our intentions clear through the medium of speech. On the comprehension side, pragmatics concerns our abilities to infer the speaker's intention in making an utterance. For example, the utterance *Is the window open?* could be a question or a request to close a window that the speaker and his audience both know to be open. Pragmatics thus encompasses rules of conversation or discourse. Children must learn how to initiate conversations, take turns, maintain and change topics, and provide the appropriate amount of information in a clear manner.

It should be evident that pragmatic difficulties can arise for a variety of reasons. Difficulties with the language system can lead to pragmatic failures of communication. But it is also the case that difficulties elsewhere in the cognitive system can lead to failures to understand the way in which a hearer makes inferences about intentions. This will result in a failure to take appropriate account of the listener's perspective in producing utterances.

The development of pragmatic skills begins before the use of language itself (McShane, 1980). Becoming an effective conversationalist is an extended process. At age 2 years children's abilities to participate in sustained conversation is limited; they rarely continue a conversation beyond two turns. Further development of pragmatic skills can be regarded from both a general and a more specifically linguistic perspective. From a general perspective we can study the development of the ability to understand how other minds work and to take account of this in communication. From a linguistic perspective we can study the development of specific verbal strategies for communicating intentions.

Pragmatic Problems

Some children with language difficulties have been described as having a semantic–pragmatic disorder (Bishop and Rosenbloom, 1987) or a conversational disability (Conti-Ramsden and Gunn, 1986). Children with such difficulties may have a good mastery of the formal aspects of language but conversation does not flow smoothly, because they express themselves in an odd fashion, produce unexpected utterances and seem unaware of the conversational needs of their partner.

Fey and Leonard (1987) review five areas of pragmatics which are of particular concern for children with language difficulties: conversational participation, speech acts, discourse regulation, code switching, and referential skills. They identify three sets of problems noted in these children:

- they are unresponsive
- they place over-reliance on back-channel responses, such as an *uhm* or a nod, made by the listener to indicate the degree to which messages are understood
- their communication may be impaired because they lack specific discourse devices such as question forms

The recent identification of semantic-pragmatic problems has raised a number of important questions for researchers and clinicians. First, it is important to assess the type and extent of the communication problems experienced by these children. Second, the extent to which such problems are the consequence of other specific language impairments must be considered. Finally, it is necessary to consider the extent to which these children's difficulties reflect a delay (that is, their performance is equivalent to younger children) or a deviant pattern of development. Work by Bishop and Adams (Adams and Bishop, 1989; Bishop and Adams, 1989) has gone some way to answering these questions.

Adams and Bishop analysed conversations between children and an adult. There were three different groups: children with semantic-pragmatic problems, children with other language difficulties, and normal children. They make the important point that the population of children with specific language problems is no more homogeneous with respect to pragmatic skills than it is with respect to semantic, syntactic, or phonological abilities. Moreover, their study suggests that conversational problems cannot simply be explained as an inevitable concomitant of expressive language impairment. Children with the most severe impairment in terms of expressive abilities were not those with the most immature or abnormal conversational skills. They note that in comparison with the two control groups, children with pragmatic problems did not generate a high rate of utterances in conversation with an adult. However, they did produce a high rate of initiations and this was shown to be a stable and abnormal conversational characteristic. The adults interacting with the children had significant problems in following the conversation and there was a frequent need for clarification. An example from our own work will help illustrate the case:

> James was talking with an adult about home. The adult asked James whether he lived in a house or a flat. James replied *A flat.* The adult then asked *Which floor do you live on?* James responded with a blank expression. The adult then asked *Do you live on the ground floor or do you have to walk up stairs?* James replied *I live in a flat.* The adult again asked *Yes but which floor? Is there a lift or are there stairs?* James replied *My floor has lovely carpets in all the rooms.*

In a second study (Bishop and Adams, 1989) an attempt was made to explore in greater detail what was inappropriate about the children's utterances. A wide range of semantic, syntactic, and pragmatic peculiarities were identified as leading to a sense of inappropriateness. Bishop and Adams claimed that the children's conversational style was not just immature for their years but included some conversational features that are not normal at any age. In addition there were examples in which the oddness of the conversation seemed less a matter of poor pragmatic skills than a reflection of underlying disturbances in the cognitive system. Whether or not this is the case remains to be established.

Problems Beyond the Language System

The language system does not exist in isolation from the rest of the cognitive system. It is possible that some language difficulties may be due to problems that arise in the non-linguistic processes on which the language system draws. In this section we shall consider three possible sources of non-linguistic difficulty: auditory processing, working memory, and general cognitive processes.

Auditory Processing

A number of writers have proposed that some specific language difficulties are caused by problems in processing the auditory input (Eisenson, 1972; Stark and Tallal, 1988). Tallal and her associates have found that children with language difficulties are poor at processing rapid or brief auditory stimuli such as tones or speech sounds (Tallal and Piercy, 1978; Tallal and Stark, 1981). This problem only occurred for auditory stimuli. When visual stimuli were used there was no difference between children with language difficulties and controls (Tallal, 1976). With auditory stimuli, the language difficulties group performed better than a group of younger controls when the interval between stimuli was long but when it was short, they performed worse (Tallal, 1976). This type of difficulty in processing the auditory input could result in a degraded signal being available for phonological representation. Consistent with this, Frumkin and Rapin (1980) showed that children who had phonological difficulties had poor auditory discrimination when stimuli were presented rapidly while children with normal phonology but with difficulties on other aspects of language, performed normally on these tasks. However, the latter group performed poorly on other auditory discrimination tasks. This suggests that there may be different types of auditory processing problems contributing to different types of language problems.

Working Memory

Gathercole and Baddeley (1989) showed that individual variation in normal children's short-term storage of phonological material in working memory was a predictor of vocabulary scores. This suggests that a poor or reduced ability to store information in working memory could be a contributory factor in language difficulties. To test this, Gathercole and Baddeley (1990) studied the performance of a group of children with language difficulties on a variety of memory tests. The children were aged between 7 and 9 years at the time of the study and had age-appropriate non-verbal intelligence. On a variety of language measures they had age-equivalent scores between one and two years below their chronological age. They were matched with two control groups: a chronological age matched group and a language age matched group. The chronological age matched group had the same non-verbal abilities, but superior verbal abilities. The language age matched group had the same vocabulary and reading skills as the children with language difficulties.

Gathercole and Baddeley found that the children with language difficulties performed less well than either control group on a task that required immediate recall of non-words. The fact that the children with language difficulties were poorer than the younger language age matched controls is of particular significance. Gathercole and Baddeley then investigated a number of possible reasons for the difference, including whether it derived from an impaired ability to analyse the acoustic input. On these tests they found no differences in the processes used by the different groups. They concluded that the children with language difficulties could retain less material in the phonological store of their working memory and suggested that this may affect the formation of a stable representation of an initially novel sound sequence in long-term memory.

Cognitive Processes

A very common hypothesis about language difficulties is that they reflect impairments in more general cognitive processes. A large number of hypotheses have been investigated about the relation between cognition and language (see Bishop, 1992; Cromer, 1991, for reviews). Many have resulted in negative rather than positive conclusions about the causal role of cognitive processes. Even when results have been positive, the methodology used has not usually been sufficiently strong to establish a causal relation. Showing that there is a correlation between poor performance on a cognitive task and a language difficulty is not sufficient to establish that the cognitive process is causally involved in language difficulties. The direction of causation could be the other way round – delayed language could be the cause of delays in cognition. To rule out this possibility, it is necessary to use a control group of younger normal children matched for language ability.

Kamhi et al. (1984) proposed that language difficulties might be due to general problems in hypothesis testing and concept formation. To test this, they compared the performance of a group of children with language difficulties and a group of normal children on a concept formation task. They found no difference between the groups. In a further study of hypothesis-testing ability (Kamhi et al., 1985), there was again no difference between

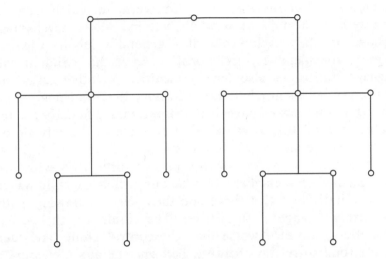

Figure 3.2   *Pattern used by R. F. Cromer to study hierarchical planning in the drawings of children with language difficulties.*
(Source: Cromer, 1983)

the groups. However, they carried out one further test (Nelson et al., 1987), which did find a difference between the groups. Despite this, the weight of the evidence suggests that a difficulty in hypothesis-testing ability is not a major cause of language difficulties.

Cromer (1978) noted that many sequentially ordered behaviours, including language, have hierarchical structure. This means that there are important structural relations between non-adjacent items as, for example, in the syntax of language. Cromer proposed that there might be a general hierarchical planning ability, which underlies a number of skills, including language structure. Cromer (1983) asked children to copy patterns of the type shown in figure 3.2. Children with language difficulties were less likely than a control group of deaf children to use hierarchical planning in their reproductions. However, these groups were not matched on verbal skills, and therefore the causal implications of the findings are not clear.

At a more general level, it has often been proposed that language difficulties are due to general difficulties in processing symbols of any type. Much of the research on this issue has been conducted within the Piagetian framework, in which language is viewed as one type of symbolic activity, whose development depends on the development of a general symbolic capacity. There is considerable correlational evidence that children with language difficulties also have difficulties on other tasks that require symbol manipulation (see Bishop, 1992) but none of the existing studies has employed an appropriate methodology to test whether the relation is causal. One example of the relation between language and cognitive processing, is Kamhi et al. (1984), which compared children with language difficulties with controls matched on mental age, on a task on which the child was required blindly to feel a shape and then select a drawing of the shape from a range of alternatives. The children with language difficulties performed worse than the control group, and there was a strong correlation between performance and a measure of receptive vocabulary. Kamhi et al. speculated that the relation arose because of common demands the tasks made on generating and interpreting symbolic representations.

Implications of a Processing Model of Language Difficulties

Although it is likely that factors outside the language system may be implicated in some language difficulties, the primary difficulty is in the comprehension and production of speech. It is these difficulties that we must seek to understand in greater detail if progress is to be maintained in understanding language difficulties.

A processing model of language difficulties requires that the language system be treated as a series of components that may be impaired to a greater or lesser extent rather than as a single system. This type of analysis allows us to dissociate the development of different components and has direct implications for classification procedures and our understanding of development.

Classification

At the beginning of this chapter we highlighted the need to constrain the proliferation of new syndromes. Given the heterogeneity

Table 3.2   *Good outcome at 5.5 years as a function of language difficulties experienced at 4 years reported by Bishop and Edmundson (1987a).*

Type of difficulty	Good Outcome
Pure phonological impairment	78%
Impairment restricted to phonology, syntax, and morphology	56%
All expressive functions impaired	13%
Receptive–expressive disorder	14%
Other	33%

of language difficulties it is difficult to devise a classification system that does justice to the various factors involved in the difficulty. At present there is still insufficient known about language difficulties for definitive classification to be possible.

Nevertheless, it is necessary for intervention purposes to attempt to determine which children have difficulties in common and are therefore likely to respond to a particular type of intervention. The best way to achieve this is to classify children on the basis of different manifestations of language problems and then to test the relative effectiveness of different types of intervention with the different groups. Effectively, what is required is a profile across the language components. This means that assessment techniques must be oriented towards differentiating among children on the basis of their processing difficulties. It also means that if a particular intervention strategy is effective with some but not all children within a particular group, then the classification, and the assessment techniques, are in need of further refinement.

We have seen in considering the information processing involved in language that there is a theoretical reason to distinguish expressive difficulties alone from difficulties with both the receptive and expressive aspects of language. Further differentiation within the language system itself can be made such as between phonological and syntactic problems. Using distinctions similar to these Bishop and Edmundson (1987a) have found that the likelihood of a good outcome varies as a function of the child's difficulties as table 3.2 shows. This suggests that the distinctions drawn are a useful basis from which to begin relating processing to intervention. But there is another aspect of the data that we must also consider: the outcome was not uniform for all children with a particular difficulty. For example, the outcome for children with a pure phonological impairment was much better than for other difficulties *for most children*. But there remains a residual group who exhibited a pure phonological impairment for whom the outcome was not good. The challenge remains to distinguish children who are likely to have persisting problems from those whose disorders are likely to be transient.

Delay Versus Disorder

A processing model of language highlights the difficulty of trying to make a simplistic distinction between delay and disorder. A delay in one component may make overall language appear deviant because of the interaction between the components. Further research is needed to establish the value of such a distinction. The key may be whether the notion of delay versus disorder has implications for the type of intervention required.

The distinction between a delayed or deviant language system has been considered by clinicians for a number of years. Menyuk (1975) outlined three explanations of different patterns of language development: some aspects of language may be acquired at a later stage than normal; some may be acquired differently from normal; some may not be acquired at all. She also drew attention to the role that compensatory mechanisms may play: some children's language may appear deviant because they are compensating for a delay. In the area of phonology, Ingram (1989: 163) points out the difficulties in distinguishing between delay and disorder because 'we have yet to establish what normal children may or may not be able to do and therefore cannot claim unique differences for disordered children.' The same point could be made in relation to the other components of the language system. Thus, while the logical distinction between a delay and a disorder is clear enough, it is extremely difficult at present to apply it in a satisfactory way to language difficulties because of our limited understanding of how the language system works. Given the range of variability that exists in the normal process of acquiring language, it may be that conceptualizing language difficulties in terms of a simple dichotomy between delay and disorder is far too simplistic to do justice to the issue.

Assessment and Intervention

Two central tenets need to guide the approach to language assessment and intervention. In the first instance it must be accepted that there is no complete and satisfactory model of language processing. Much remains to be learned but current models can serve to constrain the analysis of children's language problems. Secondly, there is no single overriding deficit that accounts for the problems experienced by *all* language impaired children. Thus, assessment must be driven both by knowledge of the child and knowledge of the language system.

As we have argued, children with language difficulties present a varied set of problems to the clinician. The child must be the primary focus of any assessment. This assessment should be informed by a processing model of the language system. In addition one needs to consider the role of the environment in modifying the acquisition process. There is some evidence that the input that a child receives can alter certain aspects of the language system. However, given the many different situations in which children receive input it is unlikely, except in extreme situations (Skuse, 1984), that variation will be the primary cause of a child's language difficulty. In fact, one of the major problems in attempting to intervene in cases of language difficulty is the fact that we do not normally have to teach children to talk in the way that we teach them to read and write. Thus, when children have difficulty in acquiring even the most basic language it is hard to know where to begin to teach them.

Assessment

The first task for the clinician when confronted with a child is to establish that the child is actually experiencing a language problem and to identify what this problem is. Norm-referenced tests and checklists can help suggest avenues of exploration which need to be pursued. The second step is to describe the child's linguistic skills. A principled approach is needed to direct this stage of the assessment. The method of description should be effective in demonstrating the child's system of rules and the complexity of the structures that have been acquired. Although it is possible to group children according to their overall pattern of language performance, to a certain extent every child represents a unique pattern of language abilities. Priorities must be set since it will not be possible to describe all aspects of the child's language skills in detail. A preliminary step is to focus on those aspects that are most debilitating to the child.

How one elicits the language sample is important. Bloom and Lahey (1978) point out that the most frequently suggested sampling contexts have focused on describing pictures, talking about toys, or responding to probes by an interviewer. The context in which language samples are collected is important because a child is not equally productive across contexts. Longhurst and Grubb (1974) investigated the effect of various contexts on the language sample obtained. They found that less structured conversational settings elicited more, and more complex, language than structured task-oriented settings or pictures, and that pictures were least effective. Lee (1974) has also reported that younger normal children used more spontaneous speech when presented with toys than with pictures.

Shriberg and Kwiatowski (1980) identify a problem with most articulation tests. They demonstrate that most of these tests typically use words that are relatively complex when compared with the words children usually use in their spontaneous speech. Thus, the children are placed at a disadvantage. They argue that for phonological analysis one should rely completely on spontaneous samples.

Assessments should lead to providing management alternatives. These management alternatives should be continuously reviewed as intervention proceeds. Thus, assessment becomes an integral part of intervention since one is continuously reevaluating one's initial assessments and the impact of various interventions.

Intervention

There are no clear guidelines as to when a child should begin therapy. The general consensus is as early as possible but there is little evaluation work to substantiate this claim. There is a range of intervention procedures (see Lees and Urwin, 1991, for examples). However, there is little work which evaluates the impact of timing of therapy, the influence of different types of therapy or whether certain types of problems are likely to be more persistent than others.

The output transcribed from a particular child is the product of complex interacting components; any one of these or a combination may be a source of the child's difficulties. Theoretically, the clinician's aim should be to move in the direction of therapy that teaches strategies enabling a child to extract rules and processes rather than just giving lots of examples of rules to practise; though the skill built up by practice must not be ignored. When the child has a language disorder it is clear that he cannot learn in the usual fashion from the environment. Language cannot be taught but it can be facilitated by creating conditions which support language use. Compensatory strategies can be taught where facilitation is not enough. Crystal (1985) has provided important general principles for language remediation and stressed the need for an individualized approach.

The emphasis must be on language and language related skills. The strategies the child learns should be applicable to processing language in normal contexts. If, for example, the focus of intervention is auditory discrimination, the emphasis should not be on simple sound discrimination, such as bells from drums, but on discriminating the type of content that will occur in language. Content is one parameter. The sequencing of the content, pacing, context and reinforcement will also need to be addressed.

One of the most important questions that needs to be addressed is whether the skills acquired in therapy or teaching settings generalize to other situations. Yet this issue is often not addressed by interventions. Leonard (1981) reviewed intervention studies over the previous 18 years. Of the 32 studies he considered, only 5 measured the occurrence of generalization and none attempted to investigate how to make generalization occur. There is a variety of ways in which the issue of generalization can be addressed (see chapter 7).

Summary

The major points of this chapter are: first, that an analysis of language difficulties must concentrate on *language*, and second that language processes are very imperfectly understood at present. We have emphasized the relevance and importance of models of language processing to models of language difficulties. There is still a great deal to be discovered both about normal language development and about language difficulties. Proposing and testing models of language processing with both normal children and with children who experience difficulties is the best way to make these discoveries. On present evidence, it makes most sense to consider the language system as a series of interacting components. A child's difficulty may be more severe in one component than another, but because of the interaction of the components it is likely that most children will exhibit a pattern of difficulty across several components. These interactions suggest that profiles of language difficulties may be more useful than classification into categories.

4
Specific Difficulties with Reading

Overview

We begin by discussing the varying estimates of the prevalence of reading difficulties and some of the reasons for variation. We then discuss the distinctions that have been drawn between different types of difficulty. Reading involves two fundamental processes: the recognition of words, which is usually called decoding, and the comprehension of what is recognized. We first discuss how reading skills develop in normal children. We then consider three types of deficit that have been proposed to account for decoding difficulties: perceptual deficits, phonological processing deficits, and memory deficits. Following this we consider a number of factors that affect text comprehension and consider their relevance to comprehension difficulties. Finally, we consider issues of assessment and intervention in cases of reading difficulty.

Reading and Reading Difficulties

Reading consists of a complex set of skills, which include recognizing printed words, determining the meaning of words and phrases, and coordinating this meaning with the general theme of the text. This requires processes that operate on many different levels of representation, including letters, words, phrases, sentences, and larger units of text. Reading difficulties typically involve a failure either to recognize or to comprehend written material. Recognition is the more basic of these processes, since a word must be recognized before it can be comprehended. Comprehension difficulties are not usually at the level of individual words but rather at the level of phrases, sentences, and integration of information across sentences (Oakhill and Garnham, 1988).

Perhaps more than other specific learning difficulties, reading difficulties hamper educational progress in a wide variety of areas because reading is the access route to a wide range of information. Failure to learn to read in the early school years effectively locks the child out of much of the remainder of the school curriculum. For example, the presentation of arithmetical problems in the school curriculum occurs largely through the written medium. If a child has reading problems then it is very likely that this will hamper the child's arithmetical progress. In fact, the co-occurrence of reading and arithmetical difficulties is common (Rutter et al., 1970). Reading difficulties will also adversely affect the acquisition of knowledge beyond the curriculum. This in its turn adversely affects reading comprehension, which draws considerably on one's general knowledge. In short, reading difficulties create a vicious circle (Butkowsky and Willows, 1980). Box 4.1 presents an illustration of the problems that may be experienced and an indication that, with help, motivation and progress can be improved.

Prevalence

Estimates of the prevalence of reading difficulties vary, depending on the definition of a difficulty, the measurement instrument used, and the geographical area sampled. A commonly used measure is a discrepancy between reading age and chronological age. However, this measure is rather crude because the distribution of reading scores is different at different ages. Gaddes (1976) has shown that if a uniform definition of a two-year gap between reading age and chronological age is used, this will lead to a wide variation in the reported prevalence of reading problems

March 8th

Dear Mr Pumfrey.
I am ten. I did not injoy life until
I got hellp because the techer say
(thinking they no evrything) you
are lase and norty...
    Now I am haveinghellp
I can rit letters and storys and
eneyfing I wont to. But speling is
stil a lital bit difacelt.
    I fink evre scool have a speshal
techer tat thchis chririn to try and
get rid of ther Broblem. When the
techer told me to rit I wood sit
thon and antil it got difelcett
and sumthing alluay cort my
alenchon and I wood mes a round
and get told off ond I did not
liok life then.
    I have riton a book and I have
folocopeed it for you. I am going
to rit a Book and it is about two
mice that go to the city and met
ampcooth   Love
                From
                    Sachary

Box 4.1 *A letter written by a 10–year-old child with literacy difficulties.*
(Source: Pumfrey and Reason, 1991)

as a function of age. Using results from a population tested with the Wide Range Achievement Test, Gaddes showed that if two years are subtracted from the reading level of 6-year-olds, less than 1 per cent of the population would be considered to have a reading difficulty; at age 7 the proportion would rise to 2 per cent, and would continue to increase until the age of 19, when 25 per cent would be considered to have a reading difficulty. Other measures compare reading age with mental age, or measure the discrepancy between reading scores predicted on the basis of IQ and those obtained, while allowing for regression effects (Yule and Rutter, 1976). Given the differences among criteria, measurements, and populations, it is not surprising to find wide variation in the reported prevalence of reading difficulties.

Probably the most thorough study of the prevalence of reading difficulties is that conducted by Rutter et al. (1970) on the Isle of Wight on the whole population of 9- to 11-year-olds. This study found that 6.6 per cent of the sample were 'backward readers', which was defined as a score on the Neale Analysis of Reading Ability test that was 28 months or more below chronological age on either accuracy or comprehension. Some backward readers, however, would have had reading skills consistent with their mental age, while others would have had scores that were below their mental age scores. Rutter et al. called this latter group 'retarded readers'. Retarded readers had scores on either accuracy or comprehension that were 28 months below the score predicted on the basis of their IQ. Rutter et al. found that 3.7 per cent of the sample were retarded readers, of whom the vast majority (88 per cent) were also backward readers. A study conducted in an inner London borough using the same questionnaire found rates that were twice as high as the Isle of Wight: 19.0 per cent were backward readers and 9.9 per cent were retarded readers (Berger et al., 1975). In a further report Rutter et al. (1975b) identified several environmental factors that were associated with specific reading retardation and that differentiated the London and the Isle of Wight samples.

Other studies of the prevalence of reading difficulties have used different criteria and reported different results. Summarizing a large number of studies Tansley and Panckhurst (1981: 178) presented the following conclusion:

There is a tendency for estimates to cluster around three levels: the highest level, running from about 20 per cent upwards, which is a very general category of which reading difficulty is one aspect, a middle group clustering around 5 to 15 per cent, depending on the precise criterion used, but including both backward and retarded readers, and a 'hard core' group of children with severe and specific reading and associated difficulties, comprising about 2 to 5 per cent. This is borne out by both British and world-wide studies, with the exception of China and Japan, whose very different writing systems put them in a separate category.... On the whole, there is a fairly even spread of incidence over the entire range of school-age children, with perhaps slightly different emphasis at the different ages. There is a tendency for studies of secondary school pupils to be aimed at determining more general reading backwardness, thus arriving at estimates ranging between 10–30 per cent. Most studies have concentrated on the age range 8 to 11, and there is considerable variation in the incidence figures given for this group, from 3 to 28 per cent, but with a greater stress on the distinction between severely retarded readers and generally backward readers, giving the usual clusters of from 2 to 5 per cent of retarded readers and between 5 and 25 per cent for the rest. There are necessarily fewer studies of the lower age range (5 to 7) as these children are still at the beginning age of learning to read and it is difficult to be sure of their relative success or failure. On the whole, the incidence for this group tends to range from 4 to 15 per cent, depending on the definitions and criteria used.

Varieties of Reading Difficulty

Do all children who have difficulty learning to read experience the same difficulty, or is there a variety of different types of difficulty? Surprisingly, perhaps, there is not a very clear answer to this question.

One group that is often distinguished is children said to be dyslexic. In addition to having a reading difficulty, dyslexic children must meet a number of other criteria, designed to rule out possible explanations for their reading difficulty. These criteria therefore function to *exclude* children for whom any of the possible explanations apply. A typical list of criteria cited by Vellutino (1979) is:

- An IQ of 90 or above on either the verbal or performance scale of the Wechsler Intelligence Scale for Children
- Adequate sight and hearing
- Absence of severe neurological or physical disability
- Absence of significant emotional or social problems
- Not socioeconomically disadvantaged
- Adequate opportunity to learn to read

Diagnosis by exclusion rules out a variety of children from being considered dyslexic, even though they may experience similar cognitive problems in learning to read as those who meet the criteria for inclusion. A major problem with the exclusionary definition is that it does not select a group of children on the basis of similarity in the problems they experience with reading. Miles (1983) has made a notable attempt to provide positive criteria for diagnosis of dyslexia. None of the criteria he proposes is either a necessary or a sufficient condition for a child to be classified as dyslexic, but Miles claims that all dyslexic children will show some of the symptoms. However, the majority of the criteria are not measures of reading skill but of variables correlated with reading. Thus, the same criticism can be applied here as was applied to the negative criteria: we do not know whether or not children diagnosed as dyslexic have a different cognitive basis to their problem than children not so diagnosed.

The concept of dyslexia carries the implication that there is a syndrome of behaviours that distinguish dyslexia from other types of reading difficulties and it also carries the implication that the syndrome is of genetic origin. Yule and Rutter (1976; 1985) have reviewed the evidence relating to a specific syndrome of dyslexia and concluded that there is no evidence to support a single special syndrome of dyslexia as distinct from other cases of specific reading difficulty. On the matter of genetic causation Seymour (1986) has pointed out that if the cause of a reading difficulty that can be termed dyslexia is genetic, then it is unlikely to affect selectively the group of children who show a discrepancy between reading achievement and intelligence but is also likely to affect children who have more general learning difficulties in addition to a reading difficulty.

There have been many attempts to group poor readers together on the basis of their performance profiles (see Hooper and Willis, 1989, for a review). Boder (1973) proposed three distinct types of dyslexia: *dysphonetic dyslexics, dyseidetic dyslexics,* and a mixcd group. The dysphonetic dyslexics were the most common among the children that Boder studied and constituted about two-thirds of the sample. This group had some ability to recognize words as wholes but were poor at breaking words up into sounds. Both of these skills, as will be seen below, are crucial in learning to read. The dyseidetic dyslexics had the reverse strengths and weaknesses: their ability to break a word up into sounds was good but their ability to recognize words as wholes was poor. They constituted about a tenth of the children studied. The mixed group were bad at both skills. They constituted about a quarter of the children studied.

Ellis (1985) considers two ways of conceptualizing the subtypes of reading difficulties proposed by Boder. The first way assumes that the children who make up the subtypes are relatively homogeneous and that the subtypes do not overlap to any significant extent with the rest of the population. This is shown in figure 4.1A. The second way, shown in figure 4.1B, assumes that reading difficulties can be represented in terms of degrees of skill along the dimensions shown. On this model groups of children with reading difficulties of the types identified by Boder occupy extremes of the distribution, but there is no discontinuity with children who have milder forms of the same difficulty in reading.

An important study by Seymour (1986) lends support ofo the dimensional model of reading skills. He conducted a very thorough study of a group of children who had reading difficulties and a group of younger children with normal reading ability for their age. Seymour obtained a variety of measures of the children's abilities to read words of different types. He found that the normal readers did not form a homogeneous group in their profile of skills and weaknesses on the various measures used. On most of these measures the children with reading difficulties performed more poorly than their age matched peers, but the same lack of homogeneity was evident: the children with reading difficulties were not uniform in the measures on which they were poor, nor were they easily separable into different subtypes.

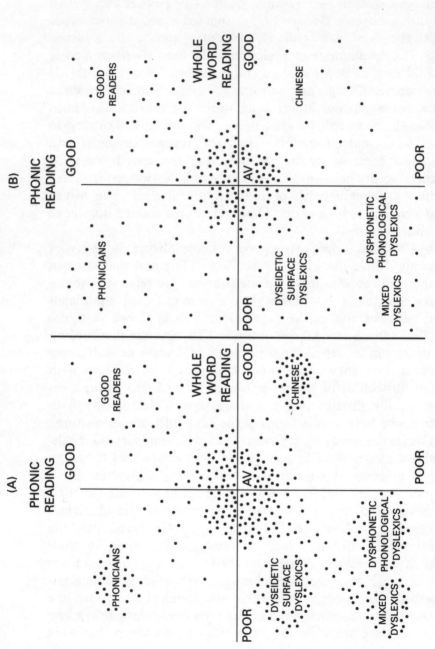

Figure 4.1 *Hypothetical distributions of the normal population of readers and populations with reading difficulties along two dimensions of reading skill on (A) a subtype and (B) a dimensional model of reading skills.* (Source: Ellis, 1985)

Different children exhibited different degrees of severity in the problems that they had experienced along a number of dimensions. Thus, although there were different profiles of difficulty, there were not distinct subtypes. Seymour concluded that the information processing system involved in reading should be regarded as a series of components, in any of which localized difficulties or inefficiencies can occur. The nature and extent of these will determine the degree of reading difficulty that a child experiences.

The Development of Reading: Identifying Words

We read both by eye and by ear. When we read by eye alone we recognize words directly; when we read by ear we transform the visual input into a phonological representation. Skilled readers recognize the vast majority of words in print directly (Henderson, 1982), but when an unusual or novel word is encountered, then it is read phonologically (Perfetti, 1985). Children learning to read are in the situation that a lot of the words they encounter are novel. Thus, it seems likely that they will place considerable reliance on using a word's phonological structure in order to read it. This process is usually referred to as *decoding* in the literature on reading development. Figure 4.2 shows a model of how written input is processed before any meaning is derived from the input.

The model shows that there are two routes by which access can be gained to the conceptual system and thereby to the meaning of a word. The first of these involves direct recognition of a word. This can be done by recognition of the complete word as a unit, or by recognition of its component letters (Johnston and McClelland, 1980). Direct recognition of a whole word, which does not necessarily require recognition of the individual letters, can be an important process in learning to read, particularly in the initial stage (Barron, 1986; Seymour and Elder, 1986). Many systems for teaching reading, in fact, begin by teaching children to recognize whole words.

However, skilled readers can read by ear as well as by eye. Reading by ear requires conversion from a written code to a speech-based code. This is the second route to the conceptual system

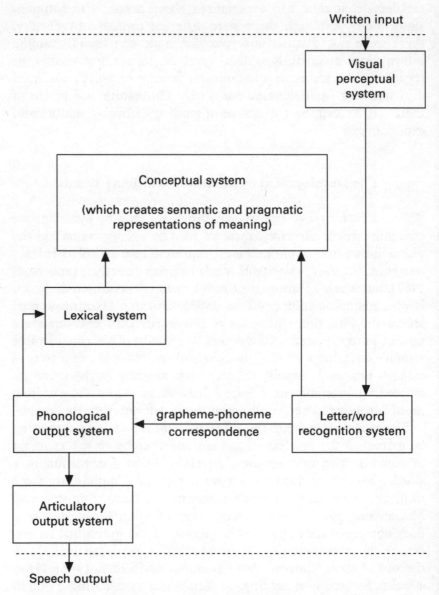

Figure 4.2 *Components involved in word recognition. The model shows that there are two routes by which the conceptual system can be accessed.*

shown in figure 4.2. Reading by ear is achieved by converting the written input to a phonological representation. The output of this process is then passed through the speech processing system and thence to the conceptual system. Figure 4.2 shows the way in which written input is processed by skilled readers. How do children arrive at this point?

Marsh et al. (1981) and Frith (1985) have proposed models of the normal process of reading development. Marsh et al. propose that children pass through a series of stages in learning to read. Frith's model proposes a sequence of strategies rather than stages, and also emphasizes the importance of the relation between reading and writing in the developmental process. The models are largely complementary, and so we shall discuss them together.

The first stage is characterized by learning to associate the visual stimulus of a whole word with the response of a spoken word. Frith calls this a logographic strategy. In terms of the model presented in figure 4.2, the child is learning to read words by direct recognition of the whole word. The assumption of initial rote learning is supported by evidence from observational studies (Torrey, 1979). A popular pedagogic method at this stage is to use 'flash cards', which present a single word on a card, to which the child is required to give an oral response. If a word is not recognized then the child will usually not respond.

The logographic strategy takes no advantage of the fact that words are built from a small number of units that can be combined and recombined in infinitely many ways. The progression towards a system that decomposes words into letters marks the next stage of development: the use of an alphabetic strategy.

The alphabetic strategy is, essentially, an elaboration of the logographic. As the size of the word set that can be recognized increases, the child comes to pay more attention to the individual letters of a word. Marsh et al. argue that the child initially only processes individual letters to the extent necessary to discriminate one word from another. The alphabetic strategy is characterized by translating from individual letters to individual sounds in decoding. With this strategy, letter order and phonological awareness play a crucial role in decoding, as they also do in Marsh et al.'s third stage. This strategy allows the reader to pronounce novel words.

The alphabetic strategy consists of simple letter–sound rules. Nevertheless, these rules bring a much greater flexibility in reading than is possible with a logographic strategy. When a new word is encountered in print, an attempt can be made to decode it phonemically. With any luck the word will be in the child's spoken vocabulary and so its meaning will be accessible. Marsh et al.'s third stage is characterized by the full-blown use of letter–sound translation in reading. Gaining access to the phonological representation of a word from its written input is probably the most important part of learning to read.

An important question for reading development is how children learn to use an alphabetic strategy. Although there is some evidence that children may naturally progress to this stage without specific phonics teaching (Barr, 1974), instruction must play a large part in further progress in view of the complex relations between orthography and phonology. A wide variety of 'phonics' teaching methods have been designed to facilitate the child's understanding of the relation between written and spoken language. Chall's (1967) detailed review suggested that these methods lead to successful reading. Experimental research on the effects of increasing children's awareness of the phonological structure of language has shown that this leads to significant advantages in reading and spelling for children who received the training over those who did not (Bradley and Bryant, 1983; Olofsson and Lundberg, 1985).

Reading does not develop in isolation. At the time that they are being taught to read, children are also being taught to spell and to write. Frith suggests that the alphabetic strategy is first adopted for spelling and writing while a logographic strategy may continue to be used for reading. Spelling requires the conversion of sounds into letters and thus practice at spelling should increase phonological awareness. However, this could, in principle, happen independently of reading. Initially it seems to do so (Bryant and Bradley, 1980). However, the act of writing what is spelled will serve to establish links between sounds and the letters that represent them. This explicit awareness of the relation, which is necessary for successful spelling and writing, can then be used in reverse to decode words while reading.

In a recent study Ellis and Cataldo (in press) provided empirical support that development in spelling affects development in reading (see also Tunmer and Nesdale, 1985). They studied the developments of reading, spelling, and of phonological awareness during the first two years at school. Obviously we would expect these skills to develop alongside each other. When skills develop in conjunction like this, it is important to try to determine what effect, if any, one is having on the other. Ellis and Cataldo took account of this in their analysis. They showed that developments in spelling ability during the first year at school had a strong influence on both improved awareness of the phonemic content of words and improvement in reading. By contrast, the contribution of developments in reading to improvements in spelling was minimal.

The fourth stage proposed by Marsh et al. builds on the third. During this stage the rules of letter–sound correspondence become context-sensitive. This constitutes what Frith calls the orthographic strategy. The orthographic strategy is one in which units larger than a single letter are recognized as wholes without individual letter by letter analysis. These units can be syllables or they can be whole words. However, the basis of whole-word recognition is now the instant recognition of letter patterns, which distinguishes it from the logographic strategy. Nevertheless, the alphabetic strategy remains available as a backup, which allows the unfamiliar to be decomposed to units that are familiar. Figure 4.3 shows an elaboration of the model presented in figure 4.2, which takes account of the developments that we have discussed.

What Causes Decoding Difficulties?

Most studies of the causes of reading difficulties have operationally defined a reading difficulty as a discrepancy between chronological age and reading age. The performance of a group thus defined has then been compared with the performance of one or more control groups. The composition of these control groups is of considerable importance in attempting to determine the causes of reading difficulties.

There have been many investigations of the causes of reading difficulties and many different causes have been reported – so many that it sometimes seems that anything can cause a reading

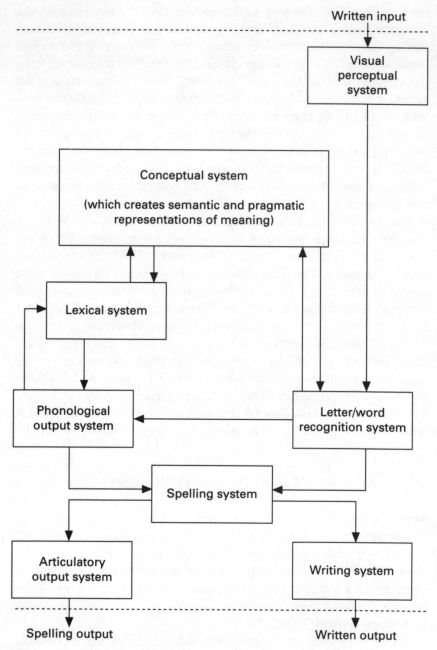

Figure 4.3 *Components involved in reading and spelling words.*

difficulty. However, this is not the case. Many studies have simply been poorly designed and have confused correlation with causation, and sometimes effect with cause. Although it is difficult to pin down definite causal factors in a single study, there are a number of requirements that, taken together, can strengthen the hypothesis that a given factor plays a causal role in reading difficulties. These include the following:

- children with reading difficulties must be shown to perform significantly worse on the factor in question than age matched controls
- it must be established that this difference is not the result of differences in reading skills
- measures of the factor in question taken before reading skills are acquired should be predictive of later reading skills
- intervention designed to improve performance on a factor presumed to be a cause of reading difficulties should lead to improved performance on reading itself

The first of these conditions is relatively straightforward to satisfy: it simply requires a comparison between a group of children with reading difficulties and a group of children of the same age who are learning to read normally. If no difference is found between these groups on the relevant factor then the hypothesis that this factor causes reading difficulties is obviously wrong. However, if a difference is found, this does not establish a causal role for the factor. It could be that the superior reading ability of the normal children is itself responsible for their superior performance on the factor we have tested. This possibility is not just a logical nicety; as we shall see below, there are a number of factors that seem to depend on the development of reading skills for their own development.

The second requirement above is designed to guard against this possibility. One way to achieve it is to compare the performance of the children with reading difficulties with a group who have the same reading ability. By doing this one can rule out the possibility that differences will be due to the two groups of children possessing different levels of reading skills. This is normally accomplished by testing a group of normal children who have the same reading age as the children with reading difficulties. Obviously this normal group will be younger. If it is found that the children with reading difficulties score more poorly on the factor hypothesized to be the cause of reading difficulties, then there is good reason to entertain a causal hypothesis, although it is not yet proven – reading and our hypothesized factor could both be under the control of some third factor, which has not been measured. Suppose, on the other hand, that there is no difference between the children with reading difficulties and the younger group of ability matched controls. What conclusions can now be drawn? None at all, unfortunately. This does not mean that the hypothesized factor can be eliminated as a possible cause of reading difficulty. Because there is an age difference between the groups, the older group of children with reading difficulties may have had the opportunity to develop some compensatory strategies to get round a real difficulty. If the two groups are using different strategies to achieve the same level of performance, then we are not comparing like with like. Thus, the ability matched comparison cannot be used to eliminate causal factors, although it can be a powerful indicator of likely causes when the reading difficulty group performs more poorly than the younger group of controls.

If there is a causal relation between some factor and reading difficulties, then it should be possible to obtain measures of performance on the factor in question before the children have learned to read and then to relate these measures to their progress in reading. Children who score poorly on the hypothesized causal factor should have greater difficulty in learning to read than children who score in the average to good range. In order to test predictive hypotheses of this sort it is necessary to carry out a different type of study from that needed to satisfy the first two requirements: it is necessary to conduct a longitudinal study, usually with a large number of children. In practice, longitudinal studies are not conducted to test a single causal hypothesis but to measure the effects of a range of factors. The children are assessed before they begin to read and are then assessed again at intervals during the succeeding years as they learn to read, with measures of reading ability added to the assessment. The initial measures can then be correlated with later measures of reading ability in order to determine which are predictive of reading ability. Suitable statistical techniques allow the researcher to determine to what extent different factors are responsible for success at learning to read. Since the initial measures were taken before the children learned to read, these studies give a clearer indication of the factors that play a causal role in the acquisition of reading skills. However, even with longitudinal studies, the causal status of any factor in the acquisition of reading skills cannot be unequivocally established. If a correlation is found between some measure taken before a child learns to read and later reading ability, then it is possible that both the initial measure and the later measure of reading are determined by a third unmeasured factor. In general, longitudinal studies cannot rule out such possibilities.

There is one final type of evidence that is relevant in relation to causes: intervention on a presumed causal factor should lead to improvements in reading performance. This type of evidence is not sufficient on its own however; reading difficulties can have negative effects on other aspects of a child's cognition, which may add to a child's delay. Intervention directed at such an effect could lead to some improvements in reading performance but this would not, of course, turn the effect into a cause of the reading difficulty.

Ultimately, establishing a factor as a cause of reading difficulties is not a simple matter. Any factor will only become compelling as a causal factor when there is a clearly-stated theoretical relation between the factor and reading and when there is convergent evidence in its favour from the different types of studies described.

Perceptual Deficits

One of the oldest theories about reading difficulties is that they are caused by a deficit in perceptual processing. This idea can be traced back to the early part of this century. Hinshelwood, a Scottish ophthalmologist, proposed in 1917 that problems in learning to read were caused by a difficulty in acquiring and storing in the brain the visual memories of words and letters. In the United States, Orton (1937) proposed that reading difficulties were due to what he called 'reversals', which could be of two types. The first type involves confusing letters with the same form but opposite orientation, such as 'b' and 'd'. The second type involved reversing, either partially or totally, the order of letters in a word as when 'was' is read as 'saw'. Orton's view encapsulates what is still a common misconception about children with reading difficulties. It is true that children with reading difficulties do sometimes make errors of reversal but so do all children, and the proportion of reversals does not differ between children with reading difficulties and those without (Vellutino, 1979).

Perceiving letters and words in reverse is just one form of perceptual deficit that has been proposed to account for reading difficulties. It would be impossible to review the various forms of the hypothesis here, but all have failed to find empirical support when tested rigorously. The evidence has been extensively reviewed by Vellutino (1979). A more recent paper (Vellutino, 1987) provides a concise summary.

The empirical evidence does not offer support for the view that reading difficulties are caused by a deficit in visual processing. One reason for the persistence of the perceptual deficit hypothesis is that studies with poor methodological designs continue to report differences between children with reading difficulties and those without. Many tests of the perceptual deficit hypothesis have employed alphabetic or linguistic stimuli, which age matched normal readers are likely to find easier to process because of their superior reading skill. As was discussed above, finding a difference in favour of age matched normal readers is not sufficient to establish a factor as a cause of reading difficulties. Studies employing reading age controls have consistently failed to find evidence for a perceptual deficit.

A more general point can be made in relation to perceptual deficit theories. If reading difficulties are caused by a perceptual deficit, then it is unlikely that this deficit will operate selectively with written material. It should therefore be possible to demonstrate the deficit with other forms of perceptual stimuli. Thus, it should be possible to demonstrate that children with reading difficulties perform less well than control groups on a task that requires perceptual abilities but does not require reading. When such experiments have been conducted the results have failed to support deficits in perceptual processing as the cause of reading difficulties. For example, Stanley (1978) investigated whether or not differences in eye movement patterns might cause reading difficulties. He found that when a reading task was used, the eye movement patterns of good and poor readers were different. However, when another task was employed, which required the children to locate a picture within a scene, there was no difference between the groups. Many other studies have similarly failed to find any evidence of a causal link between eye movements and reading (Stanovich, 1986). Thus, the differences in eye movement patterns in the reading task were the result, not the cause, of the differences in reading ability.

Ellis and Miles (1978) compared the speed with which children with reading difficulties and normal readers could judge whether pairs of letters were the same or different. This experiment is of particular interest because it employed alphabetic material but did not require the material to be read. Under these conditions there was no difference between the groups. Vellutino et al. (1973) investigated the ability of children with reading difficulties and those without to print words and letters from an unfamiliar writing system: the Hebrew alphabet. The children with reading difficulties were as good as the normal readers on this task.

The evidence is consistently against the hypothesis that children with reading difficulties have a general difficulty in processing visual information. This does not, of course, rule out the possibility that a real difficulty in processing visual information could cause reading difficulties for at least some children. What has been established is that when reading difficulties occur, they are not, in the main, the result of general perceptual deficits.

Deficits in Phonological Processing

Unlike the case of perceptual processing, there is strong evidence that phonological processing and reading ability are closely related. In this context, phonological processing refers to the use of information about the sound structure of language in processing written input. The individual letters of our writing system convey information about the sounds of our language, although the match between sounds and letters of the alphabet is far from perfect (Gleitman and Rozin, 1977).

Children must, at some point, acquire the skill of mapping the written form of a word onto its sound structure. It is generally assumed that this is done at the level of individual letter–sound correspondences, which are called *grapheme-phoneme correspondences*. Since children know many words before they begin to read, it might seem that the better their awareness of the phonemic structure of words, the easier they would find it to learn grapheme-phoneme correspondences. The only problem with this very plausible hypothesis is that children seem to have little awareness at all of the individual phonemes of a language before they begin to read, although they are aware of other units of sound, such as the syllable, which is the smallest individually pronounceable unit of a word, but may consist of a number of phonemes. Liberman et al. (1974) examined the ability of 4- to 6-year-olds to segment words by phonemes and by syllable. None of the 4-year-olds could segment by phoneme but half could segment by syllable. By age 6, 70 per cent could segment by phoneme and 90 per cent by syllable. Between 4 and 6, these children learned to read, to spell, and to write. This suggests that phonemic awareness may develop as a result of school instruction rather than precede the development of reading skills. As we suggested earlier, it seems likely that spelling and writing play the major role in bringing about phonemic awareness.

However, although awareness of sounds at the level of individual phonemes may be absent before children learn to read, awareness of larger units may be present, as Liberman et al. showed for syllables. Children also seem to be able to divide a syllable into its *onset* and its *rime* (Goswami and Bryant, 1990), which allows them to detect respectively alliteration and rhyming between words. There is evidence that if children are poor at these pre-reading skills they are likely to experience difficulties in learning to read.

Bradley and Bryant (1978) compared the abilities of a group of poor readers, who were 10 years old, and a group of 6-year-old normal readers with the same reading age, to detect rhyme and alliteration. In spite of the fact that the poor readers were, on average, 3.5 years older than the normal readers, they performed less well in detecting the word that did not rhyme with the others among a group of four words. This study thus suggests that there may be a causal relation between poor phonological awareness and reading difficulties. Other studies have come to the same conclusion using different methods to measure phonological awareness.

Children with reading difficulties have a poor awareness of grapheme–phoneme correspondences and this causes problems in reading new words. To test this, experimenters often ask children to read pseudo-words such as 'dake' or 'tepherd'. Since these will not have been encountered before, they cannot be read by direct recognition. They must therefore be read using a phonological strategy. A number of studies have shown that children with reading difficulties are poorer at reading pseudo-words than younger reading age matched controls. In one of these, Baddeley et al. (1982) gave the two groups lists of real words and pseudo-words to read. There was no difference on the real words, as might be expected since the groups were matched for reading age, but on the pseudo-words the group with reading difficulties made many more mistakes than the controls (see also Frith and Snowling, 1983; Szeszulski and Manis, 1987).

If phonological awareness is really a cause of reading difficulties, then there should be a predictive relation between measures of phonological awareness prior to reading and later reading skills. Bradley and Bryant (1983) administered a test of sensitivity to rhyme and alliteration to a group of 4- and 5-year-olds before they had learned to read and then followed up progress in reading over the next four years. They found a clear link between phonological awareness, as measured by a sensitivity to rhyme, and level of reading skill. Similar findings about the role of phonological awareness in the development of reading skills have been reported by Lundberg et al. (1981). They tested 6- to 7-year-old children in Sweden a few months before they began school. (In Sweden schooling begins at 7 years.) The children were administered a variety of tests of phonological awareness. One year later the groups were given reading and spelling tests. Lundberg et al. found that the results of the tests of awareness of sounds were good predictors of progress in learning to read. In a more recent study Bryant and his associates (Bryant et al., 1990) showed that a sensitivity to rhyme was related both to the development of reading skills and to the emergence of an awareness of the phonemic structure of words.

Thus, one type of phonological awareness, an ability to detect rhymes, helps the development of another type, an awareness of letter-sound correspondences, which is crucial to the further development of reading. As we suggested earlier, the development of an awareness of letter-sound correspondences may come about directly as a result of learning to spell and write. Thus, an early insensitivity to rhyme hinders both spelling and reading. This is consistent with the findings of Bryant and Bradley (1985) that awareness of rhyme is related to later success in both spelling and reading.

Memory Deficits

There is considerable evidence that children with reading difficulties perform worse on a variety of short-term memory tasks than age matched controls (Jorm, 1983). These difficulties are specific to memory for words; they do not occur when other stimuli are used. In one demonstration of this Holmes and McKeever (1979) compared children with a reading difficulty and normal readers of the same age on the recall of faces and of words. They found no differences between the groups on the recall of faces but differences were found on word recall. Many other studies have reported similar results (see Stanovich, 1986; Wagner and Torgesen, 1987, for reviews). Very few studies have used reading age match controls or examined the predictive relation between memory and reading. Thus, it is difficult at present to establish the causal relation between memory and reading.

We must now address a different question: in what way is memory important in the reading process? The most likely source of the poor memory performance of children with reading difficulties is their already established difficulties in phonological processing. As we discussed in Chapter 1, the working memory system includes a specialized phonological store in which verbal information is retained. Information in the phonological store fades rapidly, unless refreshed by rehearsal. This system plays an important role in storing the products of letter-sound conversions, while further processing occurs. Since letter-sound conversion is important in the acquisition of reading skills, the performance of the resources on which it draws is also of importance. In the context of reading, difficulties could arise in any of the following processes:

- converting a string of letters into sounds
- storing the sounds temporarily
- blending the stored sounds together to pronounce the word

If a printed word cannot be converted into sounds then its sounds cannot be stored; if conversion is slow, then previous sounds may be lost before further processing can occur; if the store is reduced in capacity then the information cannot be retained; if the stored sounds cannot be blended, then a pronounceable form of the word cannot be obtained. An experiment that begins to address these issues was reported by Torgesen et al. (1988). They compared three groups of children: one group had reading difficulties and a low memory span; a second group also had reading difficulties but their memory span was normal; the third group were normal readers. All groups were given a sound blending test. There was no difference between the two groups with normal memory spans, but the children with a low span were poorer at sound blending. This establishes a link between poor sound blending and a low memory span, although further research will be required to clarify the relation. The finding that one group of children with reading difficulties did not differ from the normal readers in sound blending is also of importance because it suggests that the problems experienced by children with reading difficulties may not be all the same. Determining whether or not this is the case could have important practical implications for intervention.

In summary, difficulties in the development of decoding are related to difficulties in establishing correspondences between sounds and letters. These children tend to have poor awareness of the sound structure of words before they begin to read. Some (though not all) poor readers have poor memory for auditory material, which may impede their ability to blend sounds together in sounding out a word. But decoding is only one part of the process of reading. Children must also comprehend what they have decoded.

Comprehension of Text

Deriving meaning from text requires the operation of a large number of processes. Decoding is only one of these. Several studies have found that children who are poor at decoding also tend to have poor comprehension of what they have read (Curtis, 1980; Smiley et al., 1977). However, being good at decoding is no guarantee of being a good comprehender. Oakhill and Garnham (1988) estimate that up to 10 per cent of children who can read fluently experience difficulties comprehending what they have read. As children reach the end of primary school, comprehension replaces decoding as the most important predictor of overall reading skill (Curtis, 1980; Stanovich et al. 1984).

One possible relation between decoding and comprehension is that slow recognition could disrupt the process of comprehension. Perfetti and Lesgold (1979) showed that decoding is more rapid in good comprehenders than in poor comprehenders. They argue that the reason for this is that decoding and comprehension compete for a limited amount of resources in working memory and that because of their slow recognition, poor comprehenders have less resources available for comprehension than good comprehenders. While this may be true, making more resources available does not necessarily improve comprehension skills. This was shown by Fleisher et al. (1979), who trained poor readers to recognize words as rapidly as good readers. The poor readers showed no improvement on the comprehension of prose passages that were made up entirely of the trained words.

Although decoding is a prerequisite to comprehension, there does not seem to be a direct causal relation between the two skills. On the whole, children who are good comprehenders tend to have good decoding skills and poor comprehenders tend to have poor decoding skills. But there are also children whose decoding skills are good but whose comprehension is poor and vice versa. Thus, we must consider other cognitive factors as explanations of comprehension difficulties.

One obvious factor to consider is the processing of the syntactic and semantic structure of a sentence. In order to understand the meaning of a sentence, it is necessary to understand the structure of that sentence in addition to the meaning of the individual words. Another obvious factor is the way in which information is integrated across sentences. The ability to make inferences may be particularly important when a sentence or a larger piece of text is processed because we are often required to draw upon elements of knowledge that have not been explicitly mentioned in order to comprehend text or speech. Finally, the strategies that are used in reading text may influence its comprehension. We shall discuss each of these issues in turn.

Sentence Processing

Children with reading difficulties often have difficulty in dealing with complex syntactic structures in spoken language. Newcomer and Magee (1977) found that the performance of children with reading difficulties was inferior to that of age matched controls on spoken language tests of grammatical understanding, sentence imitation, and grammatical completion. Other studies have reported similar findings (Menyuk and Flood, 1981; Siegel and Ryan, 1984; Vogel, 1974). These studies establish a correlation between measures of syntactic ability and reading difficulties.

Longitudinal studies indicate that there may be a causal relation. Children who are delayed in acquiring language tend to experience reading difficulties (Fundudis et al., 1979; Silva et al., 1987). In a recent longitudinal study Bishop and Adams (1990) followed up a sample of 8-year-olds, who had had language difficulties at 4 years of age. These children had previously been followed up at 5 years. Two of the results are of particular importance here. First, if language problems had resolved at 5 years, then reading performance was similar to an age matched control group. Second, those children who still had language difficulties at 5 years scored poorly on reading comprehension at 8 years and also continued to score poorly on a variety of language measures. Thus, persisting language problems impede the child's ability to comprehend what is read.

Is there any evidence that poor comprehenders process what they read differently from good comprehenders? Cromer (1970) found that poor comprehenders who have normal decoding skills may read text on a word by word basis, without taking advantage of larger syntactic units such as phrases. Isakson and Miller

(1976) also arrived at the conclusion that poor comprehenders process text on a word by word basis. They hypothesized that if poor comprehenders process text on a word by word basis, then they should not be affected by words that are either semantically or syntactically anomalous in a sentence. By contrast, good comprehenders, because they are constructing the meaning of what they read on the basis of syntactic and semantic information, should be affected by anomalous words. In fact, Isakson and Miller predicted that good comprehenders would be more likely to misread the anomalous word than other words, whereas poor comprehenders would be no more likely to misread anomalous words than any other word. This is what they found.

In summary, children who have difficulties processing syntactic structure in the domain of language are likely to have comprehension difficulties when reading. These children have a tendency to read on a word by word basis. This is probably the result rather than the cause of their syntactic difficulties. It should also be noted that reading on a word by word basis will place greater demands on working memory because this method does not take advantage of the chunking that can occur when linguistic structure is used.

Text Integration

There are many levels at which the integration of information in a text can occur and we can only discuss illustrative examples here (see Oakhill and Garnham (1988) for a detailed account). Text integration involves linking information about somebody or something across sentences. This relies on both explicit and implicit devices. The explicit devices are such things as pronouns, which derive their meaning from some other word in the text. The reader has to work out which word a pronoun has replaced. Thus in the sentences

Mary baked a cake.
It was delicious.

it obviously refers to the cake. Oakhill and Yuill (1986) showed that poor comprehenders had difficulty in supplying the appropriate pronoun in such sentences as

Steven gave his umbrella to Penny because ... wanted to keep dry.

Yuill and Oakhill (1988) carried out a direct test of comprehension of pronouns. They compared the ability of good and poor comprehenders to work out which words in the text pronouns referred back to. Poor comprehenders were much worse at this task than good comprehenders. They were also much worse at answering questions about the text that required them to use information provided about a pronoun when there was a medium to large amount of text between the noun and the pronoun. When the gap between noun and pronoun was small, the poor comprehenders performed quite well, which shows that they understood the task but could not carry it out all the time. Thus, some cognitive resource on which this task depends was creating a comprehension difficulty. Yuill et al. (1989) suggested that the difficulty is due to an inefficient use of the working memory system by poor comprehenders. This may be so, but it may also be that poor syntactic processing led to greater demands on working memory than it could support. This would especially be the case if the children read on a word-by-word basis. As we have seen in discussing sentence processing, word-by-word processing will place greater demands on working memory than will processing the syntactic structure.

Comprehension difficulties with reading may really be difficulties in the language system rather than difficulties specific to reading. Smiley et al. (1977) compared good and poor readers on comprehension and recall of a prose passage under both reading and listening conditions. Poor readers recalled less than good readers under both conditions. Furthermore, poor readers took less account of the structure of the passage in their recall. These findings suggest that syntactic and semantic difficulties within the language system may be a major cause of comprehension difficulties in reading. A similar conclusion is suggested from the results of experiments on children's ability to make inferences.

To make an inference is to go beyond the literal information given. This is often necessary in order to understand text as the following simple children's story illustrates:

Jane was invited to Jack's birthday party.
She wondered if he would like a kite.

She went to her room and shook her piggy bank.
It made no sound.

Despite its simplicity, the story requires the reader to infer in the second line that Jane intended to buy a present for Jack, which provides a link to the third line in which she seeks money with which to buy the present.

Oakhill (1984) compared the ability of good and poor comprehenders to answer questions about text. Some of the questions had answers that were explicitly stated in the text, while others required inferences. In one condition the children had to answer the question from memory. The poor comprehenders were poorer at both types of questions. The poor comprehenders improved to the level of the good comprehenders for the literal questions but remained poor at answering questions that required an inference. This latter condition is of particular importance because text is continuously available in the normal reading process and inference from text is frequently required for comprehension.

Executive Strategies and Metacognitive Knowledge

Most characterizations of skilled reading attribute an important role to executive strategies and metacognitive knowledge (see chapter 1 for a discussion of these concepts). There is a large number of skills that can be discussed under their rubric (see Baker and Brown, 1984; Garner, 1987, for reviews). Here we shall focus on those that have been shown to be related to poor comprehension. Before doing so it is worth observing that it is not clear whether the different strategies to be discussed are all reflections of some general executive skill or simply a collection of independent skills, to which a common label has been attached.

Interview studies reveal that poor comprehenders have less explicit knowledge about reading and reading strategies than good comprehenders. Poor comprehenders tend to emphasize the decoding aspects of reading more than do good comprehenders. For example, Garner and Kraus (1981–2) administered a questionnaire to 12-year-old good and poor comprehenders and found that poor comprehenders emphasized the importance of decoding and few mentioned comprehension, in contrast to the good comprehenders who all mentioned the importance of comprehension. Thus, poor comprehenders are slower to realize that reading consists of more than decoding. They focus more on individual words than on the text as a whole. Whether this is a causal factor in comprehension difficulties or an effect of those difficulties is not clear.

When text is easy to comprehend, reading proceeds smoothly for the normal reader. When comprehension difficulties arise the normal reader (a) detects the existence of a problem and (b) takes corrective action by implementing additional strategies such as rereading. Detecting that a difficulty has arisen requires that the reader have some monitoring system to detect difficulties and institute corrective action. There is considerable evidence that poor comprehenders do not monitor their comprehension as well as good comprehenders do (Garner, 1987). Poor comprehenders do not detect errors in text as well as good comprehenders. Baker (1984) conducted a study in which children were instructed in the use of specific criteria to employ in detecting errors in a text. There was no difference between good and poor comprehenders in the number of times a criterion was used but the poor comprehenders were less likely to use the criteria effectively; they relied more on applying a single criterion rather than using multiple criteria and they were less likely to use specific criteria when it was appropriate to do so.

Poor comprehenders also fail to take effective action when faced with difficulties. Garner and Reis (1981) asked good and poor comprehenders to read passages of text with interspersed questions that related to material on a preceding page. Only the oldest (13-year-old) group of good comprehenders spontaneously looked back to the previous page to answer the questions.

The evidence is quite consistent that poor comprehenders are less effective than good comprehenders in the use of executive strategies in reading. The question of why this is so is largely unresolved. Poor comprehension may be the result of a difficulty in deploying executive strategies. However, the relation could be the other way round: poor comprehenders may have failed to develop good strategies because of their difficulties in comprehension.

Assessment and Intervention

The ability to recognize words is of considerable importance in the early stages of learning to read. Thus, this ability should be a major focus of assessment of early reading difficulties. Later reading difficulties usually involve problems of comprehension. These are more difficult to assess. In particular, it is important to establish whether the child's comprehension problems are the result of decoding difficulties or whether they occur in spite of adequate decoding skills.

There are a number of specialized tests of word recognition, which are frequently used to determine a child's level of reading ability relative to other children. These tests use words of increasing length and difficulty, which the child is required to read aloud. While these provide a useful check in confirming, or otherwise, the existence of a reading problem they do not identify the processing difficulties that are the source of the problem. This requires further investigation. One test that allows independent assessment of decoding and comprehension skills is the Neale Analysis of Reading Ability (Neale, 1989, is the most recent revision).

Assessment of comprehension skills poses more problems than assessment of decoding. In one sense, it is easy enough to see why this is so. It is relatively obvious what should be measured in decoding, it is not so obvious with respect to comprehension. One of the major difficulties is distinguishing comprehension that is based on what was read and comprehension that is based on general knowledge. Tuinman (1973–4) showed that on a number of popular comprehension tests, students who had not read the passages in the test could answer questions about these passages at above chance level. This suggests that general knowledge may play a considerable role in determining test score. Apart from this, there is still little agreement on what it is that a comprehension test should measure (Oakhill and Garnham, 1988).

What type of intervention should occur? If much of decoding difficulties can be attributed to difficulties in the acquisition of a phonological code, then it seems reasonable to ask whether intervention techniques that try to increase a child's awareness of the phonological structure of words will help to overcome reading difficulties. There is evidence that programmes designed to increase awareness of sounds improve the reading performance of normal children (Bradley and Bryant, 1983; 1985; Goldstein, 1976). Do such programmes also help children who experience reading difficulties? It is quite possible that they may not. Children with reading difficulties might, for example, have such reduced phonological sensitivity that they are impervious to the type of training that improves the performance of normal readers. We cannot therefore simply extrapolate from the results of the studies discussed above to children with reading difficulties.

Hornsby and Miles (1980) compared three different programmes used by remedial schools for dyslexic children. The schools all used some version of a phonics approach – that is they emphasized sounds and the relation between sounds and letters. The children in all programmes made reasonable progress, which suggests that the method is effective across variation in the details of its implementation. Unfortunately, the Hornsby and Miles study does not contain any comparison data from children being taught using other methods or from children who have reading difficulties but are not receiving any specialist intervention.

Gittelman and Feingold (1983) compared two groups of poor readers. One group received a systematic phonics programme over a period of four months; the other group received the same amount of extra attention devoted to non-specific tutoring in other subjects. By the end of the intervention programme the first group had reading ages that were about 12 months ahead of the control group. Furthermore, the improvement was maintained in two follow-up assessments conducted two and eight months after the intervention programme had ended, which shows that the programme had a long-lasting effect on reading ability.

The evidence from intervention programmes strongly suggests that increasing awareness of the phonological structure of words and of the relation between phonological and orthographic representations is an effective technique both of teaching decoding and of intervening in cases of reading difficulties. It is also the case that although it seems that the methods discussed work, it is difficult to pin down why they work in a precise fashion. In order to establish this, future research will need to concentrate on a more fine-grained analysis of the relative effectiveness of the components that make up an intervention programme.

One attempt to package insights into the reading process with insights into techniques of intervention (see chapter 7) is the Direct Instructional System for Teaching and Reading (DISTAR). The programme was initially developed by Bereiter and Engelmann (1966). It consists of a carefully controlled and sequenced programme in which the teacher presents some information, children repeat the information, the teacher asks simple direct questions about the information, and the children respond. If the response is correct, the children are praised; if the response is wrong, it is corrected, and the process is repeated until the correct response is produced. Only then do children proceed to the next step of the sequence. The programme places considerable emphasis on the oral use of language and on the use of phonological strategies while reading. DISTAR has been shown to be an effective programme in increasing reading achievement (Summerell and Brannegan, 1977) and in leading to gains in comprehension which are maintained (Gersten and Carnine, 1986). The programme has also been found to be effective in improving children's understanding of language (Booth, 1979; Sexton, 1989), although not all studies have found this effect (see Sexton, 1989).

Intervention need not only occur in the classroom. In fact, the development of reading skills is a classic example of the mesosystem effects discussed by Bronfenbrenner (1979 – see chapter 1). It has been consistently found that reading achievement is linked to reading at home (Topping and Wolfendale, 1985). A parent listening to a child read is sufficient to have an effect on reading achievement (Greening and Spenceley, 1987; Tizard et al., 1982). More directed methods, such as paired reading of texts by parent and child (Morgan and Lyon, 1979; Robson et al., 1984), or teaching self-correction strategies (Glynn, 1980; Wheldall et al., 1987) have proved even more effective. In a small-scale comparison of different methods of home instruction, Leach and Siddall (1990) compared four programmes used over a 10-week period, with a group of normal 5-year-olds. The biggest gains on both reading accuracy and reading comprehension were made by children whose parents used a method of direct instruction based on DISTAR (Engelmann et al., 1983), follow by paired reading, followed by a method to teach self-correction responses, followed by simply listening to the child read. Unfortunately, no control group was used in this study against which the relative gains could be determined. However, what this study suggests, consistent with previous research, is that direct instruction may be a particularly effective method in the initial stages of reading. It seems likely that the techniques of self-correction may be more effective, once a repertoire of initial skills has been established. A study by Palincsar and Brown (1984), which we shall discuss in more detail in chapter 7, has shown that teaching monitoring skills to children who have progressed further with reading (but who had poor comprehension of what they read) led to significant improvements in comprehension.

Summary

Reading difficulties can be analysed at two levels: decoding and comprehension. Difficulties reflect inefficiencies in the underlying cognitive components that are involved in processing written input. The most important initial skill is learning to map between letters and their sounds. This requires an awareness of the sound structure of individual letters and combinations of letters. The evidence suggests that the most common cause of decoding difficulties is problems in mapping between letters and their sounds. These problems seem to be common to children who are sometimes labelled dyslexic and those who are simply regarded as poor readers. Comprehension difficulties are sometimes the result of poor decoding skills. In many cases children who have had difficulty in learning to decode, process text on a word-by-word basis rather than at the level of phrases and sentences. This leads to poor comprehension. Comprehension difficulties also occur independently of decoding skills. When they do, they usually reflect difficulties in the language system, rather than being specific to reading. Intervention designed to increase phonological awareness has had some success in improving the performance of children with decoding difficulties. In addition there has been some success in teaching poor comprehenders how to use monitoring strategies more effectively. Intervention in home settings has also been effective in leading to improvements.

5
Specific Difficulties with Number

Overview

In this chapter we shall discuss difficulties with number. We first consider the development of counting and the difficulties that can arise with this. Basic arithmetical skills develop from counting. We discuss this development and the difficulties that many children have in establishing basic skills. These basic skills provide the foundations for multi-digit addition and subtraction, which also require additional skills of borrowing and carrying. We discuss the most characteristic errors that children make here. We then consider word problems, which present mathematical problems in a verbal rather than a purely numeric form. Finally, we discuss issues of assessment and intervention in number difficulties.

Types of Number Difficulties

Number difficulties can occur in a variety of ways. Some children have difficulties in the early stages with the basic number operations of counting, adding, and subtracting (Hughes, 1986). This can sow the seeds for later difficulties both cognitively, in that the child acquires a poor grasp of the basic skills on which later developments build, and motivationally, in that the child may come to dislike number work because of his lack of success with it. A more common difficulty occurs in learning the rules for manipulating written numbers. Many children encounter problems here because they fail to relate what they know about spoken numbers to the written version. As a result, calculating with written numbers becomes an isolated activity, which is pursued by applying rules that have little meaning to the child. In these circumstances children frequently invent faulty versions of these rules. The following are all examples of this:

(a)	12	(b)	24	(c)	12	(d)	201
	+19		+53		−7		−47
	——		——		——		——
	21		68		15		154

In (a) the child has failed to carry a one to the second column from the first; in (b) the child has added the numbers within rows rather than within columns, obtaining 8 for the sum of 5 and 3, and 6 for the sum of 2 and 4; in (c) the child has subtracted the smaller from the larger number in the first column, probably operating on the principle that one cannot subtract a larger from a smaller number; and in (d) the child has subtracted in the first column by borrowing from the zero in the second column without first making this a 10 by borrowing from the third column. All of these are examples of how children have not completely mastered the procedure necessary to carry out some arithmetical operation.

All children make errors of this sort. Children with number difficulties make a lot more errors than is the norm. However, they do not seem to make different types of errors than other children; they just encounter more difficulty in mastering arithmetical operations. We need to understand why this is so.

The problems that we have highlighted all have to do with the manipulation of number symbols. Many children also experience difficulties in relating the procedures of arithmetic to real-world problems and vice versa. Sometimes, especially in the early stages of learning mathematics, a child may be able to reason about real-world quantities but be unable to perform the equivalent calculation when faced with a formal version of the problem. The following striking example of this was reported by Carraher et al.

(1985). They tested the ability of children who worked in street markets in Brazil to compute the prices of quantities of items. The following is an example of the type of question posed by the interviewer/customer, called C, and the response given by one subject, called M:

C: *How much is one coconut?*
M: *35*
C: *I'd like ten. How much is that?*
M: (Pause) *Three will be 105; with three more that will be 210.* (Pause) *I need four more. That is . . .* (pause) *315 . . . I think it is 350.*

One week later Carraher et al. tested the ability of the children to compute formal versions of problems that they had correctly solved in the marketplace. There was a dramatic difference in the results. The children had almost always been correct in computing prices in the market but were only 74 per cent correct when presented with formal word problems such as *Mary bought 10 bananas; each banana cost 5 cruzeiros; how much did she pay altogether?* and when presented with the problems in written mathematical form, such as *105 + 105*, the success rate was only 37 per cent.

We see in this example that the skills that were used to perform practical computations in the marketplace were not drawn upon when the children were presented with formal arithmetical problems. The reverse problem frequently occurs among older children who are competent at performing arithmetical calculations but are unable to use these skills effectively because they cannot translate real-world problems into an arithmetical form. The Cockroft Report (Cockroft, 1983) found that most children aged 11 to 13 years were able to perform calculations involving the four basic arithmetical operations of addition, subtraction, multiplication, and division but in many cases their abilities to apply these skills to practical problems was severely limited. This suggests that, for many children, the arithmetical operations learned in school constitute a detached skill: one that can be applied in the classroom but is of little relevance in everyday situations. The Cockroft Report (1982: 73) commented:

Mathematics is only 'useful' to the extent to which it can be applied to a particular situation, and it is the ability to apply mathematics to a variety of situations to which we give the name 'problem-solving'. However, the solution of a mathematical problem cannot begin until the problem has been translated into the appropriate mathematical terms. The first and essential step presents very great difficulties to many pupils – a fact which is often too little appreciated.

Number difficulties usually become evident in the classroom when a child produces incorrect answers to arithmetical problems. These incorrect answers are the data on which an initial diagnosis of number difficulties is made. To explain the child's difficulty and design an effective intervention programme, it is necessary to discover the pattern of the child's strengths and needs so that the strengths can be built on (both cognitively and motivationally) and the needs addressed. The errors that children make with number are usually systematic and have an underlying set of principles, albeit incorrect ones. The first task in assessment must be to discover exactly what set of principles the child is using. Our aim in this chapter is to review what has been discovered about the principles that underlie children's mathematical reasoning and about how difficulties can arise in the acquisition of these principles.

Prevalance

Number difficulties often occur in the context of reading difficulties, but they can also occur independently of reading difficulties. Figure 5.1 shows the prevalence of literacy and numeracy problems from the National Child Development Study at age 23 years (ALBSU, 1987). The data in figure 5.1 constitute 13 per cent of the 12,534 adults who were sampled. Thus, a sizeable proportion of adults report continuing difficulties with numeracy and literacy. Of these, almost 40 per cent reported a difficulty with number, either alone, or in combination with reading, writing, and spelling difficulties. It is evident that many children leave school with an inadequate grasp of the mathematics

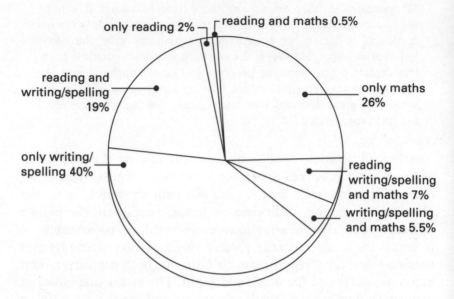

Figure 5.1   *Distribution of basic skills difficulties reported at age 23 years by 1,676 respondents in the National Child Development Study.*
(Source: ALBSU, 1987)

necessary for everyday life. Despite the frequency of number problems, they have received much less research attention than other problems such as reading difficulties. It is only in recent years that theoretically-driven models of number have been applied to the study of number difficulties.

Number and Quantity

Numbers represent quantitative information about the world. Children possess a natural understanding of quantity. Research with infants has shown that they can make certain judgements based on numerosity, long before they could have been taught anything about number. For example, infants can discriminate between two rows of dots that differ only in number, provided that the number of dots in a row does not exceed about four (Antell and Keating, 1983; Starkey and Cooper, 1980). This

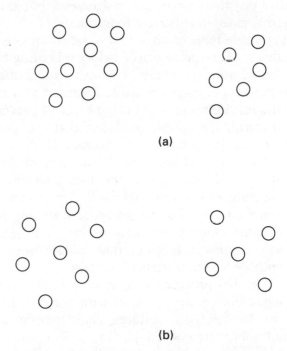

(a)

(b)

Figure 5.2 *Types of groups about which young children can judge which contains the greater number. In (a) the groups differ in size and number; in (b) they differ in density and number.*

establishes that infants are sensitive to quantity and quantity differences as a basic property of objects. This provides the child with a starting point for number judgements.

One of the earliest spontaneous uses of quantity concepts is the judgement that one group of objects contains more than another. Children can make this judgement in a variety of ways. Figure 5.2 shows examples of two groups with different numbers of objects in each, which many children aged 3 to 4 years can solve (Estes and Combs, 1966). These judgements are often based on the relative size of the two groups, or on their density if size is similar. These are not, of course, perfectly reliable indicators of quantity, but they are good approximations and use criteria for judgement that do not themselves have to be learned. The main point is not the reliability or otherwise of the judgements but the fact that children readily make quantitative judgements.

The most reliable basis of quantitative judgements is counting. Children often learn number words before schooling begins – in fact a number of nursery rhymes are built around the sequence of number words. The words are often learned as a memorized sequence, without their role in counting being of concern. This is an excellent learning principle (and one that can profitably be applied to children who have poor mastery of the sequence of number words) because it detaches the mastery of the sequence itself from the task of using it to count objects, which, as we shall see, requires a number of additional skills. This means that when the child comes to carry out counting, at least one part of the task – uttering the sequence of count words – can be carried out in a relatively automatic fashion, thus making more cognitive resources available for other parts of the task.

Hughes (1986) has provided a range of examples of the ability that preschool children often exhibit with number. In one demonstration he showed how children could reason about basic addition and subtraction when playing a 'box game' with the investigator. In this game the investigator shows the child a small number of bricks and then puts these bricks into a box. The child is asked how many bricks there are in the box. Further bricks are then added to or subtracted from the box. The child is asked questions about these additions and subtractions. Hughes found that children could solve problems that involved small numbers (up to about four), but were much less good when larger numbers were involved. He also found that children who were successful on the box task were much less successful when presented with formal versions of the same problems, such as *what does one and two make*? An example of the interchange between the investigator (MH) and one child who was particularly adept at the task is the following (Hughes, 1986: 25–6):

MH: *How many in the box now?*
Gordon: *Two*
MH: (Adds one brick in such a way that Gordon sees it going in but cannot see into the box.) *How many now?*
Gordon: *Three*

MH:	*I'm putting one more in.* (Adds one more, the same way.)
Gordon:	*Four. Four!*
MH:	*And now I'm putting in two more.* (Does so.)
Gordon:	*Six! Six!*
MH:	(Takes one brick out.) *How many now?*
Gordon:	(Pause.) *Five. Five!*
MH:	(Takes two out but does not have to ask the question.)
Gordon:	*Three!*
MH:	*Do you want to see if you're right?* (Opens the box.)
Gordon:	(Throws arms open wide.) *See.*

Basic Counting Skills

Counting is the most basic number skill but it is itself composed of a number of component skills. Children must know the sequence of number words. They must then be able to apply these words to objects being counted. To do so they must match each number word with one object and only one object. Thus, they must keep track of which objects have been counted and which remain to be counted. That much allows a child to perform the operation of counting. But still more is required. The child must also know that the last number word represents the number of objects in order to make use of the result. Thus, the simple skill of counting requires three components:

- knowledge of the sequence of number words
- one-to-one matching of count words and objects being counted
- knowledge that the product of counting represents the numerosity of the collection of objects that were counted

Studies of children's counting have shown that one-to-one matching is something with which children often have difficulty initially. There is usually an initial tendency to recite the number words without ensuring that each word has been matched with an object to be counted. When counting, the child must distinguish those objects already counted from those that remain to be counted. Fuson (1988) found that in the early stages of counting children make frequent errors, especially as set size increases.

By age 4, the error-rate drops considerably. This seems to be due to the fact that children learn to use pointing to regulate the matching of number words to objects to be counted. In teaching children to count, the task of one-to-one matching can be made easier by arranging the objects to be counted in a row. When the objects are in a row, pointing also serves to separate counted from to-be-counted objects (Beckwith and Restle, 1966). When objects are not arranged in a row, pointing is not such an effective means of separating the counted from the to-be-counted. An alternative method is to move objects as they are counted. Fuson (1988) found that it was not until they were more than 5 years old that the majority of the children she studied moved a pile of blocks while counting them.

Difficulties with Basic Counting

Establishing one-to-one correspondence while counting is an area of difficulty for some children. Baroody (1986) found that children with a moderate learning difficulty made matching errors at the beginning and end of counts. McEvoy and McConkey (1990) studied a similar group of children with a mean chronological age of 15 years and a mental age of 4 years. They found that the children were able to count small set sizes (up to 5) fairly accurately, but when asked to count large sets (between 9 and 20) they were much less accurate. In particular, there was a marked deterioration in establishing one-to-one correspondence. A major reason for this may have been that these children did not use effective strategies to establish correspondence: they were reluctant to count aloud and many failed spontaneously to produce points in the execution of a count. McEvoy and McConkey found that a major source of difficulty for these children was in coordinating the production of number words and pointing – a task with which normal children have relatively little difficulty (Fuson, 1988).

Basic Arithmetical Skills

Counting is the basic skill used in the initial acquisition of arithmetic. When presented with arithmetical problems, young children use a variety of counting strategies to solve these problems.

It also seems to be the case that poor counting skills underlie a number of the difficulties that children have with number.

The most basic addition strategy is to use physical objects or fingers to represent each of the addends (that is, the numbers to be added) and then to count the complete set of fingers. This is a popular strategy with young children. It is called the *counting-all strategy*. A more sophisticated strategy is to take one of the two addends as the starting point and to count on from there by the amount of the other addend. Thus, to add 4 + 3, the child would start from 4, display 3 fingers, and count these as *five, six, seven*. This is called the *counting-on strategy*.

Children progress from counting using fingers to counting in their heads. A further strategy dispenses with counting and retrieves number facts from memory. This strategy obviously requires that the facts be stored in memory in the first place.

Children use all of the above strategies in solving addition problems. Moreover, there is a shift from counting both addends to counting-on and then to retrieval. In a longitudinal study of children aged between 6 and 9 years, Carpenter and Moser (1984) found that children initially tended to solve problems with a counting-all strategy, and that this gradually gave way to counting-on, which in turn gave way to recall of number facts. There is also a shift from external representation of the problem by objects or fingers to counting without external support.

Two things seem worth particular emphasis in this developmental progression. The first is that some of the strategies seem to be invented by the child himself rather than being the result of instruction (Groen and Resnick, 1977). This is particularly true of counting strategies, which are rarely taught explicitly in school but are much used by children (and sometimes by adults). The second point of emphasis is that children do not simply replace one strategy with another, strategies co-exist for long periods of time. Different strategies are used for different problems. We shall briefly discuss each of these issues in turn.

The Use of Counting to Solve Arithmetical Problems

One of the first reports on the development of counting strategies was that of Groen and Parkman (1972). They gave children all possible combinations of addition problems that sum to 9 or less. Children saw the problems on a screen and had to indicate the correct answer as quickly as possible by pressing a numbered key. By measuring how long the children took to solve the problems Groen and Parkman were able to determine the technique that children used to solve these problems. They discovered that children found the sum by taking the larger of the two numbers and counting on from there by the smaller. It made no difference in Groen and Parkman's study whether the larger or smaller number was presented first.

These experiments on adding numbers are of interest because they tell us what cognitive operations children find naturally easy. These procedures may thus be of particular use in beginning instruction with a child who is experiencing difficulties with basic arithmetical operations but who knows the sequence of number words. Finger counting is often discouraged by educators, but it is a powerful aid to the child: it is a natural way to represent numerosity and it reduces the demands on memory when working out a solution. Geary (1990: 380) suggests that for children experiencing difficulties learning arithmetic 'the use of strategies which reduce demands on working memory resources, such as counting on fingers, should be encouraged rather than suppressed'.

Children also use counting strategies to solve subtraction problems. When subtracting by counting, children usually either count down from the larger number or count up from the smaller (Svenson and Hedenborg, 1979; Woods et al., 1975). Thus, 8 − 2 is solved by counting *eight* . . . *seven, six* and obtaining the answer directly and 8 − 6 is solved by counting *six* . . . *seven, eight* and keeping track of the number of digits counted after 6.

It is worth stressing again that the majority of children observed using these procedures had not been taught to use them; they spontaneously invented them. To do so, they not only needed to be competent at counting, they also needed to be able to reason about counting. Resnick (1983, 1986) has suggested that for children to solve such problems they must understand that a number can be decomposed into parts. In the case of 8 − 2 this means that 8 can be decomposed into two numbers, one of which is given as 2. The task is to find the other one. To do so it is possible either to count up from 2 to 8 or to count down from 8 by 2. If we also assume that children's knowledge of number allows them to reason that 2 is the smaller part of the decomposition of 8 then the obvious strategy is to count down from 8. By a similar process of reasoning, the obvious strategy for 8 − 6 is to count up from 6.

The analysis of these simple tasks shows the extent to which children can reason about number without being explicitly taught to do so. When these skills are present in cases of number difficulties it makes sense to encourage the child to use them in his problem solving.

Retrieving Number Facts

As children become more familiar with number facts (often as a result of classroom instruction) the tendency to retrieve the result of simple addition from memory increases. Retrieval is more likely initially for addition that involves the smaller numbers (Geary, 1990). When numbers are larger, children use counting strategies. Thus, at any point in time, a child will have some facts that can be retrieved and some that need to be calculated. If we assume that, other things being equal, retrieval is the easier strategy for the child to use, then the use of counting strategies for larger numbers implies that children know that they are less likely to retrieve the correct answer when larger numbers are involved. Ideally, children would use retrieval where it could be executed accurately and use counting strategies where it could not.

Siegler and his associates (Siegler and Robinson, 1982; Siegler and Shrager, 1984) have proposed a model of how number facts are acquired, which helps account for whether or not a retrieval strategy is selected. The model proposes that as children learn number facts, associations of different strengths are established between a problem and a range of answers (only one of which is, of course, correct). For this reason, the model is called the *distributions of associations* model. In the initial stages of learning, many answers may be associated with a problem with more or less equal strength. However, as a result of instruction and learning, the association between the problem and the correct answer becomes stronger and other associations become weaker.

How do children decide whether or not to use a retrieval strategy? Siegler and Shrager propose that children first try to retrieve an answer, but only use it if it exceeds a confidence criterion. If an answer exceeds the confidence criterion on retrieval then it is stated by the child, otherwise it is not. If several attempts at retrieval fail to yield an answer, then another strategy will be used. Thus, in the early stages of acquiring number facts, when there are many similar associations to a given problem, it is less likely that any will exceed the confidence criterion, and a counting strategy may be implemented. As the correct association is selectively strengthened then the likelihood that it will exceed the confidence criterion increases and thus the probability of retrieval increases.

One important aspect of Siegler and Shrager's model for number difficulties is that the production of incorrect answers strengthens the association between the problem and that answer. Thus children who initially make many errors may subsequently make more retrieval errors because the incorrect associations will be established between a problem and its result.

Difficulties with Basic Arithmetic

Number difficulties are defined by inaccuracy in carrying out number tasks. In what ways do children who experience difficulties with number differ from their peers? First, by definition, they will be less accurate than their peers. It is the basis of these inaccuracies that we are seeking to understand.

Mastery of computation with single-digit whole numbers is a necessary condition for further arithmetical achievement. Because these problems are a necessary component of more complex arithmetical computations, the accuracy and speed with which they are computed is important. A number of studies have found that children with number difficulties are slower than age matched controls at solving simple addition problems (Goldman et al., 1988; Hamann and Ashcraft, 1985; Svenson and Broquist, 1975). With development, normal children move from reliance on counting strategies to a retrieval strategy for addition and subtraction problems. This is not just a matter of one strategy replacing another. A mix of strategies is employed for some time, with retrieval eventually coming to dominate as the strategy of choice.

However, children with number difficulties use retrieval less frequently and continue to rely on the more time-consuming counting strategies (Geary et al., 1987). Moreover, when they use a retrieval strategy, they are less likely than normal children to retrieve the correct answer (Geary, 1990).

Geary et al. (1991) compared how the strategies used by normal children and children with number difficulties changed over a ten month period. The children were administered the same set of problems at the beginning and end of this period and the strategies used to solve the problems were compared. The normal group showed increased reliance on memory retrieval and decreased reliance on counting to solve addition problems, as well as an increase in the speed of counting and of retrieving facts from memory. By contrast, the number difficulties group showed none of these changes: the mix of strategies did not change nor did the speed of counting or of retrieval from memory. This group did, however, show some improvements: they made fewer counting errors and they relied less on a counting-all strategy.

Although children with number difficulties progress to using a counting-on strategy in solving basic addition problems, there are some circumstances in which they fall back on the more cumbersome counting-all strategy. When two addends are close together in value, such as 7 + 8, children with number difficulties often use a counting-all strategy rather than the counting-on strategy used by normal children (Geary, 1990; Goldman et al., 1988). Since these children were capable of using a counting-on strategy at other times, this suggests that they may have had difficulty in identifying which was the greater and which the smaller of the addends, which blocked the execution of the strategy.

This last failure suggests that the children's problems may derive from a weak representation of the sequence of numbers. Consistent with this interpretation, Geary (1990; Geary et al., 1991) found that children with number difficulties made more errors when using counting to solve basic arithmetic problems than did age matched controls. The nature of the errors is interesting: they were not 'wild' errors, but more often than not involved over- or under-counting by one.

It thus seems that children with number difficulties may be caught in a vicious circle as far as progressing with addition is concerned. Their execution of strategies is neither efficient nor accurate. The underlying reason for this possibly lies in the fact that their mastery of the basic sequence of counting is itself poor. The inaccurate execution of strategies will lead to the associative strength of incorrect answers for a particular problem being increased. Thus, when they execute a retrieval strategy there is an increased probability of retrieving the wrong answer.

Multi-Digit Addition and Subtraction

Being able to retrieve the basic number facts is the basis on which multi-digit arithmetic is built. However, there are additional skills to be mastered. The primary skill is that of transferring units from one column to another in the operations usually referred to as 'carrying' in addition and 'borrowing' in subtraction. As we shall see, these operations frequently give rise to errors. The errors that we shall illustrate are errors that any child is likely to make. Often the errors only persist for a short time, but sometimes they become entrenched and lead to difficulties.

When numbers to be added have more than a single digit, then procedures are required for what to do when the sum of any column is greater than 9. Children learn what to do by being taught the procedure of carrying. Thus, if the total of a column is 15, the 5 is written down and 1 is carried to the next column. Children frequently have difficulty with this procedure. Usually they find a way round this difficulty by inventing a procedure, which is often incorrect. However, these incorrect procedures have sensible origins: they are good rules badly applied or distorted in some way.

An important study in the analysis of the faulty procedures invented by children was carried out by Brown and Burton (1978), who analysed a data-base of 19,500 problems performed by school children. Let us consider the following examples of one child's addition:

41	32	989	66	216
9	917	52	887	13
50	1345	1141	1053	229

The errors may appear random but they are in fact the result of a faulty carrying procedure. If the calculations above are examined it will be found that the sum for the units and tens columns is correct in all cases. Errors only occur in the hundreds columns, and they also only occur when a carry has occurred from the units to the tens column. This suggests that the child *accumulates* the amount carried across columns. Thus, in the second problem a value of one is carried from the units to the tens column and correctly added to this column. The same value continues to be carried to the hundreds column and is incorrectly added to it. This is a case where the child has invented an incorrect procedure. It is also evident that the child fails to understand the meaning of carrying: that the 'one' being carried from the units to the tens column is one unit of ten.

The procedures for multi-digit subtraction are a little more complicated than the procedures for addition because they introduce the notion of borrowing, when a larger number has to be subtracted from a smaller in any given column. Children frequently have difficulties with this procedure, especially when it is necessary to borrow from zero. Brown and Burton found that 40 per cent of the children made consistent procedural errors in subtraction. The most common erroneous procedures that the children had invented were:

- Borrowing from 0 in order to subtract a larger from a smaller number but failing to continue the borrow to the column to the left of 0. Thus, *103 − 45 = 158*.
- Subtracting the smaller from the larger digit, regardless of which one is on top. Thus, *253 − 118 = 145*.
- Borrowing from zero without further borrowing, unless the 0 is part of a 10 in the left part of the top number. Thus, *803 − 508 = 395*, but *103 − 45 = 58*.
- Writing the bottom digit in a column as the answer whenever the top digit is 0. Thus, *120 − 53 = 73*.

The demonstration by Brown and Burton that many arithmetical errors are due to the child following faulty procedures is an important one to bear in mind when considering mathematical learning difficulties. Brown and Van Lehn (1980) argued that these faulty procedures originate when the child reaches a point in trying to carry out some calculation without knowing the correct procedure at that point. They propose that children invent their own procedures in these circumstances. These invented procedures are not derived out of the blue, but are often misapplications of procedures the child already knows. A further point to stress is that the errors reveal that children think of these procedures as mechanical operations on symbols, without reference to the quantities that the symbols represent. Box 5.1 illustrates the difficulties a child can have when reasoning with number symbols, even though the child has a good informal understanding of the relevant procedures.

I: If you had ninety-eight dollars and you gave away twenty-nine, how many would you have left?
B: OK, 88, 78 and 9 would be 67.
I: Almost.
B: I mean 69.

Bob had transformed 98 − 29 into [(98 − 10) − 10] − 9. He first subtracted or counted back by tens–98, 88, 78– and then counted back by ones to subtract the final 9. At first he made a minor error in the last step, but he soon corrected it.
Asked to do written subtraction, Bob did poorly.

I: If you had 158 and you took away 96, how many would you have left?

Bob wrote

$$\begin{array}{r} 158 \\ \underline{96} \end{array}$$

Then he corrected it to

$$\begin{array}{r} 158 \\ \underline{96} \end{array}$$

He did 8 minus 6 by counting backward from 8. Then he said, '9 minus 5 is 4.' This gave him

$$\begin{array}{r} 158 \\ \underline{96} \\ 142 \end{array}$$

Next the interviewer gave him a simpler problem.

I: Let's see, now, 21 take away 5.

Bob did

$$
\begin{array}{r}
21 \\
-5 \\
\hline
24
\end{array}
$$

I: Do you think that's the right answer?
B: [He checked his work.] Yes.
I: If you had twenty-one candies and gave away five, how many would you have left?
B: Oh! I think I added.

He seemed to mean that since he got more than 21 he must have added.

I: Do you still think that's the right answer?
B: No. 'Cause five take away from 21 is 16.
I: [He pointed to his written 21 − 5 = 24.] But why isn't that the right answer?
B: I don't know.
I: You had 21 and you took away 5, and you had 24 left. What's wrong with that?
B: Oh! I know! It's from this one [the 1 in 21] that it was supposed to be taken away from.

In other words, Bob recognized that he should have subtracted the 5 from the 1 rather than the 1 from the 5.

In brief, Bob first used an incorrect written procedure for subtraction. This gave him 21 − 5 = 24, where the result is larger than the number he started with. He could easily do the same problem in his head by counting backwards and in this way got the right answer. Bob then realized that his written answer was wrong. 'Oh! I think I added.' This shows that he knew that in subtraction you should end up with less, not more, than you started with. Then he saw why he was wrong in the first place: he had reversed the order of subtraction.

Box 5.1   *Bob is an 11-year-old who has difficulties solving written problems even though he has a good understanding of number and can solve problems when they are presented orally.*
(Source: Ginsburg, 1977)

Word Problems

One of the important findings of the work that we have surveyed is that children often treat arithmetical operations purely as manipulations of symbols without relating the numbers to concepts of quantity to which the numbers refer. For many children arithmetical failure lies not in the absence of the basic skills but in being able to relate these skills to the world. Being skilled at manipulating numbers is not an end in itself. The real power of numbers is that they permit everyday problems to be represented in the language of mathematics for purposes of computation. Children frequently have difficulty in representing real-world quantitative problems in mathematical form, which is the necessary first step in solving these problems.

Word problems are common in the mathematics curriculum. These problems describe situations in which quantities are manipulated. They are used with the intention of linking practice in arithmetical calculation to situations in which arithmetic might be applied. The extent to which they meet this goal is not clear but they nevertheless provide a valuable insight into the child's ability to translate a problem into the language of mathematics.

Word problems can be classified in terms of the problem type, and within that in terms of the level of difficulty. Thus, Riley et al., (1983) propose four basic types of word problems: combine, change, equalize, and compare. The following are examples of each type:

Combine: Jane has 7 marbles. John has 5 marbles. How many marbles do they have altogether?
Change: Joe had 8 marbles. Then he gave 5 marbles to Mary. How many marbles does Joe have left?
Equalize: Rose has 10 marbles. Emily has 7 marbles. How many marbles must Emily get to have as many as Rose?
Compare: Lucy has 11 marbles. Jack has 3 marbles. How many marbles less than Lucy does Jack have?

In order to solve problems such as these children must first understand the problem; then plan a method for solving it; then carry out the plan. Understanding is based on the child's cognitive and linguistic skills; planning a method involves constructing a mathematical representation of the problem; carrying out the plan involves executing the mathematical procedures that have been selected. When the structure of the problem can be directly translated into arithmetical procedures, then children as young as 4 years have no difficulty with the problems (Riley and Greeno, 1988). Thus, in the combine problem above, the question can be directly translated into addition, and in the change problem into subtraction. However, when there is no direct translation, children have much greater difficulty, as in the following example:

> Mary went shopping for groceries. She spent £2.70 and had £2.30 left when she returned home. How much did she have when she left home?

In this example, the two quantities must be added to obtain the answer, but the problem does not specify addition at all. Thus, the child must translate the problem into a representation that decomposes an unknown initial amount into a part that is spent and a part that is left and then combines these parts to obtain the initial amount. This example illustrates the relatively complex relation that can exist between a verbal statement of a problem and its mathematical representation.

Difficulties can arise in the comprehension of the problem, the construction of a mathematical model, or in the execution of strategies in solving word problems. However, it seems to be the complexity of the text of the word problem and the availability of a suitable basis for its mathematical representation that are the major determinants of performance.

Children can lack the linguistic and conceptual knowledge necessary to understand the problem. This is evidenced by the fact that young children can often solve problems phrased in one way, but will fail to do so when the problem is phrased differently (Hudson, 1983). Even if the problem is comprehended, children may not represent it in the appropriate mathematical form. Solution of a word problem requires the availability in memory of an appropriate framework for representing the problem. The verbal statement of the problem must be translated into this framework (Kintsch and Greeno, 1985). (In the examples of problem types above, a *combine* framework would specify that the quantities mentioned should be added together.) Finally, the solution to the problem must be computed. If a child has acquired a faulty procedure for carrying out any of the arithmetical operations, then this will lead to an incorrect solution.

The performance of children with number difficulties on word problems is of particular interest, since these problems test the child's understanding of the relation between number and the world. However, there is relatively little research on this issue (see Montague and Bos, 1986). It may well be the case that a child who has difficulty with basic computational procedures has no particular additional difficulty on word problems, but this needs to be established by empirical research. Conversely, it may be the case that some children who have good computational skills are nevertheless poor at word problems.

Assessment and Intervention

Assessment

In chapter 2 we observed that much educational assessment uses norm-referenced tests and we noted that, although these tests can be useful in helping to confirm a suspicion that a child is currently performing below the norm, they do not identify the processing problems that the child experiences. As we have attempted to illustrate in this chapter, there is a variety of difficulties that may occur with number, many of which are the result of a misconception or a faulty procedure. It must be part of the purpose of assessment to discover these. At the same time it is necessary to discover also what the child's strengths are with number.

Ginsburg (1977) discusses an approach to mathematical assessment, which we shall call a structured interview. This follows a systematic process of posing problems for the child designed to assess his abilities and difficulties. The child is encouraged to 'think out loud' when solving the problem. As difficulties are uncovered, the interviewer asks further questions in an attempt to discover the child's underlying strategy. This is the most difficult part of the technique because it must be tailored to the individual child. However, there is some commonality in the faulty procedures that different children acquire, and knowledge of these can serve as a basis for probing. In what follows we shall review the skills that might be considered for assessment.

The domain of number is built on a small number of component skills, some of which can be assessed in a relatively straightforward way. To begin with a child must know the sequence of number words up to 20 in English, and thereafter the rules for forming the decade and century structure. Whether or not a child possesses this knowledge can be determined in a straightforward way.

Next, the child must be able to apply these words to the act of counting, maintaining one-to-one correspondence between number words and the objects being counted. This also can be easily determined. It is useful to determine at this stage the child's proficiency at counting fingers as well as counting objects, especially if finger counting is employed in solving arithmetical problems.

Retrieval of number facts is the basic skill that replaces counting for simple addition with most children. While it is not essential that a retrieval strategy be used, it is important to determine the child's skill here, because most children employ both counting and retrieval strategies in solving basic problems. Thus, any errors in retrieval may become self-perpetuating if the child employs this strategy. It is not too difficult to devise and administer either a verbal or a paper and pencil test of all the basic single-digit number facts for addition, subtraction, and multiplication, in order to determine a child's strengths and needs. There are 81 possible pairings of digits for basic addition and multiplication and 45 for subtraction if problems with a zero solution are included. Any test should, of course, have the items randomized. The test results should be examined for problems that are incorrect and any patterns that may be evident among these problems. These problems can then be assessed further, especially with respect to the strategies employed for their solution. It is also important to bear in mind that a child who appears to be unable to solve written problems may very well be able to solve the

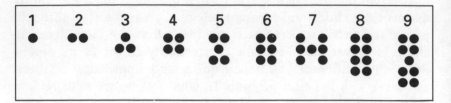

Figure 5.3 *A board on which the numerals are matched with countable groups. If suitable materials are used, then internal spatial arrangement of the countable groups can be varied.*

equivalent problems when presented in a verbal form. It is important to determine whether or not this is the case.

The errors that occur with multi-digit problems are more difficult to diagnose because many errors are the result of the systematic application of incorrect procedures. It is necessary to detect these procedures in assessment. The research of Ginsburg (1977) and of Brown and Burton (1978) and Young and O'Shea (1981) has gone some considerable way to providing an indication of the likely errors, and Burton (1981) has devised a test for detecting faulty subtraction procedures. It is worth reiterating here that the vast majority of errors in multi-digit arithmetic involve operations on zero. Thus, any assessment of multi-digit skills should contain a heavy weighting of problems that require operations on zero.

Intervention

The focus of intervention with number difficulties should be the numerical basis of the tasks with which the child has problems. We have seen that strategies based on counting provide the basis for the initial solution of number problems. Learning number words is not usually the problem, but if it is, the task can be embedded within rhymes and games. Mastering the subskills of counting, such as one-to-one matching and ensuring that each object is counted once and only once can be facilitated by encouraging children to partition a collection being counted, or even to place each object into a container as it is counted. Michie (1984a) makes a number of proposals for improving counting skills, including the use of visual displays as shown in Figure 5.3, which shows the relation between a countable collection and the numeral that represents that collection. Children are often discouraged from using strategies such as counting fingers in solving arithmetic problems. Yet the findings reviewed above suggest that it may be useful to encourage such strategies in children with basic arithmetical difficulties for two reasons: first, that it is a strategy that most children find relatively natural, and second, that the more often a correct answer to a problem is produced the greater the strength of association will be between that problem and that answer. Thus, the ultimate likelihood of correct retrieval may be increased by encouraging the use of accurate counting strategies (VanDevender, 1986).

There is evidence that the frequency of problem presentation affects the likelihood of retrieval (Siegler and Shrager, 1984). Thus, repeated exposure to basic arithmetic facts may also be a useful intervention strategy. It may be difficult to implement repeated exposure for children with number difficulties in the context of a full classroom and scarce resources. However, computers can readily be used to present such facts repeatedly (and in interesting formats).

Being able to use a strategy is one thing; knowing when to use it is another. Very often children do not use a strategy because they are unaware of its effectiveness in relation to a particular problem. Michie (1984a, 1984b), for example, has shown that 3- and 4-year-old children when presented with two rows of objects and asked such questions as *which row has more?* did not usually count even though they were able to do so. However, when encouraged to count *and given feedback that the strategy was effective in solving the problem*, the children adopted a counting strategy for other problems. Similar results about the effects of feedback on strategy use have been found in other domains of cognition (see chapter 7). As a general rule, feedback that a strategy has a positive effect leads to increased use of the strategy. A further factor that seems to help in the acquisition of strategies is verbalization of the procedure as it is being carried out (Resnick and Omanson, 1987; Schunk and Cox, 1986).

When a student has acquired an incorrect procedure, it may be necessary to make the student aware of this as well as providing instruction in the correct procedure. Drucker et al. (1987) investigated the effects of providing normal students with information about their consistent procedural errors in multicolumn subtraction, which had been diagnosed using a computer-based diagnosis modelled on the methods of Brown and Burton (1978). The experimental group were told the nature of their errors, had the correct procedure demonstrated, and practised using the procedure, with the teacher gradually withdrawing support. After instruction, the experimental group made fewer errors than a control group who had only received normal classroom instruction.

In chapter 7 we emphasize the importance of setting objectives in designing an intervention programme. The tasks that we have discussed above might be embedded in the context of an educational programme designed to teach basic number facts and their applications. As an example of the application of these skills, box 5.2 shows a set of objectives proposed by Ainscow and Tweddle (1979) that could be used in teaching the child to apply arithmetical skills to the manipulation of money.

In order to solve word problems it is necessary to create a representation of the problem that mediates solution. Goldman (1989) has discussed a number of methods of instruction related to this. While most methods have proved to be effective during training, generalization of the effects over time and to related problems has not always been achieved (see chapter 7 for a more detailed discussion of generalization). Goldman argues that it is necessary to teach the student both *what* to do and *how* to do it. The emphasis on *what* is an emphasis on the relevant task skills. The emphasis on *how* is an emphasis on using executive strategies in regulating task strategies. For example, van Lieshout (1986) employed a strategy training procedure for simple addition and subtraction word problems that emphasized the following steps:

- identify the goal
- identify the givens
- define the solution required
- carry out the computation
- produce a response
- check the answer

ARITHMETIC AND MONEY

Goal: To teach manipulation of money up to totals of £1.

It is probably advisable to delay the formal teaching of money until the slow-learning child is reasonably conversant with the computation of numbers. Most children will have had contact with coins outside school, and it can be useful to have some coins as an aid to the learning of addition and subtraction, but the problems of dealing with groups of different coins are likely to be more confidently approached when the child has a reasonable competence level in dealing with numbers. The following programme assumes such a level and is intended as a basis for structuring a variety of activities involving the manipulation of money, including classroom shop play.

(1)   States all the numbers up to, and including 100;
(2)   Counts by 5s and by 10s up to 100;
(3)   Gives instant correct responses for addition and subtraction bonds up to 20;
(4)   When presented with single coins of any denomination, writes down their value, including the 'p' symbol;
(5)   States that 100p = £1;
(6)   Given sufficient coins, makes up any required amount up to £1;
(7)   Given 3 items costing various amounts but with total value less than £1, works out total cost;
(8)   Given totals up to £1, gives appropriate change.

Box 5.2   *Objectives to teach the application of arithmetical skills to the manipulation of money.*

Using this six-step procedure, van Lieshout secured substantial performance improvements on word problems for two girls with general learning difficulties to whom he taught the strategy.

In order to carry out a sequence such as that described it is necessary to be able to carry out each of the individual steps. For example, in order to identify the goal and the given information, it is necessary to know what to look for in the problem. A number of programmes have been developed to train word problem skills

(Charles and Lester, 1984; Derry et al., 1987). Goldman (1989) provides an account of these and a number of other instructional strategies currently under investigation.

Summary

Children have a natural aptitude for number. They readily learn to count and to solve problems using counting. However, some children have difficulty in learning to count. Number problems start here. If they are not overcome, then they can lead to a vicious circle in the acquisition of more advanced arithmetical skills that rely on counting for their establishment.

Children with basic number problems differ from their peers in their ability to use number strategies effectively and efficiently. They often continue to employ inefficient and time-consuming strategies when their peers have advanced to more efficient strategies. Their own perception of their inefficiency can be discouraging to these children leading them to lose interest in mathematics.

With multi-digit arithmetic, the area of greatest difficulty is in the acquisition of the correct procedures for borrowing and carrying, especially when the numeral 0 is involved. Children's errors here are not usually random but are the result of the application of an incorrect procedure. Detecting these procedures can be difficult, but major advances have been made in describing the most common ones, which can provide the basis of an investigation into any particular child's problems.

Word problems require that verbal statements are first represented in a form suitable for mathematical manipulation and then the arithmetical procedure carried out. At present this is a much under-researched area of number difficulties.

6

Mild, Moderate, and Severe Learning Difficulties

Overview

In this chapter we focus on the problems experienced by children with general learning difficulties (sometimes called mentally handicapped). General learning difficulties are conceived of in terms of specific cognitive processes and structures that, if absent or inefficient, lead to poor performance on a number of cognitive tasks. We first consider the way in which these difficulties have been defined and the ways in which they can be classified. In doing so, we raise the question of whether children with general learning difficulties comprise a homogeneous group. We then discuss whether general learning difficulties constitute a delay in development or a different pattern of development from normal. We evaluate the evidence implicating particular cognitive mechanisms as the causative factors underlying problems in learning. We conclude by outlining the implications of our analysis for assessment and intervention.

What are General Learning Difficulties?

In the previous chapters we have been concerned with the types of difficulties children experience with particular cognitive tasks. By contrast, there is a group of children who appear to experience difficulties across a wide range of tasks. Traditionally children who experience such problems have been called *mentally handicapped*, *mentally retarded*, or *developmentally delayed*. These children have often been described as 'slow' or 'dull' in their abilities to learn and respond to the problems of everyday living (Zigler and Hodapp, 1986). For some children these problems only become evident when they enter school and their progress is contrasted with that of their peers. For others, as the case example below illustrates, the problems will have been evident very early on.

> Charles is 4;1. He was first brought to the attention of the consultant paediatrician at the age of 18 months. At this point he was diagnosed as developmentally delayed. Regular assessments have continued. His most recent assessment indicates that his cognitive and social skills are equivalent to those of a 2-year-old and his language and communication skills are further delayed. His IQ score is 55 and it has been recommended that he attend a developmental nursery.

The above example will be very familiar to professionals who work with children who have special needs. General problems of development, similar to Charles's, are typically identified and defined on the basis of an IQ score. However, there are a number of limitations with this approach. An IQ score fails to identify the precise nature of the child's difficulty. Since the cognitive skills which are involved in the child's problem are not specified there is limited information that can be used in an intervention programme. Further, there is an implicit and often explicit assumption that all children with similar IQ scores will have similar cognitive skills. In this chapter we shall address the problems experienced by children with general learning difficulties. In particular we shall consider the assumptions of homogeneity such a diagnosis implies and evaluate the evidence which implicates different cognitive mechanisms to account for the problems experienced by these children.

There is no consensus about which term should be used to describe children experiencing general learning difficulties. Many attempts to establish an agreement on terminology have been made (see Heron and Myers, 1983). Descriptive terms are necessary for communication among professionals and with parents.

The Warnock Report (Warnock, 1978: 43) advocates the use of the term *learning difficulties* to describe children who have previously been described as *mentally handicapped* or *educationally subnormal*. 'We recommend that the term "children with learning difficulties" should be used in future to describe both those who are currently categorized as educationally sub-normal and those with educational difficulties who are often the concern of remedial services.' This description can be further elaborated into mild, moderate, or severe learning difficulties.

In this chapter we have opted, where possible, to use the terminology recommended by the Warnock Report to describe the problems experienced by these children. The term *learning* describes the characteristic limitation with which we are dealing without discriminating among such functions as memory, attention span, language, or spatial abilities. The term *difficulties* focuses attention on the nature of the problem without specifying a priori whether patterns of development are characterized *only* by delay or *only* by differences. Moreover, the term *learning difficulties* is preferred by those who experience such problems (King's Fund, 1980). However, the terms *mentally handicapped* and *mentally retarded* are still in common usage in medical circles and in the experimental literature when reporting the results of studies. These terms will be used, where necessary, to refer accurately to the conclusions of empirical work.

Diagnosis

The American Association on Mental Deficiency (AAMD) has defined mental retardation as 'significantly subaverage general intellectual functioning existing concurrently with deficits in adaptive behaviour, and manifested during the developmental period'. Subaverage general intellectual functioning is defined by a score on an intelligence test. According to the AAMD a person's IQ score must be at least two standard deviations below the mean of the population (that is, less than 70) to be considered 'retarded'. The rationale for selecting this particular cutoff point is more a pragmatic statistical decision than one based on sound classification procedures. Until recently this was the common cutoff point in Britain to warrant education in special schools.

However, the actual allocation of a child with mild learning difficulties to special educational facilities depends as much on regional provision, in Britain, as it does on a child's performance on psychometric tests (Tomlinson, 1982).

The observation that many academically disadvantaged individuals functioned adequately in society after their school years led clinicians in the 1960s to a redefinition of 'retardation' to include social as well as academic difficulties. For example, the President's Committee on Mental Retardation (1973) defined the mentally retarded as children and adults who, as a result of inadequately developed intelligence, are significantly impaired in their ability to learn and adapt to the demands of society. More recently, Zigler et al. (1984) have argued that because social adaptation is a vague concept and difficult to measure, it should not be included in a definition of 'mental retardation'. In reality, adaptive behaviour is rarely used as a criterion by researchers or in the diagnosis process by clinicians.

For researchers and clinicians alike the diagnosis of a learning difficulty is intimately linked to a child's performance on a standardized test of intelligence. A number of implications follow from the assumption that the main factor distinguishing children with general difficulties from those with no problems or only with specific learning difficulties is *the extent or level* of an individual's measured intelligence:

- no specification of aetiology is made
- there is an assumption that we are dealing with a fixed, immutable, biological characteristic present at or soon after birth
- intellectual functioning is being defined in terms of an IQ score but no explanation for the performance is identified other than low IQ

The link between possessing 'intelligence' and being successful at learning is a powerful one and has pervaded both psychological theories and society for a long time. Teachers, parents, and professionals often refer to children as 'intelligent' or 'quick to learn' on the one hand, or 'slow' or 'delayed' on the other. It was around the end of the nineteenth century that scientists such as Galton (1883) and Cattell (1890) argued that high intelligence was associated with faster perceptions, faster reactions, and general superiority. By corollary, scientists and the general public alike began to view the 'mentally retarded' as inferior in all ways. This inferiority began to be both explained and described by an individual's performance on standardized tests of intelligence. There continues to be some support for the position that 'retarded' people are best differentiated by IQ alone (Ellis and Cavalier, 1982). The two most popular classification schemes (that of the AAMD and DSM-III) essentially classify on the basis of IQ and these schemes were rated as more reliable than others by clinicians (Seltzer, 1983). However, intelligence test scores provide a measure of current functioning which describes the rate of intellectual development; they do not identify the cognitive processes by which this intellectual level is achieved. An account of these latter processes is required in order to understand general learning difficulties.

Although common understanding tends to conflate cognition and intelligence, the distinction between the two is important. If we adopt the position that IQ is a measure of intelligence, then intelligence is the ability to perform well on school-like and test-like tasks. Cognition is the set of mental skills that underlie performance on these and other tasks. To understand the child's skills and to intervene appropriately we need to discover the representations, processes, and strategies that are used in performing tasks. The goal of contemporary research on intelligence is to provide a theoretical basis for intelligence (see Anderson, 1992). This is done by identifying the basic information processing components that, in various combinations, account for performance on tasks requiring intelligence (Carroll, 1976; Simon, 1976; Sternberg, 1978). From this perspective there is an attempt to break down the learning chain and identify those processes that are critical in cognitive tasks.

Intelligence is a measure of how well individuals perform tasks. However, the continuity implied by the normally distributed IQ score serves to mask any possible qualitative differences that may exist in children's processing skills and it does not tell us what aspect or aspects of the child's cognitive system is causing problems. A serious limitation of intelligence test measures is that they do not offer an explanation of how cognition develops, nor what the processing requirements are for successful completion of items on an intelligence test. Therefore, a diagnosis in terms of IQ *alone* tells us a child is having problems but it tells us little about what constitutes the problem. Moreover, such measures are too widely and too rigidly applied without the benefit of a clearly defined understanding of their limitations or a recognition of their inability to explain the child's cognitive problems.

Prevalence and Aetiological Considerations

Prevalence studies need to consider the population at large, not simply children in special schools or hospitals. A number of studies have used standardized assessment devices and considered the population at large (Drillien et al., 1966; Rutter et al., 1970). The general population estimate of children with IQs less than 70 is somewhere between 2 per cent and 2.5 per cent. It has been estimated that half of these show a severe language deficiency, articulation disorder, or a combination of the two (Endeby and Davies, 1989; Rutter et al., 1970). However, there is a significant difference between the levels of observed and predicted incidence of severe learning difficulties (Fryers, 1984).

While there is a general consensus about which individuals are experiencing severe learning difficulties, the situation with respect to milder problems is not always clear cut (Gillham, 1986). The National Child Development Study (Kellmer-Pringle et al., 1966) found that at the age of 7 years, 0.4 per cent of the children in the survey were attending special schools; 5 per cent were receiving help in the ordinary classroom because of educational or 'mental' backwardness; while there were a further 8 per cent who, their teachers considered, would benefit from some help. The Warnock report (Warnock, 1978) suggests that children who have 'limited ability' and children who are 'retarded' by other conditions, both defined by delays of more than 20 per cent from their expected score given their age, would amount to approximately 10 per cent of the school population. This figure excluded those with severe learning problems. Thus, the range of children who might be included in such a category is broad, and harder to define than a criterion based on IQ would suggest.

A distinction is frequently drawn between those individuals whose difficulties are of organic origin and those whose difficulties are of unknown aetiology. Over the last 30 years advances in biomedical research have greatly increased our ability to identify some of the causes of general learning difficulties. Grossman (1983) notes that there are now 200 identified causes of 'mental retardation'. For those individuals experiencing *severe* learning difficulties (roughly IQ of less than 50) aetiological causes can be identified in 85–90 per cent of the cases (Fryers, 1984). Organic insults are generally of three kinds: those occurring prior to birth, such as genetic abnormalities or problems in utero; those occurring at the time of birth, such as anoxia; those occurring postnatally, such as childhood encephalitis.

By contrast, for those individuals experiencing *mild* or *moderate* learning difficulties aetiological implications are less clear. For the majority of individuals who are diagnosed as 'mentally retarded' there are no obvious organic aetiologies. In general, IQ levels of this group tend to fall in the moderate to mild range (50–70). Zigler and Balla (1982) state that at least 70 per cent of those identified as having learning difficulties show no evidence of organic brain dysfunction whereas a later study by Zigler and Hodapp (1986) estimated that only 45 per cent were of unknown aetiology. This figure is continually changing due to advances in identification procedures and the increased numbers of infants being kept alive despite serious central nervous system damage.

Persons who show no evidence of organic brain dysfunction are referred to by the AAMD as suffering from retardation due to psychosocial disadvantage. The older and more widely used description is cultural–familial disadvantage, which reflects the combination of environmental and genetic factors that might account for individuals who had no definite organic pathology (Zigler, 1969). Thus, the mild level of learning difficulty (IQ in the range 50–70) is viewed primarily as academic dysfunction, or a deficiency in learning ability with aetiology unknown, while the conceptualization of severe learning difficulty (IQ below 50) is viewed as a serious physiologically caused handicap.

Classification

Children with general learning difficulties can be subdivided in three different ways: IQ score, aetiology, and curricular

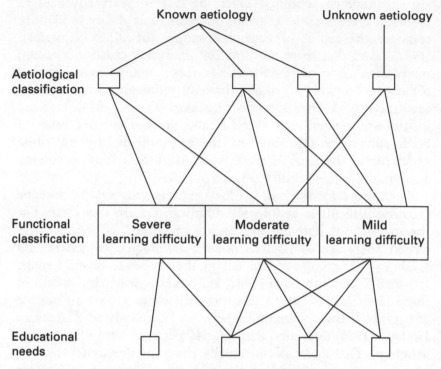

Figure 6.1 *Illustration of how different classification systems could cross-classify the population with general learning difficulties.*

requirements. As figure 6.1 shows, these different levels will cross-classify the population. They serve different purposes and the relations between the different levels may have important implications for understanding learning difficulties. The figure highlights that we are dealing with a range of reactions; that is, a specific IQ does not map onto a specific set of educational needs. Rather, the IQ offers an upper and lower limit to the types of special educational need that a child might experience. This range can be quite large and will be influenced by environmental conditions. The majority of empirical studies continue to segment research groups by level of intellectual functioning and not aetiology. Researchers either compare the functioning of children with mild to moderate learning difficulties to mental age (MA) or chronological age (CA) matched controls. Such studies attempt to document common deficits across the range of children with learning difficulties and little attempt is made to consider how the range of difficulties might vary among individuals of different aetiologies. Distinguishing along the continuum of IQ scores provides one with a tool for diagnosis, but it is less clear that this links directly to intervention or adequately reflects the cognitive skills that are necessary to learn.

Aetiology offers a different perspective on classification. Aetiological classifications, although accounting for only some children with learning difficulties, can provide important information about both the similarities and differences across the range of learning difficulties. The problems manifested must then be translated to a cognitive profile for appropriate intervention to occur. The extent to which this will guide intervention is unclear at the present but there are important implications for assessment (see Dockrell and Henry, in press). It is not clear to what extent aetiological variation leads to cognitive variation, although there are indications of different strengths and weaknesses among different groups (see Hodapp and Dykens, in press). Research work is now trying to identify the nature of the difficulties experienced by children with specified conditions, such as Down's syndrome. Data about specific handicaps should help clarify the nature of the types of problems experienced by children with general learning difficulties.

A number of classification systems that include more than one level have been proposed. For example, Zigler and Hodapp (1986) propose four groups in their attempt to subclassify children with general learning difficulties. In this case children are classified both on the basis of level of IQ and additional criteria, such as aetiology:

- 'mental retardation' with known organic aetiology
- familial 'retardation' with an IQ between 40 and 70 and one parent with an IQ score below 70
- polygenic isolates, who receive a poor genetic draw
- environmentally deprived children

Classification systems based on aetiology, IQ, or both provide a framework for identifying children who are likely to experience general learning difficulties. However, no explanations of the types of learning difficulties that an individual child may have are presented, nor does the classification have direct implications for intervention.

The Warnock report placed greatest emphasis on curricular requirements, that is, the type of educational provision best suited to the child's needs. In taking the emphasis away from categorization based on aetiology and IQ, Warnock places the emphasis on what the child requires rather than the child's limitations per se. To devise appropriate interventions we must be able to identify an appropriate curriculum for the child. To do so we must understand the nature of the child's problems and this requires an understanding of the child's cognitive abilities. This should assist professionals in deciding whether a child can benefit from a normal curriculum or whether it is necessary to recommend a modified or different curriculum (see chapter 7).

Types of Difficulties Experienced by These Children

While IQ has served as the basis for classifying children with general learning difficulties, many researchers have attempted to be more precise about the types of developmental problems these children encounter. A central question is whether children with learning difficulties are delayed in their development or whether they present a different developmental pattern. Children with general learning difficulties display a slower rate of learning and reach a lower ceiling. A lower ceiling indicates that there are limits on the extent of cognitive development; therefore upper limits on performance exist.

Is this learning process best explained by a model which invokes the same principles and mechanisms of development that apply to ordinary children, or is it necessary to invoke specific differences over and above the slower rate and lower ceiling? Attempts to answer such questions have resulted in two main foci in the studies of these children:

- establishing the extent to which children with general learning difficulties follow a *similar sequence* of development to normal children

• establishing the extent to which performance differences on cognitive tasks can be explained by underlying processing differences

In general, studies that investigate the similar sequence hypothesis (sometimes called the developmental approach) have tended to consider children's progress through the Piagetian stages of cognitive development. Research has supported the similar sequence hypothesis both across large stages and within the sub-stages (Weisz and Zigler, 1979; Weisz and Yeates, 1981). This is true regardless of aetiology, with the possible exception of children with severe seizure disorders. Children progress through the Piagetian stages at a slower rate and there is a lower ceiling.

Studies from the Piagetian perspective are predominantly concerned with what stages the child has mastered and in what order. An alternative perspective is to consider how the child's cognitive system processes information. One suggestion is that children with general learning difficulties actually process information in a different manner from ordinary children and that this accounts for the difficulties that they experience on a wide range of tasks. From this perspective general learning difficulties are conceived of in terms of specific cognitive processes and structures that, if absent or inefficient, lead to poor performance on a number of cognitive tasks. Processing difficulties need not, however, imply fundamental cognitive differences.

An important question to address is how might the cognitive system of children with general learning difficulties function differently? There are at least three possible ways in which this might occur: the system might produce different patterns of performance across cognitive domains; there might be a particular processing difficulty which is not domain specific; there might be reduced efficiency in one particular component but the difference is manifested on other tasks which depend on this component. While these different interpretations are not mutually exclusive, determining which is the major cause in any particular case could have important implications for intervention. For example, if a child cannot process a particular type of input, interventions would need to take this into consideration.

The first possibility is that the relation between cognitive domains is different from the commonly expected pattern in development (Anderson, 1992). From this perspective the cognitive system could be considered to function differently in terms of the pattern of performance across different domains, and thus the relation between different domains of knowledge may not be the same as we might expect in normal patterns of development (Hodapp and Burack, 1990). Children with Down's syndrome, for example, may have specific problems with language over and above their general problems.

The second possibility suggests that a particular cognitive mechanism may not function appropriately. Research on this issue began at least 30 years ago with cognitive psychologists attempting to identify where the breaks in the learning system might occur such as in attention (Zeaman and House, 1963); in short term memory (Ellis, 1963); or in cross-modal coding (O'Connor and Hermelin, 1963). Such research attempted to account for a general learning difficulty by identifying a specific deficit. Recently, Dykens et al. (1987) noted that males with fragile X syndrome are particularly impaired on tasks involving sequential processing or those requiring short-term memory. In such cases it is important to decide what is an acceptable variation in processing (as one finds ranges of abilities in the normal population) and what is truly exceptional.

The third possibility is that due to skills being acquired more slowly the child is unable to build up the requisite knowledge and strategies to perform a task successfully. This might give the appearance of a different cognitive structure. For example, if children have difficulties in identifying the appropriate strategy to use in a problem solving situation, it may appear as if the cognitive system is functioning differently, but the behaviour may simply reflect an inappropriate basis for responding. Children with mild to moderate general learning difficulties are more helpless in problem solving situations (Weisz, 1978). These young people do not behave in a proactive way in problem solving situations, rather they are passive. There is a danger of interpreting such passivity as indicating a different cognitive structure when it does not necessarily do so.

To date, more similarities than differences have appeared when children with general learning difficulties have been compared with children matched for MA on cognitive tasks. General reviews of the relevant research conclude that children categorized as 'familial' do on the whole have similar cognitive structures where as organically retarded children do not (Weisz et al., 1982). Such conclusions are still contentious (Weiss et al., 1986). Children with mild, moderate, and severe learning difficulties are a heterogeneous group. The only assumed underlying commonality is a cognitive problem. It is unclear whether the same cognitive difficulty is the underlying cause in all cases. Moreover, as Siegler and Richards (1982) note, the lack of disparities may be due to the fact that most studies focused on the children's spontaneous performance rather than on their ability to learn. They argue that it seems plausible that the major difference between more and less 'intelligent' children lies in the rapidity and completeness with which they acquire new information. The emphasis on children's ability to learn implies that we must consider the strategies involved in the learning process and the ways in which strategies interact with the knowledge that the children possess.

Methodology

There are three key factors which must be considered when attempting to investigate the delays or problems experienced by children with general learning difficulties;

• the control group with whom a comparison is being made
• the homogeneity of the sample of individuals with learning difficulties
• the assumptions that are made about the problems causing the difficulties

If we wish to identify the cause(s) of a general learning difficulty we must be able to show (1) that ordinary children require a particular cognitive skill, strategy, or set of knowledge successfully to complete a task and (2) that this is lacking in individuals with general learning difficulties. But what comparison group of children is appropriate? If children of a similar chronological age are used as a comparison group, differences in performance

Table 6.1 *Implications of MA comparisons for gaps in experience.*

Chronological age	4	8	16
Mental age	4	4	4
Additional years of experience	0	4	12

between the groups will be noted. Moreover, these differences will be large since by definition children with general learning difficulties are functioning below what is consistent with their chronological age by at least two standard deviations on an IQ test. If we are interested in any specific differences in information processing, children of an equivalent MA should be used. This, in theory, allows a comparison between similar levels of cognitive skills. Matching on MA is an important control. However, in interpreting differences between groups it is important to be aware of two problems. Firstly, the larger the chronological age gap between children and their MA comparisons the more difficult it becomes to draw conclusions. As table 6.1 shows, a child of 16 years with an MA equivalent of 4 years has 12 years of additional experience to influence performance on tasks. Whether this learning history has any *significant* implications for cognitive skills will not be clear. There will be a likely impact on motivation (Zigler, 1969) and the strategies that a child might apply to solving tasks. When there are large gaps it cannot simply be assumed that the two individuals are comparable. Secondly, MA equivalents are constructed by summing over a number of subscales on an intelligence test (the precise number and combination varies according to the test). Thus, two people can have the same MA for entirely different reasons. In fact matching on MA or IQ is particularly problematic for information processing models since we do not know which skills are being matched and which are not. Ideally children need to be matched on the basis of the cognitive skills under investigation as well as CA.

We must also consider who should be included in the group of children with general learning difficulties. Conducting studies that include unspecified groups of subjects with general learning difficulties seems to be justified only if the guiding view of intelligence and cognition is such that 'retardation' is conceptualized as a homogenous entity. Zigler and Hodapp (1986) suggest that children who show a clear organic aetiology are not easily defined in terms of their 'nonretarded peers': 'These children may not be part of the normal (Gaussian) distribution of intelligence because their intellectual apparatus has been damaged.' By contrast, other researchers are happy to assume that all children traverse the same developmental path. This is, of course, an empirical question.

An additional problem for studies in this area is identifying the critical dimension in performance. A child may fail a task because some ability, other than the ability under investigation, has interacted with task variables to produce a performance deficit. For example, a child might score poorly on a digit recall task for reasons other than a poor memory; attention or language skills are possible factors influencing performance on such a task.

There are no simple answers to these problems. An important first step should be to create models of the range of developmental patterns evidenced by children with general learning difficulties. To this end studies which focus on particular diagnostic groups will be helpful. In addition we must be clear about which specific skills are required to solve a task so that the key dimensions can be identified when comparisons are being made.

The Cognitive System

In order to understand the types of problems experienced by any child with a learning difficulty we must have some understanding of how information is normally processed and what factors inhibit or support the working of the cognitive system. Any information processing model is concerned with the factors that shape or underlie cognition. Guilford (1967) argued that a theory of tasks is a prerequisite for a theory of intelligence. However, unlike the domains considered in other chapters in this book, general learning difficulties force us to consider the cognitive demands of a range of tasks.

In chapter 1 we outlined the structure of the cognitive system from an information processing perspective. This included the cognitive architecture, mental representations (the knowledge base), task processes, executive processes and metacognitive knowledge. Together, these provide the basic building blocks by which the cognitive system acquires, stores, and retrieves information. In the attempt to identify the causal factors for general learning difficulties the focus has been on mechanisms that are general and operate across domains.

The architecture is the basic innate structure of the cognitive system. This basic structure is assumed to be common among individuals. However, it may be subject to neurological damage, as in many cases of severe learning difficulties. More generally, there may be differences among individuals in the efficiency with which the architecture functions. Accordingly, the basic speed and efficiency of information processing has been seen as one possible cause of general learning difficulties.

A second possible factor that has been widely studied in relation to general learning difficulties is attentional processes. In order for information to be processed at all, it must be received by the cognitive system as input. We selectively attend to some input, while ignoring a huge amount of other possible information from the environment.

Information being processed is held temporarily in working memory. If there are any deficiencies in either the capacity of working memory or in the processes used to manipulate information in working memory, then this is likely to have general effects on cognitive performance. The memory system and memory processes have also been widely studied in relation to general learning difficulties. Of particular importance here is the role that executive processes may play in deploying lower-level memory strategies.

Finally, the way in which information is represented will affect its storage and retrieval. Individuals can vary quantitatively (they may know more) or qualitatively (their knowledge may be organized in different ways). In one way or another each of the above has been postulated to account for the difficulties experienced by children with general learning difficulties. However, it is unclear whether there is a single common causal mechanism for these difficulties. There may be a range of factors which, in various combinations, can account for the problems in learning.

What an information processing approach allows is the decomposition of intelligent behaviour into components that can serve as the locus for intervention.

Efficiency and Reaction Time Measures

It has been argued that the speed with which individuals can execute a number of basic cognitive processes on tasks which, in theory, do not demand knowledge or problem solving skills, may explain the problems experienced by children with general learning difficulties. Many of these studies have focused on basic reaction time tasks. While early attempts to link individual differences in mental ability with reaction time measures were unconvincing (Brewer, 1987), more recent studies have supported a consistent correlation between low IQ scores and slower reaction times. However, the explanation of why differences in processing speed occur is still unclear. One possibility is that the slower reaction times actually imply a fundamental architectural deficit either in terms of slower perceptual, motoric, or decision making processes. For example Anderson (1986: 303) argues that the 'retarded' are characterized by low efficiency (e) perhaps as a result of speed of operation: 'Low e constrains the use and development of knowledge systems (a qualitative effect) and also the efficiency with which task solutions, generated by knowledge systems, are executed (a quantitative effect).'

Such an analysis implies that the cognitive deficit is general. However, it might be possible to obviate some of the effects of this general deficit by training specific activities which allow the formation of processing strategies. There is evidence that the differences in speed of responding, between individuals with general learning difficulties and those without, can be reduced to some extent (Nettelbeck and Brewer, 1981).

The crucial question is whether speed is the problem or whether it is the manner in which cognitive resources are deployed. The slower rate of processing may reflect differences in learning strategies. In this case the pattern of response becomes critical in the analysis and not the absolute magnitude. For example, Campione (1986) argues that the reaction time behaviour of individuals with general learning difficulties is due as much to lack of consistency as to a general lower level of responding. As Brewer (1987: 43) notes: 'Despite the emphasis on the speed of basic processes it has become clear that considerable care must be exercised when interpreting the available evidence, because most tasks appear to reflect the influence of higher order cognitive processes.' Brewer suggests that failing to use past experience effectively in terms of judging the right balance of accuracy and speed can account for many of the problems experienced by individuals with general learning difficulties. Training and practice can reduce differences between normals and individuals with general learning difficulties on particular tasks. The fact that differences are not completely eliminated indicates that we are dealing with a system that has limits to its modifiability.

The complexity of the cognitive processes under investigation and the analysis required to identify the sources of the problems should not be underestimated. Each task involves a range of processing skills. As figure 6.2 shows, simply responding to the presence of a particular stimulus requires a complex series of operations. Nettelbeck and Brewer (1981) conclude that less efficient processing has been identified at each stage in the serial processing task presented in figure 6.2. They believe this to be the result of less efficient operations in the central executive processes that direct or mediate other processing operations. The balance between speed and accuracy is critical. Thus, one gets effects at all levels and stages. The view that a dominant difficulty for people with general learning difficulties is with the executive processes that control information processing will recur when we consider attention and memory. Until one can rule out the possibility that other strategies are not involved, the inference that speed is the central and overriding influence on cognitive performance must be questioned.

Attention

Poor attentional processes have frequently been considered to be the main barrier to adequate intellectual functioning (Zeaman and House, 1979). There have been suggestions that a deficit exists in the perceptual and attentional system of children with

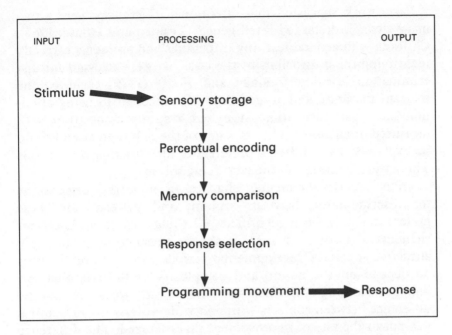

Figure 6.2 *Schematic representation of processing operations between a stimulus input and a response output.*

general learning difficulties and there is considerable evidence to support this claim (Detterman, 1979).

Two central questions need to be addressed to understand the importance of attentional mechanisms: What is attention and what are poor attentional processes? Attention refers to the selective processing of inputs from the range of stimuli that impinge on our senses. In the context of a task this raises the question of why children attend to certain task dimensions in preference to others. Attention may be poor because the child does not attend to the task at all or because the child has not realized what the relevant dimensions are. For example, a child may fail to distinguish between reading the words *pat* and *bat* because he has not looked at the words or because the child does not know that the *p* and *b* are the relevant dimension for distinguishing between the two words.

Early work suggested that attentional differences were a primary factor in 'retarded intelligence' (Zeaman and House, 1963). Children with general learning difficulties had problems correctly identifying the dimensions of the task that were relevant for discrimination learning. Zeaman and House (1979) reviewed the relevant literature and argued that differences in focusing attention on a particular dimension had a strong association with measured intelligence. That is, some of the failure to attend could be explained by children's preferences for stimulus dimensions which were irrelevant to the task being solved.

There are developmental changes in preferred dimensions for discriminating between stimuli, and patterns for these preferences have been identified. All things being equal certain elements of a stimulus, such as shape, appear to be particularly attractive at certain developmental periods. However, preferences do depend on the nature and complexity of the stimulus. An important finding of Zeaman and House's early work was that the difference between subjects with and without learning difficulties was not in the rate of improvement that occurred. The difference in performance arose before learning had begun. There was a longer initial period of chance level performance before identifying the correct dimension.

The role of attention will be critical in terms of what information enters the memory system. Which dimensions a child focuses on in more complex tasks will be determined by a range of factors outside the attentional system. For example, there is an interaction between what the child already knows (that is his knowledge base) and attention. Attentional subprocesses can be seen as part of a wider range of processes (including retention and learning) related to cognitive functioning in children with general learning difficulties.

Recently, research has suggested that infants' performance on habituation tasks reflects a measure of attention (Bornstein, 1989). The performance of infants on such tasks is significantly related to verbal proficiency at 1 year of age and performance on tests of intelligence at 4 years of age (see chapter 2). While there is considerable debate about what sorts of models best explain this correlation, there is the indication that a measure of attention contributes to later performance on a range of tasks. For example,

infants with Down's syndrome habituate to criterion in the same
number of trials but they spend longer processing the stimuli
(Wagner et al., 1990). It is not clear whether this is best explained
by the inadequacy of the children's representations, their inability to identify the relevant target dimensions, or a problem in
storage.

Current reviews of the effect of attentional processes on
performance have highlighted the fact that children with learning
difficulties perform worst on the most cognitively demanding
tasks, particularly tasks with distracters. In complex tasks the
children appear to have great difficulty in monitoring the task
requirements. On some simple tasks, differences can be minimal
(Krupski, 1986). It may be more parsimonious to consider difficulties in processing particular types of information as a failure
of executive processes rather than as a failure of attention. The
problem with these tasks appears to be one of resource allocation
rather than difficulties in attending per se. Thus, we should be
identifying the processing requirements of particular tasks when
planning interventions. For example, Borkowski et al. (1983)
point out that subjects with learning difficulties show much more
off-task glancing on a range of reaction time and discrimination
tasks. In a test situation the subjects may not orient themselves
appropriately or scan arrays in a systematic fashion.

Memory

Poor memory performance characterizes children with general
learning difficulties. All the stores and processes of memory
systems have been thought to be deficient to a greater or lesser
extent in individuals with general learning difficulties (Detterman, 1979). Ellis (1963) proposed one of the first explanations
of the memory deficit in these children. He suggested that
memory traces decay more rapidly. In general the recent research
does not support this view (Kail, 1990). While children with mild
and moderate learning difficulties remember less well than their
peers, the rate of forgetting appears to be similar in both groups.
In fact there is no compelling evidence to suggest that either the
capacity of short term memory or the durability of items in short
term memory varies with either age or intelligence.

Memory is not a unitary construct. For a child to be able to access information from memory it must be initially encoded, stored and then retrieved. If information on memory processes is to be useful in an applied fashion it needs to be framed in a way that has implications for intervention.

Component Processes in Working Memory   As we argued in chapter 1, working memory supports complex cognitive behaviours. Working memory can be considered to be the cognitive space in which attentional mechanisms reside. It has two functions:

• storage of information as it is being processed
• regulation of the operation of executive routines

Torgesen et al. (1987) review studies of working memory and conclude that children with general learning difficulties scan the information present in working memory more slowly than individuals of average intelligence. However, the scan rate differs between children of different aetiologies and varies according to the nature of the stimuli presented. Torgesen et al. (1987: 58) conclude:

> if search and comparison processes can be considered to be elements of basic processing efficiency, then the evidence ... suggests that most mentally retarded children will be limited in performance on complex verbal tasks by the inability to examine the stored contents of working memory as rapidly as normal children.

Structure and Organization in Memory   A critical aspect in memory performance is the fact that variations in the use of mnemonic strategies contribute to performance differences among special children on many kinds of memory tasks (Torgesen et al., 1987). Memory tasks that are influenced by strategy use are those that allow sufficient time for the conscious execution of an appropriate strategy or give the subject some control over the way stimuli are presented. Poor strategic processing appears to be a ubiquitous characteristic of individuals with general learning difficulties. These individuals are more passive during encoding and show little spontaneous use of strategies such as rehearsal (Borkowski and Kurtz, 1987). Strategic problems have been identified at both the encoding and retrieval stages (Butterfield and Ferreti, 1987).

The critical question then becomes why strategies are not used. Children with mild and moderate learning difficulties can be taught to use mnemonic strategies and enhanced performance can be obtained and maintained for appreciable time periods (Brown et al., 1974). Thus, it is not the case that the children are unable to use strategies; they have the requisite skills. However, Butterfield et al. (1973) suggested that in the case of rehearsal it is not simply a failure to rehearse spontaneously that causes the difficulties. They used a task which involved increasingly explicit training on probed serial recall. Individuals with general learning difficulties had problems in actually coordinating the necessary components to rehearse; that is, the process of rehearsing itself caused problems. This implies, of course, that not only will these children need to be told to rehearse, they will have to be shown how to do it.

Although training studies show positive effects within the training situation, generalization of specific strategies to new situations is almost never obtained (Borkowski and Cavanaugh, 1979; Borkowski and Peck, 1986; Campione et al., 1984). If it were simply the case that the children were not aware of the need to engage in such cognitive activities prior to training then one would predict that training might lead to generalization. Since this is not the case other processes must be implicated.

Several researchers have argued that the central problem for those with general learning difficulties rests in the understanding of their own cognitive system and the ability to control strategic processing. Consistent with this view is research indicating that individuals with general learning difficulties are not skilled at the phase in memory problems which involves identifying appropriate strategies to aid recall (Lukose, 1987). For example, children with general learning difficulties are very poor at estimating the difficulty of memory problems (Brown et al., 1977). A number of studies have begun to investigate the effects of training people with learning difficulties on the use of processing strategies relevant to remembering. This has led to an emphasis on informing the individual about the value of using a strategy and opportunities to apply the strategy in a variety of tasks. As in the case of speed and attention, executive processes are highlighted as major contributory factors to the child's learning difficulties. It is as yet unclear to what extent these difficulties can mainly be explained in terms of a lag in the development of metacognitive processes.

Storage and Knowledge Bases   Deciding on strategy use or re-deploying cognitive resources is determined by the knowledge that one possesses. There is evidence that the state of the learner's knowledge affects both the speed of processing information and the manner in which strategies are selected. If new information to be remembered is meaningful, comprehension and subsequent memory for the essential features will occur more easily. If a child is asked to learn some vocabulary items for reading and he knows the meaning of these items, more will be recalled than if the child is asked to learn vocabulary items where the meaning is unknown. Thus, the match between the information to be remembered and what a child knows is critical for memory.

Children with general learning difficulties have smaller and less elaborately organized knowledge bases than CA matched controls (Butterfield et al., 1985; Chi, 1981; Holzman et al., 1982, 1983). Inadequate knowledge bases do not support memorial processes to the same extent that well organized knowledge bases do (see chapter 7). McFarland and Weibe (1987) argue that the semantic representations are less elaborate and less inter-connected for children with general learning difficulties and this is the basis for the semantic processing deficit. For example, let us assume that two children are being tested, both know a lot of dinosaur names, and both are asked to recall a list of dinosaur names which they have previously learned. Let us assume in addition that one child knows a lot about dinosaurs and the relationships between various types of dinosaurs and the other does not. It is the child who knows a lot about dinosaurs who will remember more dinosaur names. By contrast, when children generate their own lists, memory difficulties are not as obvious. Therefore, the extent to which various semantic relationships are activated during stimulus encoding is potentially a major factor in this deficiency.

Information Processing and General Learning Difficulties

Information processing models allow the decomposition of intelligent behaviour. In the previous sections we have highlighted some of the dimensions which can contribute to general learning difficulties. Each dimension could serve as a locus for intervention but clearly learning to extract the relevant dimensions to store information efficiently is important. The challenge for researchers is to specify the interactions among these basic processes. For practitioners the challenge is to incorporate these models in intervention.

It is as yet unclear to what extent structural features play a role in the behaviour of some or all children with general learning difficulties. There are ceilings in performance but the 'reaction' range of variability is as yet unspecified. An important aspect in cognitive performance is the selection and execution of strategies that optimize task performance. Transfer of training seems to depend, in part at least, on training of executive processes as well as training of task strategies. It is for this reason that a theory of intelligence must take care to specify in detail the strategy or strategies that are used in solving various classes of problems. Thus, from a cognitive perspective, general learning difficulties refer to a developmental process in which strategies for storing, acquiring, or using knowledge develop at a slower rate and ultimately reach lower levels than for normal students. The implications of these difficulties can be made explicit for the teaching situation. Specifically, these children may:

- have difficulty remembering new information
- find it difficult to generalize what they have learned to new situations
- have great difficulty in understanding complex or abstract ideas
- finish their work more slowly and not complete tasks

Assessment and Intervention

Assessment

There are at least two issues that need to be addressed when assessing children thought to have general learning difficulties. Firstly, it must be established whether or not the child experiences a pervasive problem with learning. Secondly, it is important to isolate whether there are any specific difficulties that are hindering the child's performance. To establish that a child has a general learning difficulty we must be able to demonstrate that the child's performance lies outside the normal range of development. Developmental schedules are often used to identify preschool children who are experiencing difficulties. In these cases the child's behaviour is contrasted with that of an age-matched control group on a range of developmental tasks. Children in school are generally assessed by considering their performance on a standardized measure of intelligence. This initial attempt to determine cognitive skills needs to be supplemented to provide a profile of strengths and needs. Ideally criterion-referenced tests, which aim to identify the exact level and content of development, should be used.

There is a range of tools to assess children who are not coping with the school curriculum or who are in the preschool years. For example the Wessex revised Portage Checklist (White and East, 1983) extends the original Portage and is organized in small steps. A baseline is identified and interventions are planned which are task specific and geared to the child accomplishing a further task on the checklist. This is an ideal way of providing a detailed profile of a child's strengths and needs and is directly linked to intervention. The lack of items at the lower end of the checklist required for many children with severe learning difficulties has been addressed by the program devised by McBrien and Foxen (1981).

Older children who are falling behind at school can be assessed on specific aspects of the school curriculum to establish their present level of performance. Effectively one is creating a profile of the child's special educational needs across a range of domains. Careful observation of the types of tasks which cause the child difficulty will be required. Detailed information of the child's approach to the tasks should identify any general difficulties, such as failure to attend to relevant task dimensions.

Neither norm-referenced nor criterion-referenced tests successfully assess strategies generally or executive processes in particular. Standardized intelligence tests cannot begin to sort out the influence of various information processing factors on performance, nor can they offer direct predictions of what sorts of competencies or difficulties might exist. The information processing approach suggests directions for training intelligent performance because of its emphasis on processes and strategies. However, there are very complex implications of these models for assessment (Detterman and Sternberg, 1982) and it is not clear how these can be easily transferred from the laboratory to the clinical setting. Presently, the strength of this approach lies in the guidelines which are set for intervention rather than in ways of assessing children's performance.

Intervention

The term *modified curriculum* is sometimes used to describe the type of curriculum required for children with mild to moderate learning difficulties. It refers to the fact that these children require modifications to the main-stream curriculum if their educational needs are to be met. In practice it should at least mean that learning objectives are more carefully graded and broken down into smaller steps. The term *developmental curriculum* is sometimes used for individuals with severe learning difficulties. Here the curriculum is usually conceived of in terms of the acquisition of developmental skills such as fine and gross motor, language and communication, emotional, social and self-care (see Clements, 1987, for a discussion of severe learning difficulties).

The goal of intervention should be to develop whatever skills the individual possesses to the highest level possible. Asking for normality only leads to frustration for the child, the child's family and for those trying to intervene. However, we do know that children with general learning difficulties tend to follow normal developmental patterns. Thus, if one knows that skill A precedes skill B, and the child does not possess skill A the best way to train skill B is to train skill A first. Kiernan (1981) has demonstrated that an objectives approach can be successfully applied to multiply handicapped children. The objectives must be set in consideration with the types of general problems that we have identified in this chapter. There are two important factors which need to govern approaches to intervention: the tasks will be learned at a slower rate and there will be specific difficulties with generalizing what is learned.

The issue of generalization is central. Butterfield and Belmont (1971) point out that for these children learning is more passive and it needs to be made active. Campione and Brown (1978) describe the learning of these children as being 'welded' to the context in which it was first learned, and the children certainly do not appear to have flexible access to cognitive structures to enable them to learn more efficiently. Strategies must be identified at the appropriate level. For example, Brown and Campione (1977) trained learning strategies for free recall. Their results again showed that information processing deficits can be assessed and remediated but that students must be taught strategies appropriate for their level of cognitive functioning. Teaching generalization strategies is likely to be of importance since generalization does not readily occur across time, situations, and persons (Brown et al., 1983; Campione et al., 1982; Paris et al., 1982).

The particular task chosen for training needs to be identified on the basis of task centrality. For example, Sugden (1989) discusses the need to build generalization into the national curriculum. He proposes general guidelines in terms of cognitive strategies. These involve the promotion of perceived similarity between tasks, an analysis of the context in which tasks are learned, the use of expert scaffolding, and the detailed planing of practice schedules. All of these strategies allow the child to make links between skills learned in different situations and reinforce the learning process by making the links explicit.

Effectively what an information processing approach indicates is that initially a task analysis of the problem at hand is required and then training can occur on the basis of the task analysis. Generalization needs to be maximized by focusing on components rather than the tasks as such.

Summary

In this chapter we have discussed the problems of defining general learning difficulties on the basis of IQ. We then high-lighted the difficulties in classifying children with general learning difficulties. We have argued that they do not constitute a homogeneous group. Children with general learning difficulties display a slower rate of learning and reach a lower ceiling of performance than their age-matched peers. We then discussed whether this difference in performance is best seen as a delay in development or a different pattern of development from normal. We reviewed a number of cognitive difficulties experienced by children with general learning difficulties, including speed of information processing, attentional mechanisms, and memory processes. The implications of these difficulties for learning were discussed. In conclusion we discussed problems of assessment and intervention.

7

Principles of Intervention

Overview

In this chapter we shall discuss the principles of intervention. We distinguish between what needs to be taught and how this information should be imparted. In identifying what to teach, it is necessary to consider both the task and the child. Cognitive task analysis is a procedure whereby an overall task is decomposed into subtasks and the information processing requirements of each subtask identified. An analysis of the child's knowledge base and strategies is also required. In deciding how to intervene it is necessary to set aims and objectives and consider how to manage learner errors. Special attention needs to be paid to generalizing learning from the training task to other situations. Finally, we consider how to identify teaching requirements.

Issues of Intervention

Intervention in the preschool period involves supplying some type of specialized provision. In school, intervention to reduce children's learning difficulties is the provision of something over and above the normal curriculum. It is a set of actions designed to influence the anticipated course of development. The central concern for anyone involved with children who are experiencing learning difficulties is to help the child. Ideally one would wish to remedy the problem(s) but reducing the impact of the difficulties may often be the more practical goal. Identifying a child's particular difficulty, diagnosing its constituent components, and understanding the cognitive prerequisites of a task are of little avail to the practitioner if these cannot be translated into appropriate intervention programmes. As we stated in chapter 2, all intervention is theory driven but the theories may sometimes be implicit rather than explicit. Practitioners often intervene in a way they consider to be 'natural' or to make 'teaching sense'. In these cases the theories that guide teaching and intervention are implicit. The cognitive theories that drive our analysis have been explicitly stated and we have attempted to be explicit about their ramifications. To what extent can the framework constructed in the previous chapters guide intervention?

In the four preceding chapters our aim has been to establish the cognitive basis of learning difficulties. We have discussed the cognitive basis of these difficulties by asking the question: in what ways do children with learning difficulties differ from those who develop without difficulties? In this chapter we shall extend our analysis to address issues of intervention. We are now concerned with the questions that must be considered in planning and organizing an intervention programme, and in monitoring and measuring the results of intervention in order to determine its effectiveness.

In this chapter we are primarily concerned with planning appropriate learning opportunities for individual children. However, the planning and implementation of any programme requires communication and collaboration among a range of individuals. Moreover, the way in which a particular programme is implemented will depend on organizational structures both within the classroom and within the school. Wolfendale (1987) addresses some of these issues and figure 7.1 shows the intervention options for key people that she proposes.

In chapter 2 we argued that the assessment process is critical in any attempt to identify and diagnose a child's problems. Assessment forms the first step in the test-teach-test process. As figure 7.2 illustrates, the process is a cyclical one, which requires evaluation of one's hypotheses throughout the cycle. Intervention is the central part of the process since attempting to teach a child new knowledge and skills serves as a test of our initial hypotheses about the cause of the child's difficulty. If the intervention proves

Devise individual programmes
examples:
Direct instruction; Precision
teaching; Parental
involvement in reading;
Peer tutoring

Classroom organisation
Room management
Seating arrangements
Groupwork
Timetable

Children's self-monitoring & recording

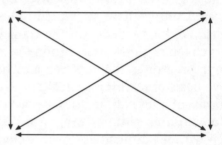

Work with other teachers
Peripatetic/visiting advisory
teacher
School-based advisory/special
needs co-ordinator

Work with support agencies
Educational psychologists
Advisors
Remedial and resource teachers
Community languages
Parents

Figure 7.1   *Intervention: options for key people.*
(Source: Wolfendale, 1987)

successful, then this provides support for the hypothesis. If the
child's performance does not improve, the intervention will not
have served its purpose. Thus, if initial intervention techniques
do not lead to success a return to assessment is required. In this
case, either the initial target of the intervention was not the cause
of the problem or the target is not amenable to current attempts
to intervene and alternative approaches will need to be considered. It is important that both the impact of a programme and
the implementation are evaluated. Children may fail to learn
because a programme is misconceived or because it is badly
implemented.

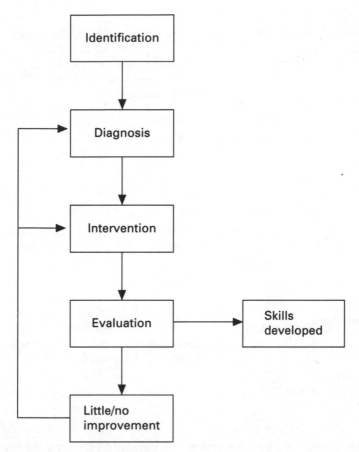

Figure 7.2   *The test–teach–test cycle.*

We have argued that in initial attempts to diagnose the child's difficulties it is necessary to consider the child, the task, and the environment. In many cases it will be difficult to specify the unique contributions of each of these factors. Problems should not be assumed to be the property of the child alone or the task in isolation. Rather the problem lies in the interaction between the two within a particular environment (see chapter 1). However, even when it is evident where the major source of the difficulty lies, it may not be possible to intervene at that level. Elimination or modification of a problem can occur in many different ways.

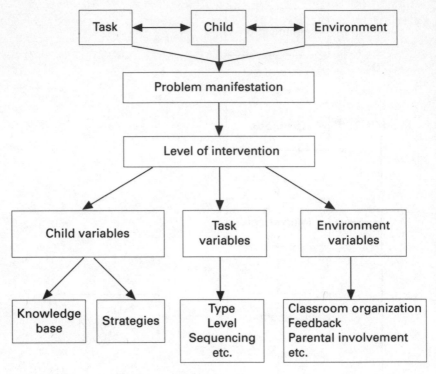

Figure 7.3   *Possible foci for intervention.*

Interventions can be targeted at the child, the parents, or teacher. Alternatively, aspects of the task can be targeted for change. Figure 7.3 outlines the possible foci for intervention and highlights the fact that there need not be a direct mapping between the origins of the problem and the level of intervention. Our aim in this chapter is to discuss a framework for intervention, not to present specific prescriptions. This framework should help determine and organize an approach to a set of very complex issues.

The intervention process requires both an analysis of *what* needs to be taught and *how* this information should be imparted. To do this we need to identify both the task components and the child's strengths and needs. Unless both of these are established by an adequate analysis of the task and assessment of the child, intervention will be unlikely to succeed. There are other factors, particularly at the level of the environment, which need to be considered. For example, decisions need also to be made about where the intervention should take place, who should carry it out and when it should be started.

The *what* and the *how* are intimately linked to the issues that we have discussed in the preceding six chapters and as such we focus on these elements in this chapter. *What* and *how* are not independent concepts; they are different perspectives on the same problem. The nature of the problem will often determine how the intervention proceeds. However, while bearing this close link in mind, it is important to separate *what* and *how* analytically because they often draw on different data sets and procedures.

Identifying *What* Needs Must be Addressed by Intervention

Learning difficulties must necessarily come to light in learning situations. Initially the child's difficulties will be identified through failed or partially achieved milestones. For example, a child may fail to combine words together in speech by the age of 3 years (see chapter 3). As the child develops, milestones are replaced by educational criteria. Thus, the interaction between the child and the educational curriculum will now be the critical situation in which learning difficulties manifest themselves. In the school situation the child is continually presented with new tasks and activities which must be accomplished. The child's performance will be monitored and contrasted with other children's performance. Problems will arise when the child is trying to master a particular task and fails. Such failures to learn will readily be apparent. In seeking to identify the problem, most would agree that the current difficulties in learning should serve as the focus for investigation.

The first step is to understand the nature of the task that is causing the child problems. We can then consider the individual child's particular difficulties. Unless a comprehensive and valid description of the task exists, a test-teach-test strategy will not be possible. An appropriate task analysis of the particular skill or aspect of the curriculum must be developed to provide the basis for assessment. An adequate description of the task allows for an informed assessment of the child's progress and continual adjustment of instructional objectives, materials, and strategies. Thus, the first issue to address is the cognitive components of the task. As Engelmann (1977: 61) notes in discussing the relation between task analysis and instruction:

> There is no magic to instruction. If the instruction is carefully designed, if demonstrations are consistent with only one interpretation, if operations are initially overt and perfectly clear, if preskills are identified and taught without teaching other skills that 'may be' important you will succeed. Remember don't start by observing the child. Start with the task.

Cognitive Task Analysis

Cognitive task analysis is a procedure whereby an overall task, such as talking or reading, is decomposed into subtasks, and the information processing requirements of each subtask determined. Task analysis involves breaking a task down into its component subtasks, and then breaking each subtask in turn into its components until the subcomponents are of an appropriate size. There is no absolute answer to what an appropriate size is; this will vary with the task and the learner who is to be trained on the task. Gagné et al. (1962:1) summarize the procedure for performing a task analysis thus:

> Such an analysis is executed by asking the question of the final task, 'What would the individual have to know how to do in order to perform this task, after being given only instructions?' and successively asking the same question of the learning sets so defined, until one describes a 'hierarchy of knowledge' containing very simple and general learning sets at its lowest level.

Figure 7.4 shows a learning hierarchy for subtraction as depicted by Gagné et al. (1962). The hierarchy is the result of the type of analysis outlined above, but it must also be validated empirically. The hierarchy can be critically evaluated by observing whether

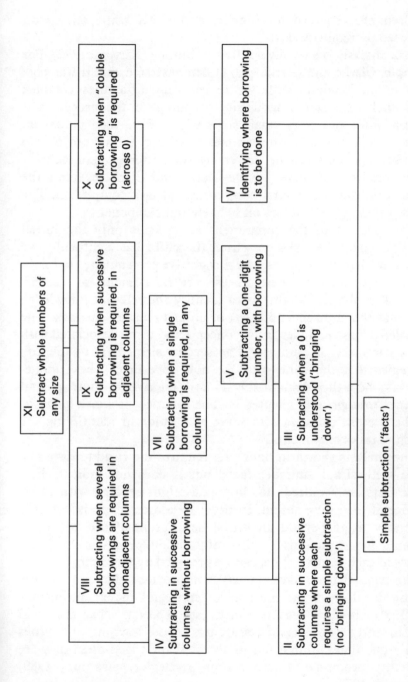

Figure 7.4 *Learning hierarchy for subtraction.*
(Source: Mayer (1987) based on Gagné *et al.*, 1962)

children ever succeed on higher level skills while failing on proposed prerequisite skills.

Task analysis is a widely applied technique (Kirwan, 1992). For example, Clarke and Clarke (1974) demonstrated that it was possible to teach adults with severe learning difficulties complex tasks such as assembling a bicycle pump, if the process was broken down into very small steps which were then taught on a carefully monitored programme. Breaking a task down into its subcomponents can be driven by two different approaches – behavioural or cognitive. In the Clarke and Clarke example the focus is on the behavioural components of task completion. The Gagné example also focuses on behavioural components.

Identification of the component subtasks is only the initial step; for cognitive tasks on which the child has a difficulty we must now determine the essential cognitive prerequisites to carrying out the subtasks. There are two central elements to a cognitive task analysis. The first is to identify the relevant knowledge base that the child must possess in order to master the task. The knowledge base includes facts, concepts and terms associated with particular tasks or domains. The second element is to identify strategies that the child must be able to utilize. These strategies may be either domain specific *task strategies* or more general *executive strategies* (see chapter 1). The function of a task analysis, in the present context, is to serve as a guide in identifying the essential task components.

The analysis shown in figure 7.4 requires the child to have as a basic skill 'simple number facts' but it does not indicate how these facts are acquired, nor how one might proceed with intervention if they were absent. In order to address these issues, it is necessary to go beyond an initial description of the task components to an analysis of the information processing requirements of each subtask. This can be provided by theoretical models of the types that we have discussed in previous chapters. Models of this kind highlight the role of strategies in explaining our abilities to perform cognitive tasks (see especially chapters 5 and 6). Currently a number of researchers in the learning difficulties field argue that children fail to access knowledge unless they are explicitly prompted to use certain strategies (Swanson, 1989; Torgesen, 1977).

We can distinguish between strategies that are task specific and those that can be applied to a wide range of tasks independently of the content of the information. Executive strategies of attending, of putting effort into a task, of monitoring the effects of one's learning, are all general strategies. Task specific strategies, on the other hand, can only be employed with material of appropriate content. Thus, strategies for addition can only be applied to numbers, and should only be applied if the task is one of adding the numbers.

As an example of a task that requires both specific and general strategies, let us consider the task of writing an essay. At the most general level, the student must *plan* the essay, then *decompose* the plan into discrete steps, then *write* a draft for each step, then *review* what has been written, and finally *revise* the draft, which may involve iterating through the previous steps for sections of the essay. Each of the steps discussed can be broken down into a finer analysis. Englert et al. (1991) developed a writing programme based on the six steps below and implemented it as part of normal classroom activities for 9- to 11-year-old children with and without a learning difficulty. The intervention lasted from October through April. At the completion of the study the writing of the students who participated in the programme had improved significantly more than that of controls who had not participated in the programme. This held for children with and without learning difficulties alike. The steps taught by Englert et al. were as follows:

Plan: The student is taught to consider who the audience is, what the purpose of the essay is, what knowledge the student has about the topic, and how this knowledge can be organized into groups of related ideas.
Organize: In this step the student organizes the ideas gathered during the planning into a sequence of steps and chooses an appropriate text structure for each idea (such as whether to explain, compare and contrast, and so forth).
Write: The student then writes a first draft by fleshing out the previous steps and adding introductions and conclusions.
Edit: The students were taught to edit their own and each other's papers by considering the content and the organization. They

were encouraged to identify content that was regarded as good and content that was considered unclear, and to consider the extent to which relevant text structures had been used. This step concluded with a discussion between the author and the peer editor on how the paper might be improved.

Revise: This step involved first listing the suggestions generated and received and deciding which of the editing suggestions to implement. The student then wrote a final draft of the essay.

Recently, there has been increased attention to cognitive strategies designed to teach individuals how to learn. Effectively, these are general strategies which should enhance the child's performance on a wide range of tasks. Such approaches have been termed cognitive intervention programmes and aim to promote general learning and performance. Cognitive intervention in learning difficulties occurs mostly in the area of reading comprehension although a few studies have involved vocabulary training and writing. A number of commercial programmes have been developed but few have an empirical base and their effectiveness has yet to be determined. The central issue that such general approaches need to address is the extent to which the knowledge base is crucial for the development of appropriate strategy use. As we shall see there is considerable evidence that the two interact.

Problem Manifestation: The Child and the Task

Having outlined the cognitive prerequisites for accomplishing the task, one must then consider the cognitive skills of the child and identify the mismatch between the two. Here we are concerned with *what* the child's level of functioning is. It is important to consider the potential interactions between the child's knowledge and skills and the tasks that the child is required to complete. Identifying the child's cognitive strengths and needs is achieved through a thorough assessment of the child's current cognitive performance (see chapter 2). If a child appears to have a general problem, as in the case of general learning difficulties (see chapter 6), interventions will need to address the most important task for that child's performance in both school and home situations. In essence a hypothesis is being made about what desired learning has not occurred given the tasks and settings the child has already confronted. Interventions will need to be prioritized.

The Importance of the Child's Knowledge Base The specific questions asked during the assessment will be based on the understanding of the task. We will need to assess both the extent of the child's knowledge base, that is the range of facts about a given domain at the child's disposal, and the strategies which the child possesses and uses. The importance of the child's knowledge base to performance has been demonstrated in a number of studies. For example, Chi (1987) found that children who were skilled chess players had superior recall for patterns on a chess board to adults who were unskilled at chess. However, when the task was the recall of digits, the adults were superior. In the first case, the children were using their superior knowledge of chess to encode the patterns while in the second the adults were using their general strategic superiority. In another study, Chi (1985) found that when a child's knowledge is well established and stable as, for example, when the child knows the names of her classmates well, she could learn to use a new strategy, which was retrieving her classmates' names according to alphabetical order. Prior to the introduction of this strategy the child had used classroom seat arrangement as her retrieval strategy. However, when the child had to learn new information (a list of unfamiliar names), the same newly acquired strategy (alphabetization) was not as effective in retrieving the names. Thus, there is a clear interaction between the knowledge base and the use of strategies. A learned strategy may fail to promote performance unless the child receives a concurrent increase in domain knowledge.

The child's existing knowledge base is an important determinant of the strategies that can be learned and applied. As the knowledge base in any domain increases, the types of strategy that can be applied may change. The knowledge base must contain the information required by the strategy. Thus, as the size of the knowledge base increases, larger chunks of related information are stored together, and the relations between different items of knowledge become more organized. As a result of this, the child becomes less reliant on the use of simple strategies because the relevant information can be retrieved from the knowledge base and this, in turn, allows for the use of more complex strategies. For example, young children usually do not cluster related items together on memory recall tasks, such as clustering all food words together when these have been presented interspersed among other words. One of the major reasons why they do not is that their knowledge base is not strongly organized in a hierarchical fashion (Ornstein et al., 1975). Until this organization is well-established in the knowledge base, clustering cannot be used as a strategy.

As a further example, let us consider a child who is required to learn a list of three-letter words for spelling. The list contains ten words, which can be divided into two sublists – one set consisting of five words that end in – *at* as in *cat, mat, bat, flat, hat* and one set consisting of five words that end in – *et* as in *pet, met, get, set, let*. The task is simplified if the child can organize the list into two groups, that end in *et* and *at* respectively. If, in contrast, the child is not aware of this organizing principle then the strategy cannot be implemented for aiding recall and thus the task becomes one of learning ten individual items.

These examples demonstrate that there is a dynamic relation between a knowledge base and strategies. Strategies often play a vital role in establishing a knowledge base, but once acquired, the role of strategies may become less important within the domain, because the relevant knowledge is available for retrieval. In cases of learning difficulties it is often the case that the acquisition of knowledge is at issue. Thus, the use of strategies becomes a critical factor. Strategies require a knowledge base that provides the appropriate information on which the strategy can operate. In considering strategy training it is important to consider, as a first step, whether or not the child's knowledge base contains the information required for successful execution of the strategy.

Strategies   Strategic behaviours should be taught as they are needed as methods to solve problems, not as isolated skills. The purpose and function of the intervention needs to be transparent to both pupils and teachers. The child's existing knowledge base is an important determinant of the strategies that can be learned and applied, as we have shown.

A large number of studies have shown that children with learning difficulties use strategies less effectively than their peers without learning difficulties. It would seem, therefore, that much of the focus of intervention should be on training relevant strategies. This is almost certainly true, but attempts to train strategies have not always had effective outcomes. Children with learning difficulties who are taught new learning strategies often do not transfer these strategies to tasks similar to the training task. This failure to generalize the use of a strategy to similar tasks has been a recurrent finding of the literature on intervention. We shall discuss the issue of generalization in more detail below.

In search of the further factors that account for strategy transfer, or its failure, researchers have turned to other variables. In addition to possessing an adequate knowledge base and relevant strategies, children must know when, where, and how to apply a strategy. This knowledge is often termed metacognitive knowledge.

Metacognitive knowledge is knowledge about one's own cognitive states and processes. This is one source of influence on the strategies that an individual employs. Many children with learning difficulties lack an awareness that planned strategic behaviours are necessary and beneficial (Torgesen and Kail, 1980). One common suggestion is that generalization failure is due to a lack of knowledge about the strategy's effectiveness. Often children do not understand the relation between strategy use and level of performance on a task. Thus, in addition to training task-based strategies, it is often necessary to provide children with explicit information about the effectiveness of the strategy and when, where, and how to apply it. However, although some studies have had success using this approach with normal children (Black and Rollins, 1982; Lawson and Fuelop, 1980; O'Sullivan and Pressley, 1984), it has been less effective in promoting generalization among children with learning difficulties (Gelzheiser, 1984). Thus, while provision of knowledge about the effectiveness of a strategy may be a necessary condition for achieving generalization, it is not always a sufficient condition, especially in the case of children with learning difficulties.

In chapter 1 we distinguished between metacognitive knowledge and metacognitive beliefs. Metacognitive beliefs are the
attributions that children make about the causes of their success
and failure when attempting to learn. Many children with learning difficulties have acquired a set of self-defeating beliefs about
their own ability to learn. These beliefs are often a major impedi-
ment to the acquisition and use of strategies.

The Child's Learning History

In addition to understanding the child's cognitive skills it is
important to understand the child's learning history and the
implications this may have for the approach taken to tasks. When
children believe that they can tackle an academic task they
will learn given time and appropriate educational opportunities
(Kistner et al., 1988).

Children with learning difficulties are often inattentive and
seem to put little effort into tasks in the domain in which they
have difficulty (Licht, 1983). This is sometimes interpreted as a
problem within the child's attentional system. However, it is also
possible that lack of attention and effort are the result rather than
the cause of the learning difficulty.

Children may put little effort into a task because they have
doubts about their capacity to perform well. Children with learning difficulties have all experienced academic failure and it has
been proposed that, as a consequence of these failures, the children learn to doubt their intellectual abilities and come to view
their efforts at achievement as futile (Dweck and Licht, 1980;
Torgesen and Licht, 1983). This in turn results in frustration
and/or giving up very quickly, which contributes to further failure and the reinforcement of the belief that the child does not
have the ability to succeed. With experience this cycle is strengthened and even successes can be viewed as luck or understood by
conceiving the task as an 'easy' one (Licht and Kistner, 1986).

This vicious circle is not inevitable and it is important to
understand the process if it is to be minimized. When children
believe that their failures are due to insufficient ability, this leads
to a deterioration in performance on difficult tasks. By contrast,
when children view their failures as an indication of insufficient

effort or an indication that they did not use the proper strategy, they are more likely to maintain or even improve their performance in the face of difficulty (Licht, 1983).

On the whole, younger children (less than 7 years of age) view task success in a different light than older children do. They often view successes that have been achieved with a great deal of effort as evidence of higher ability than when the same success is achieved with very little effort. Moreover, social comparisons are less prominent in the judgements of younger children. Even between the ages of 7 and 10 years children still view ability as modifiable by effort. The direct implication is that learning problems are likely to have the most debilitating effects after the age of 10 (Licht and Kistner, 1986).

The developmental evidence suggests that early identification and remediation of learning difficulties should prevent this negative cycle. However, in dealing with a child who has had a history of failure, a major effort must be expended on changing the child's causal attributions of failure. A number of studies have shown that an effective method of doing this is by linking past failures with insufficient effort and past successes with the expenditure of effort (Andrews and Debus, 1978; Dweck, 1975; Schunk, 1985). This helps to promote current effort and persistence.

Reid and Borkowski (1987) showed the effectiveness of attributional intervention with children who had been labelled 'hyperactive'. They compared three types of intervention on the acquisition of a memory strategy. One group were simply taught the task strategy; the second group were taught the task strategy together with self-control strategies; the third group received the same strategy training as the second group but were also given training on attributions. This included an initial discussion with the child on the causes of success and failure and feedback during training about the relation between strategic behaviour and performance. In addition, these children were given the opportunity to perform previously failed items during the training. Three weeks after the training had ceased, the children were tested for strategy maintenance and generalization. The children in the third intervention condition were superior to the children in the other two conditions. Moreover, the use of strategies was maintained on a 10-month follow-up.

A final factor which must be addressed is the teacher's role in setting up and maintaining such negative attributions. The data concerning the consequences of teacher feedback are complex but there are some initial conclusions which should be considered. There appears to be a developmental difference in the ways children respond to praise. Young children and children with learning difficulties appear to be motivated by praise for an attempt. By contrast, when adults, teenagers, and cognitively advanced primary school children are praised for poor work they interpret the praise as implying they are low in ability (Meyer et al., 1979). Thus, the older children do not take praise at face value. However, it seems unlikely that simply praising children with learning difficulties, irrespective of the task difficulty, will have a positive effect. Obviously, to be effective in the long term, praise should be contingent on effortful attempts and should convey specific information about what would lead to further improvements.

Selecting What to Teach

In the assessment of the *what* in relation to the task, we have identified: the relevant task content, the specific task strategies, the metacognitive knowledge about a strategy's effectiveness, and the metacognitive beliefs about the effectiveness of one's own efforts. The identification of which particular aspect to teach will depend in part on the child and in part on the particular task with which the child is having problems. The five guidelines provided by Engelmann and Carnine (1982) are a useful basis for the development of a functional programme content:

- The items taught should include only those for the final competency
- An item should only be included when foundation skills have already been taught
- Each item should be of direct relevance to performing the task
- An item should only be included when the learner has achieved mastery on preceding items
- Any item on which the learner has persistently made errors will also need to be included

Let us consider a child who is having difficulties learning the colour lexicon. In this case we would only teach colour terms, since these are the relevant items for final competence. One foundation skill we would expect the child to have mastered is the ability to sort colours. It would not be possible to learn new colour terms if, for example, a child is unable reliably to discriminate between colours. We would initially teach common colours (red, blue, yellow) rather than less common ones (violet, indigo, aquamarine). The numbers of items (colours) taught would need to be sufficiently large for the child to grasp the concept without being so large as to cause confusion. New colours would only be taught once the child had learned most of the initial set.

A Framework for *How* to Conduct Intervention

In the *what* section we identified the basic determinants for selecting valid programme content. In this section we consider how to sequence, manage, and measure rates of learning. The problem that needs to be addressed is what teaching input will support the internal processing required to learn. In order to effect improvement in children with learning difficulties it is usually necessary to be quite explicit about what is required.

Setting Aims and Objectives

The aims are the general goals of the intervention programme. The objectives are the steps that must be taken to reach the goal. The objectives model seeks to evaluate pupil performance in any curriculum area against an agreed list of teacher or pupil curriculum objectives. This requires the previously completed task of agreeing, clarifying, writing down, and sequencing specific objectives in a curriculum. Such an evaluation informs the teacher of the component skills within an area of learning that the child has not yet mastered and the precise skills that need to be taught.

Aims and objectives thus differ in their level of generality. But the difference is more than simply this. Aims are not theory-driven; objectives are. Thus, in the case of a child with a reading difficulty, the aim of anyone concerned with intervention will be to improve the child's reading skill. The objectives that are set to achieve this aim would differ, however, between someone who believes that a perceptual problem is the cause of the difficulty and someone who believes that the difficulty is caused by problems in phonologically encoding written material.

Objectives are statements about what the child should be able to *do* following intervention. Objectives should be set in the light of two pieces of knowledge: the information processing skills required for performance on the task and the current abilities of the learner. Cognitive task analysis is the means by which the information processing requirements of the task are determined. The task analysis also serves as a basis for assessing the current abilities of the learner. By approaching the child's learning difficulty from the viewpoints of the demands of the task and the child's own abilities, it is possible to determine which of the necessary components of skilled performance are currently possessed by the child and which are lacking. Objectives can now be set for tasks that require a combination of skills that the child currently possesses and some that he does not possess.

Objectives need to be set in terms of pupil performance and instructional procedures need to be carefully organized. Thus, a good objective states what it is that a child is expected to do and under what conditions he is expected to do it. Moreover, objectives need to be explicit in terms of how well a task must be done so that they provide measurable indices of performance. For example, an objective that states that a child should **know the meaning of** *more* **and** *less* is inadequate since it fails to specify what criteria would constitute 'knowing'. On the other hand, an objective that states that a child, when presented with two arrays of different numerosities, should **identify without error the array which contains more items and identify the array which contains less items** clearly specifies which responses are required from the child. In this case it would also be possible to devise more complex situations for demonstrating comprehension of *more* and *less*. In addition, the teacher might wish to include production of the words *more* or *less* as an objective.

The level of precision with which an objective must be specified will vary according to the child and the task. For example, an objective of **write one's own name** is loosely defined and might be acceptable either for a child who is not having problems or who is in the early stages of learning to write. By contrast, an objective which states that the child must **print name clearly with all letters the same size and each one touching the line** is much more precise and might be required for a child who is having problems and requires explicit instruction with fine motor skills.

There is increasing evidence that children taught by teachers using objectives benefit significantly more than children taught by teachers who do not use objectives (Becker et al., 1981). Many educational programmes which include precisely stated objectives have now been developed (see Wolfendale, 1987). The added benefit of such an approach is that objectives provide the teacher with a basis for continuous assessment and review.

Sequencing of the programme is very important. To promote efficient learning, material must be presented in a way that activates the necessary knowledge structures and is consistent with them. Advance organizers such as a verbal overview of the lesson, outlines, headings, or topic questions help unlock appropriate knowledge structures enabling the learner to understand newly presented material more quickly and thoroughly (Mayer, 1979). However, in familiar tasks, repetition of well established information may interfere with the acquisition of new information. A specialized therapy setting needs no introduction if the child is familiar with it and the aims of the therapy.

Initially the child's first steps in the intervention programme should be easy, so as to gain success at the first attempt, but these early items should be drawn from relevant material. Ainscow and Tweddle (1979) emphasize the importance of ensuring that the first two or three objectives are ones that have been at least partially mastered by the child. The steps between objectives need to be small enough to allow optimum transfer. Engelmann (1977) notes that when children are only accurate about 70 per cent of the time further specification of the task prerequisites is needed. Such a criterion allows for the identification of 'sticking points' and highlights the importance of ensuring that the material is well learned.

Tasks which differ markedly in content, form of presentation, or response type will add irrelevant demands to the child's performance. If the presentation of a task allows for more than one interpretation some learners will fix on the irrelevant dimension. There is a tension between loosely structured tasks which allow for multiple interpretations and highly structured tasks which lead the learner to infer that the skill is specific only to a particular context or set of materials. This problem will be discussed in greater detail in the section on generalization.

In constructing programmes with a graded sequence, every item in the sequence may not be essential for every child. For some children, it will be possible to chunk together particular objectives, while for others the objectives may need to be broken down further. Thus, objectives are broken down into smaller steps and the selection of what will be taught is a primary consideration in getting a learning programme together. Whether the child sees the relation between tasks and transfers what is learned from one task to another will need to be determined.

Through practice, the process of recognizing conditions and selecting appropriate performance components becomes automatic. In the performance of new tasks, execution of information-processing components can be expected to be largely under the conscious control of the individual. Controlled execution of these components requires large amounts of attentional resources, which are then temporarily unavailable for other uses. Controlled processing is believed to be largely serial and centrally executed. Over the short run, it is needed for adaptation to new tasks and task environments. Over the long run, it is inefficient if it is not eventually replaced with a form of information processing that requires less attention. Practice is important in establishing skill automatization.

Managing Learner Errors

Errors are an inevitable part of learning. Teachers will want to keep errors at a minimum to prevent negative effects of failure. Ault et al. (1989), in their review of the literature on teaching techniques for children with mild and moderate learning difficulties, suggest that prompting is a more effective means of reducing errors than trial and error learning. Moreover, they suggest that providing a high level of prompts initially and gradually reducing these is an effective means of intervention.

However, errors, when they occur, can serve as a major source of information about the child's strengths and needs. When a child performs a task *without* error we cannot identify either *how* the task has been solved or *why* the correct solution was obtained. The errors children make can be helpful in revealing the way a child reasons about a task (see chapter 5 for a discussion of error analysis in number work). The discrepancy between the responses requested and the actual errors made will be the indication of what needs to be remedied.

There are some standardized tests which include details of interpretation of the types of errors that a child makes (for example, the Neale Analysis of Reading). However, often a teacher will have to construct an individualized assessment tool. In this case a teacher might sample the child's performance on a task which is a little difficult for the child. This will allow for the identification of learned as well as unlearned material. For example, in a spelling task the teacher might identify errors where a child uses the phonic alternative rather than the correct letter (*k* for *c*) or in reading where the child fails to process the last letter (*the* for *they*). For a child experiencing difficulties with writing, the teacher might observe how the child forms a letter and consider the position of the child's hand and arm, sitting posture, and the position of the paper, how the pen or pencil is held and the pressure the child exerts to form the letter. In each of the above examples it is the problems the child has in executing the task that informs the teacher about the target for intervention.

In contrast to their function for the teacher, errors are only useful for the *child* if the reason for failure is obvious and the child can identify the possible ways of preventing failure in the future. A page of calculations returned with crosses through many incorrect items does not allow the child to learn from the errors made. Feedback from the child's teacher is often necessary to make the source of the error obvious to the child. Direct correction and feedback can form an important component of an intervention programme. A correction procedure can be one that actively guides the child towards accurate performance by the same kind of demonstration and practice routines used in initial teaching.

Expert scaffolding is a means of providing children with direct demonstrations of the prerequisite skills. Expert scaffolding refers to a situation in which someone who is more skilled at a task ('the expert'), for example a peer or a teacher, guides the child ('the novice') to greater levels of participation. Initially the expert takes major responsibility for solving the task and the novice is the on-looker. The expert models and explains the task relinquishing responsibility as the novice becomes more competent. The activity of paired reading outlined in chapter 4 is an example, but there are many others.

An elaborated feedback and correction procedure provides information on why change is needed and what the change should be. Skills are selected for instruction because the teacher believes that if the child uses them the result will be improved performance on a particular task. It does not follow that the child is aware of the utility of the particular skills. If a child is not aware either that he is using a particular skill or of the utility of that particular skill, then there is no reason for the child to maintain the skill once the social pressure of the teaching situation is removed. Explicit feedback teaches the child the effectiveness of the intervention. There is growing evidence to indicate that generalization requires demonstrating to the learner the usefulness of a new strategy.

Designing for Generalization

When training occurs on a task or a component of a task, the aim is usually to provide the child with a skill that can be generalized to instances that are similar to the examples used in training. Unfortunately, it is a well-documented fact that generalization of training does not automatically occur with children who have learning difficulties. This failure to generalize to similar tasks has been a recurrent finding of the literature on intervention. In view of this obvious difficulty, it would seem wise for a teacher to give consideration to factors that are known to promote generalization in the design of an intervention task. Although this may seem an obvious enough point, it is often neglected in practice. We shall consider three types of factors in relation to generalization:

- the task examples presented and their manner of presentation
- environmental factors that can be manipulated to promote generalization
- training metacognitive knowledge in conjunction with task strategies

Let us consider, first of all, the task factors that tend to promote generalization. One of the easiest principles to implement is that training should occur on a diversity of instances (Stokes and Baer, 1977). This diversity should be representative of the instances to which the skill is to be applied. However, the range of examples must also be carefully chosen. Gick and Holyoak (1987) point out that, although variability of examples promotes generalization, it can hinder initial learning, especially if the number of examples is small and the variability high. Unfortunately, the literature on generalization does not provide a clear answer to what is the optimal combination of sufficient examples and sufficient diversity to yield the most valuable generalization. Since skills will differ considerably in the range of instances to which they are relevant, it may not, in any case, be possible to state a general law of what constitutes sufficient examples. The most useful practical approach may be to ensure adequate initial learning (to some criterion) on a small number of examples and then to introduce more examples gradually while continually testing for the desired amount of generalization. When this has been achieved, it may be presumed that sufficient examples have been presented.

Given that the examples for training have been selected, to what extent should training focus specifically on these examples? Very specific training seems to lead to poor generalization. Stokes and Baer (1977) suggest that it is desirable to train not only different examples, but also to vary the instructions given, the settings in which training occurs, and the reinforcements provided. This must, of course, be carefully managed so that diversity docs not lead to confusion.

Apart from attending to the task factors, attention can also be paid to environmental factors in order to maximize generalization. The greater the similarity between two situations, the greater the likelihood of generalization. Thus, if it can be arranged that similar environmental cues occur across different settings, then this will act to promote generalization beyond the intervention setting itself. These cues can be physical or social, or both. Physical cues can be manipulated by using similar materials initially in the training and other environmental settings. Social cues can involve ensuring that a person present during training is also present in other settings to which generalization is desired, at least until the generalization is achieved. Other children may be particularly effective in this respect as a means of promoting generalization.

One method of using other children is that employed by Koegel and Rincover (1974), who started off with a teacher-pupil ratio of one-to-one in an intervention setting designed to improve social behaviour and then changed the ratio by introducing several of the child's classroom peers, thus blurring the distinction between the training and the classroom setting. Reliable generalization of social behaviour was achieved. It remains to be determined whether the method is also effective for cognitive skills.

Stokes and Baer (1976) employed peers in a different way. They taught two children with learning difficulties several word-recognition skills. Each child was taught these skills and concurrently shown how to teach them to the other child, thus acting as a peer-tutor. It was found that both children reliably learned the skills but neither generalized them to settings in which the other child usually was absent. However, when the child's peer was brought into those settings stable generalization to that setting was achieved.

The third set of factors that we shall consider apply particularly to strategy training. A number of studies have shown that providing feedback to the student on the effectiveness of using a strategy achieves better maintenance of the strategy than training without such feedback. The majority of such studies have been conducted on memory strategies (Black and Rollins, 1982; Kennedy and Miller, 1976; Ringel and Springer, 1980) but one exception is a study by Michie (1984b), which demonstrated the effectiveness of feedback in the maintenance of a counting strategy in judging which of two rows contained the greater number. The central importance of providing feedback seems to be twofold: first, it provides the student with information that using the strategy is having an effect on performance (which the student may not necessarily be able to monitor independently of this feedback), and second, it promotes the direct attribution of success to the use of the strategy.

Possibly the most elaborate attempt to train both task strategies and metacognitive awareness of the utility of these strategies is a series of studies reported by Palincsar and Brown (1984). These studies incorporated a number of the principles discussed above. Palincsar and Brown's subjects were 13-year-old students who had poor reading comprehension. The students were taught the strategies of summarizing, questioning, clarifying, and predicting while reading text. These strategies were taught through one-to-one student/teacher dialogues about a piece of text. The student and teacher each took turns leading the dialogue. Thus, when a new passage was presented the learner was asked to predict passage content based on the title, as well as how the passage might relate to his prior knowledge. After presentation of the text, the learner recalled the topic and the main points of the text. Students were frequently prompted to guess which questions a teacher might ask. The students were provided with extensive metacognitive feedback on the effectiveness of the strategies. The strategies trained were successfully generalized to the classroom setting and the students also achieved substantial improvements in reading comprehension scores. Of particular importance was the fact that the method of intervention was successful when it was conducted by regular classroom teachers in natural group settings.

Measuring Learning

No single instructional strategy works all the time. Even with careful screening and diagnostic assessments to match a programme to the initial needs of the child, the programme will often lose its effectiveness as the needs and the abilities of the child change. This means that children's progress should be monitored regularly to assess changes.

There are two major parameters that can measured: accuracy and the speed of learning. While accuracy measurement is a commonly used pedagogic tool, speed is less so. The speed with which a task is completed offers a time-scaled index of competence on the part of the child. Frequency measures are more sensitive and precise than per centage correct measures (White and Haring, 1980). One of the strengths of such measures is that the teacher can discriminate between fluency (that is, the rate at which the child achieves success) and proficiency (that is, whether the child is correct or not). Often, recently acquired skills will be less fluently executed. For example, a child might read a number of words correctly, but recently acquired words will be read more slowly than familiar ones. Since children with learning difficulties can be slow to respond, rate measurements can provide important information about the extent to which the children are able to accelerate their performance.

A way of measuring learning is precision teaching. Precision teaching is not a method of teaching, but rather a way of trying to identify which methods of teaching are most effective. It is a method for matching tuition to performance data from the learner (Pennypacker et al., 1972). It offers continuity and sensitivity to change. Precision teaching does not dictate what should be taught or how instruction should proceed. Rather, it represents an approach to the systematic evaluation of the programme. Teachers using this instructional method define the behaviours to be taught, count or measure the behaviours, chart the behaviours, establish aims or desired outcomes, and evaluate students' progress on a regular basis (usually daily). Many precision teaching advocates suggest that a high response rate should be an instructional objective (Koorland, 1986). Table 7.1 outlines the key stages. Various skills and tasks can be taught successfully in this way (White, 1986). Precision teaching has been successfully applied to all levels of ability, even with learners who have multiple disabilities and a severe learning difficulty. Oral reading, vocabulary, arithmetic and writing are all possible aspects of the school curriculum that could be approached with precision teaching. Lovitt and Fantasia (1983) found that teachers of elementary school children with learning difficulties who used precision teaching techniques secured significantly higher gains in reading than teachers who did not use the technique. However, it is important to note that the collection of data on its own is not

Table 7.1 *The key stages in precision teaching.*

STEP	RATIONALE METHOD
Identify major skill deficiency	This is achieved through a detailed assessment of the child's weaknesses and the central nature of the skill for future performance
Select learner's response	A specific response helps identify when proficiency has been reached
Define baseline	The baseline provides a measure against which future performance can be judged
Measure performance	Rate per minute is a common measure
Chart baseline	Chart both correct and error rates
Predict future performance	Prediction may be based on self or peer performance in relation to the specific task
Intervene	Intervention is based on the theoretical understanding of the task i.e. a task analysis
Evaluate outcome	

sufficient. The data should be used to help address the students' needs.

Identifying Teaching Requirements

In the preceding section we have identified a range of issues that will influence how an intervention programme should be managed. We have emphasized the importance of a detailed analysis in both guiding children's learning and measuring their output. It would not be possible, neither should it be necessary, to use such approaches for all learning tasks. Precise behavioural objectives in terms of what a pupil will be able to do, and

Table 7.2 *Planning the level for intervention.*

Level 1 Minimum teaching requirements	1	Long term objectives
	2	Short term targets
	3	Occasional feedback
Level 2 Obvious difficulty in acquiring skills: requirements for direct teaching	1	Specified long term objectives
	2	Specified short term objectives
	3	Specified feedback for pupils
	4	Specified teaching strategy
Level 3 Major difficulty in acquiring skills: requirements for precision teaching	1	Planned long term objectives
	2	Planned and sequenced short term objectives
	3	Planned feedback for pupils including specified success procedure and teaching procedure
	4	Planned teaching strategy including what to do and say and also including specificed materials, specified place of teaching and specified practice trials
	5	Planned recording of effectiveness of teaching strategy

detailed task analysis, are not usually necessary for the majority of children who are making steady progress. Teaching requirements will vary both among children and within a child for different tasks. As Weinberg (1989: 102) remarked: 'Those who devote professional efforts to educational and child-care enterprises must appreciate individual differences, accepting the challenge to create educational environments that effectively match a child's abilities and talents.' Cameron (1982) distinguishes three levels of teaching requirements according to the level of need manifested by the child. Table 7.2 shows a summary of these.

So far we have not addressed the issue of where intervention should take place and who should be responsible for the intervention. To a large extent this is a political policy issue (Tomlinson, 1982). On the whole, policy makers decide when an intervention will be implemented and where this will occur (special class, mainstream, residential). However, the analysis in this book has some implications for policy makers. Firstly, the criteria used to identify a learning difficulty are often based on arbitrary cut-off points along a continuum of abilities. It is therefore inappropriate to use such cutoff points as the basis for specialized provision. Secondly, our analysis places great emphasis on the assessment process being carried out through teaching in a test-teach-test framework. This requires time and expertise and will therefore require resources. Thirdly, our analysis of children's cognitive skills highlights the similarities between children who learn these skills slowly and those who proceed at an average rate. Finally, many of the procedures we have discussed in this chapter can and have been implemented on a school wide basis. It is possible to assess the extent to which a class or subgroup in the class has reached the objectives. Similarly, it is possible to monitor types of errors made by groups of pupils and target the appropriate group for intervention.

Elimination of the Learning Difficulty

Learning difficulties may well be a life-long problem. However, the impact of these difficulties can be reduced. In this chapter we have tried to identify the ways in which a cognitive analysis can have a positive impact on interventions. Childhood learning difficulties are not a trivial condition that can be ignored. Rather, a thorough analysis of the child's strengths and needs can positively promote learning. Such an approach is the starting point for:

- promoting the child's confidence
- providing the teacher with an entry point to intervention
- designing intervention programmes to address all levels of performance
- addressing the task factors necessary for improved performance

Learning difficulties will always be with us. It is important that we understand these difficulties so that we can lessen the impact

that they have on an individual's life. This requires the interaction of theory and practice. Theory can inform practice by
suggesting the relevant cognitive dimensions for assessment and
intervention. Practice can inform theory by providing a critical
test of the implications of a model. In this book we have concentrated on the cognitive aspects of learning difficulties, but
have tried where possible to make links between cognitive models
of learning difficulties and the tasks of assessment and intervention that practitioners face.

Summary

In this chapter we have considered the importance of separating
the analysis of what needs must be addressed by intervention
from the methods used to effect intervention. Cognitive task
analysis is a method by which a task can be decomposed into
appropriate component parts. We have highlighted the importance of the interaction between the child's knowledge base and
the strategies used in performing a task. To plan an intervention
programme aims and objectives must be set and attention must be
paid to methods for securing generalization. We have discussed
ways in which learning can be measured and the levels at which it
can be implemented. Finally, we considered the impact of this
model for positively promoting learning.

References

Adams, C., and Bishop, D. V. M. (1989). Conversational characteristics of children with semantic–pragmatic disorder. I: Exchange structure, turntaking, repairs and cohesion. *British Journal of Disorders of Communication*, 24, 211–39.

Ainscow, M., and Tweddle, D. A. (1979). *Preventing Classroom Failure: An Objectives Approach*. Chichester: Wiley.

ALBSU (1987). *Literacy, Numeracy and Adults: Evidence from the National Child Development Study*. London: Adult Literacy and Basic Skills Unit.

Alexander, P., and Judy, J. (1988). The interaction of domain-specific and strategic knowledge in academic performance. *Review of Educational Research*, 58, 375–404.

Algozzine, B., and Ysseldke, J. E. (1981). Special education services for normal children. *Exceptional Children*, 48, 238–43.

Algozzine, B., Ysseldyke, J., and Christenson, S. (1983). An analysis of the incidence of special class placement: The masses are burgeoning. *Journal of Special Education*, 17, 141–7.

Anastasi, A. (1988). *Psychological Testing*. (6th ed.). New York: Macmillan.

Anderson, M. (1986). Understanding the cognitive deficit in mental retardation. *Journal of Child Psychology and Psychiatry*, 27, 297–306.

Anderson, M. (1992). *Intelligence and Development: A Cognitive Theory*. Oxford: Blackwell.

Andrews, G. R., and Debus, R. L. (1978). Persistence and the causal perception of failure: Modifying cognitive attributions. *Journal of Educational Psychology*, 70, 154–66.

Antell, S. E., and Keating, D. (1983). Perception of numerical invariance by neonates. *Child Development*, 54, 695–701.

Aram, D. M., Ekelman, B. L., and Nation, J. E. (1984). Preschoolers with language disorders: 10 years later. *Journal of Speech and Hearing Research*, 27, 232–44.

Aram, D. M., and Nation, J. E. (1982). *Child Language Disorders*. St. Louis: C. V. Mosby Company.

Aram, D. M., and Nation, J. E. (1980). Preschooler language disorders and subsequent language and academic difficulties. *Journal of Communication Disorders*, 13, 159–70.

ASHA Committee on Language, Speech and Hearing Services in the Schools (1980). Definitions for the communicative disorders and differences. *Asha*, 22, 317–18.

Aslin, R. N., Pisoni, D. B., and Jusczyk, P. W. (1983). Auditory development and speech perception in infancy. In P. H. Mussen (Ed.), *Handbook of Child Psychology, vol. II: Infancy and Developmental Psychobiology*. New York: Wiley.

Atkinson, R. C., and Shiffrin, R. M. (1968). Human memory: A proposed system and its control processes. In K. W. Spence and J. T. Spence (Eds), *Advances in the Psychology of Learning and Motivation, vol. 2*. New York: Academic Press.

Ault, M. J., Wolery, M., Doyle, P., and Gast, D. L. (1989). Review of comparative studies in the instruction of students with moderate and severe handicaps. *Exceptional Children*, 55, 346–56.

Baddeley, A. D., Ellis, N. C., Miles, T. R., and Lewis, V. J. (1982). Developmental and acquired dyslexia: A comparison. *Cognition*, 11, 185–99.

Baddeley, A. D., and Hitch, G. (1974). Working memory. In G. H. Bower (Ed.), *Recent Advances in Learning and Motivation, vol. 8*. New York: Academic Press.

Baker, L. (1984). Spontaneous versus instructed use of multiple standards for evaluating comprehension: Effects of age, reading proficiency, and type of standard. *Journal of Experimental Child Psychology*, 38, 289–311.

Baker, L., and Brown, A. L. (1984). Metacognitive skills and reading. In P. D. Pearson (Ed.), *Handbook of Reading Research*. New York: Longman.

Banks, M. S., and Salapatek, P. (1983). Infant visual perception. In P. H. Mussen (Ed.), *Handbook of Child Psychology, vol II: Infancy and Developmental Psychobiology*. New York: Wiley.

Barr, R. (1974). The effect of instruction on pupil reading strategies. *Reading Research Quarterly*, 10, 555–82.

Baroody, J. J. (1986). Counting ability of moderately and mildly handicapped children. *Education and Training of the Mentally Retarded*, 21, 298–300.

Barron, R. (1986). Word recognition in early reading: A review of direct and indirect access hypotheses. *Cognition*, *24*, 93–119.

Bauer, R. H. (1982). Information processing as a way of understanding and diagnosing learning disabilities. *Topics in Learning and Learning Disabilities*, *2*, 33–45.

Becker, W., Engelmann, S., Carnine, D., and Rhine, W. (1981). Direct instruction model. In W. Rhine (Ed.), *Making Schools More Effective, New Directions from Follow-Through*. New York: Academic Press.

Beckwith, M., and Restle, F. (1966). Processes of enumeration. *Psychological Review*, *73*, 437–44.

Bereiter, C., and Engelmann, S. (1966). *Teaching Disadvantaged Children in the Preschool*. Englewood Cliffs, NJ: Prentice Hall.

Berger, M., Yule, W., and Rutter, M. (1975). Attainment and adjustment in two geographical areas: II. The prevalence of specific reading retardation. *British Journal of Psychiatry*, *126*, 510–19.

Bishop, D. V. M. (1987). The causes of specific developmental language disorder (Developmental Dysphasia). *Journal of Child Psychology and Psychiatry*, *28*, 1–8.

Bishop, D. V. M. (1992). The underlying nature of specific language impairment. *Journal of Child Psychology and Psychiatry*, *33*, 3–66.

Bishop, D. V. M., and Adams, C. (1989). Conversational characteristics of children with semantic–pragmatic disorder. II: What features lead to a judgement of inappropriacy? *British Journal of Disorders of Communication*, *24*, 241–63.

Bishop, D. V. M., and Adams, C. (1990). A prospective study of the relationship between specific language impairment, phonological disorders and reading retardation. *Journal of Child Psychology and Psychiatry*, *31*, 1027–50.

Bishop, D. V. M., and Edmundson, A. (1987a). Language impaired 4-year-olds: Distinguishing transient from persistent impairment. *Journal of Speech and Hearing Disorders*, *52*, 156–73.

Bishop, D. V. M., and Edmundson, A. (1987b). Specific language impairment as a maturational lag: Evidence from longitudinal data on language and motor development. *Developmental Medicine and Child Neurology*, *29*, 442–59.

Bishop, D. V. M., and Rosenbloom, L. (1987). Classification of childhood language disorders. In W. Yule and M. Rutter (Eds), *Language Development and Disorders*. London: Mac Keith Press.

Black, M. M., and Rollins, H. A. (1982). The effects of instructional variables on young children's organization and free recall. *Journal of Experimental Child Psychology*, *31*, 1–19.

210 REFERENCES

Bloom, L., and Lahey, M. (1978). *Language Development and Language Disorders*. New York: Wiley.

Boder, E. (1973). Developmental dyslexia: A diagnostic approach based on three atypical reading–spelling patterns. *Developmental Medicine and Child Neurology, 15*, 663–87.

Booth, A. (1979). Making retarded children literate: A five year study. *Australian Journal of Mental Retardation, 5*, 257–60.

Borkowski, J. G., Carr, M., and Pressley, M. (1987). 'Spontaneous' strategy use: Perspectives from metacognitive theory. *Intelligence, 11*, 61–75.

Borkowski, J. G., and Cavanaugh, J. C. (1979). Maintenance and generalization of skills by the retarded. In N. R. Ellis (Ed.), *Handbook of Mental Deficiency, Psychological Theory and Research*. (2nd ed.). Hillsdale, NJ: Erlbaum.

Borkowski, J. G., and Kurtz, B. E. (1987). Metacognition and executive control. In J. G. Borkowski and J. D. Day, (Eds), *Cognition in Special Children: Comparative Approaches to Retardation, Learning Disabilities, and Giftedness*. Norwood, NJ: Ablex.

Borkowski, J. G., and Peck, V. A. (1986). Causes and consequences of metamemory in gifted children. In R. Sternberg and J. Davidson (Eds), *Conceptions of Giftedness*. Cambridge, England: Cambridge University Press.

Borkowski, J. G., Peck, V. A., and Damberg, P. R. (1983). Attention, memory, and cognition. In J. L. Metson and J. A. Mulick (Eds), *Handbook of Mental Retardation*. New York: Pergamon.

Bornstein, M. H. (1989). Sensitive periods in development: Structural characteristics and causal interpretations. *Psychological Bulletin, 105*, 179–97.

Bradley, L., and Bryant, P. (1978). Difficulties in auditory organization as a possible cause of reading backwardness. *Nature, 271*, 746–7.

Bradley, L., and Bryant, P. (1983). Categorizing sounds and learning to read: A causal connection. *Nature, 301*, 419–21.

Braine, M. D. S. (1976). Children's first word combinations. *Monographs of the Society for Research in Child Development, 41*, (1, Serial no. 164).

Brennan, W. K. (1979). *Curricular Needs of Slow Learners*. Schools Council Working Paper, no. 63. London: Evans-Methuen.

Brewer, N. (1987). Processing speed, efficiency, and intelligence. In J. G. Borkowksi and J. D. Day (Eds), *Cognition in Special Children: Comparative Approaches to Retardation, Learning Disabilities, and Giftedness*. Norwood, NJ: Alex.

Broman, S., Nichols, P., Shaughnessy, P., and Kennedy, W. (1987). *Retardation in Young Children*. Hillsdale, NJ: Erlbaum.

Bronfenbrenner, U. (1979). *The Ecology of Human Development: Experiments by Nature and Design*. Cambridge, MA: Harvard University Press.

Brooks-Gunn, J., and Weintraub, M. (1983). Origins of infant intelligence testing. In M. Lewis (Ed.), *Origins of Intelligence: Infancy and Early Childhood*. New York: Plenum Press.

Brown, A. L. (1978). Knowing when, where, and how to remember: A problem of metacognition. In R. Glaser (Ed.), *Advances in Instructional Psychology, vol. 1*. Hillsdale, NJ: Erlbaum.

Brown, A. L., Bransford, J. D., Ferrara, R. A., and Campione, J. C. (1983). Learning, remembering, and understanding. In P. H. Mussen (Ed.), *Handbook of Child Psychology, vol. 3: Cognitive Development*. New York: Wiley.

Brown, A. L., and Campione, J. C. (1977). Training strategic study-time apportionment in educable retarded children. *Intelligence, 1,* 94–107.

Brown, A. L., and Campione, J. C. (1986). Training for transfer: Guidelines for promoting flexible use of trained skills. In M. G. Wade (Ed.), *Motor Skill Acquisition for the Mentally Handicapped: Issues in Research and Training*. North Holland: Elsevier.

Brown, A. L., Campione, J. C., and Murphy, M. D. (1974). Keeping track of changing variables: Long-term retention of a trained rehearsal strategy by retarded adolescents. *American Journal of Mental Deficiency, 78,* 446–53.

Brown, A. L., Campione, J. C., and Murphy, M. D. (1977). Maintenance and generalization of trained metamnemonic awareness by educably retarded children. *Journal of Experimental Child Psychology, 24,* 191–211.

Brown, J. S., and Burton, R. R. (1978). Diagnostic models for procedural bugs in basic mathematical skills. *Cognitive Science, 2,* 155–92.

Brown, J. S., and Van Lehn, K. (1980). Repair theory: A generative theory of bugs in procedural skills. *Cognitive Science, 4,* 379–426.

Brown, R. (1973). *A First Language*. Cambridge, MA: Harvard University Press.

Bryant, P., and Bradley, L. (1980). Why children sometimes write words which they cannot read. In U. Frith (Ed.), *Cognitive Processes in Spelling*. London: Academic Press.

Bryant, P., and Bradley, L. (1985). *Children's Reading Problems*. Oxford: Blackwell.

Bryant, P., MacLean, M., Bradley, L., and Crossland, J. (1990). Rhyme and alliteration, phoneme detection, and learning to read. *Developmental Psychology, 26,* 429–38.

Burack, J. A., Hodapp, R. M., and Zigler, E. (1988). Issues in the classification of mental retardation: Differentiating among organic etiologies. *Journal of Child Psychology and Psychiatry, 29,* 765–79.

Burden, R. (1981). The Educational Psychologist as an instigator and agent of change in schools: Some guidelines for successful practice. In I. McPherson and A. Sutton (Eds), *Reconstructing Psychological Practice*. London: Croom Helm.

Burton, R. B. (1981). DEBUGGY: Diagnosis of errors in basic mathematical skills. In D. H. Sleeman and J. S. Brown (Eds), *Intelligent Tutoring Systems*. London: Academic Press.

Butkowsky, I. S., and Willows, D. M. (1980). Cognitive motivational characteristics of children varying in reading ability; evidence of learned helplessness in poor readers. *Journal of Educational Psychology*, 72, 408–22.

Butterfield, E. C., and Belmont, J. M. (1971). Relations of storage and retrieval strategies as short term memory processes. *Journal of Experimental Psychology*, 89, 319–28.

Butterfield, E. C., and Ferretti, R. F. (1987). Toward a theoretical integration of cognitive hypotheses about intellectual differences among children. In J. G. Borkowski and J. D. Day (Eds), *Cognition in Special Children: Comparative Approaches to Retardation, Learning Disabilities, and Giftedness*. Norwood, NJ: Ablex.

Butterfield, E. C., Nielsen, D., Tangen, K. L., and Richardson, M. B. (1985). Theoretically based psychometric measures of inductive reasoning. In S. Embretson (Ed.), *Test Design: Contributions from Psychology, Education, and Psychometrics*. New York: Academic Press.

Butterfield, E. C., Wambold, C., and Belmont, J. M. (1973). On the theory and practice of improving short-term memory. *American Journal of Mental Deficiency*, 77, 654–69.

Byers Brown, B. (1976). Language vulnerability, speech delay and therapeutic intervention. *British Journal of Disorders of Communication*, 11, 43–56.

Byers Brown, B., and Edwards, M. (1989). *Developmental Disorders of Language*. London: Whurr Publishers.

Cameron, R. J. (1982). Teaching and evaluating curriculum objectives. *Remedial Education*, 17, 102–8.

Campione, J. C. (1986). Reaction time and the study of intelligence. In M. G. Wade (Ed.), *Motor Skill Acquisition of the Mentally Handicapped: Issues in Research and Training*. North Holland: Elsevier.

Campione, J. C., and Brown, A. L. (1978). Toward a theory of intelligence: Contributions from research with retarded children. *Intelligence*, 2, 279–304.

Campione, J. C., Brown, A. L., and Ferrara, R. A. (1982). Mental retardation and intelligence. In R. J. Sternberg (Ed.), *Handbook of Human Intelligence*. Cambridge: Cambridge University Press.

Carpenter, T. P., and Moser, J. M. (1984). The acquisition of subtraction concepts in grades one through three. *Journal for Research in Mathematics Education, 15,* 179–202.

Carraher, T. N., Carraher, D. W., and Schliemann, A. D. (1985). Mathematics in the streets and in schools. *British Journal of Developmental Psychology, 3,* 21–9.

Carroll, J. B. (1976). Psychometric tests as cognitive tasks: A new 'structure of the intellect'. In L. B. Resnick (Ed.), *The Nature of Intelligence.* Hillsdale, NJ: Erlbaum.

Cattell, J. M. (1890). Mental tests and measurement. *Mind,* 15, 373–81.

Chall, J. (1967). *Learning to Read: The Great Debate.* New York: McGraw–Hill.

Charles, R. I., and Lester, F. K. (1984). An evaluation of a process-oriented instructional program in mathematical problem solving in grades 5 and 7. *Research in Mathematics Education, 15,* 15–34.

Chazan, M., and Laing, A. (1982). *The Early Years.* Milton Keynes: The Open University Press.

Chazan, M., Laing, A., Shackleton Bailey, M., and Jones, G. (1980). *Some of Our Children.* London: Open Books.

Chi, M. T. H. (1978). Knowledge structures and memory development. In R. S. Siegler (Ed.), *Children's Thinking: What Develops?.* Hillsdale, NJ: Erlbaum.

Chi, M. T. H. (1981). Knowledge development and memory performance. In M. Friedman, J. P. Das, and N. O'Connor (Eds), *Intelligence and Learning.* New York: Plenum.

Chi, M. T. H. (1985). Interactive roles of knowledge and strategies in development. In S. Chipman, J. Segal, and R. Glaser (Eds), *Thinking and Learning Skills: Current Research and Open Questions, vol. 2.* Hillsdale, NJ: Erlbaum.

Christianson, S., Ysseldyke, J., and Algozzine, B. (1982). Institutional constraints and external pressures influencing referral decisions. *Psychology in the Schools, 19,* 341–5.

Cicchetti, D., and Wagner, S. (1990). Alternative assessment strategies for the evaluation of infants and toddlers: An organizational perspective. In S. Meisels and J. Shonkoff (Eds), *Handbook of Early Childhood Intervention.* New York: Cambridge University Press.

Clahsen, H. (1989). The grammatical characterization of developmental dysphasia. *Linguistics, 27,* 897–920.

Clahsen, H. (1991). *Child Language and Developmental Dysphasia.* (Trans. by K. Richman.) Amsterdam: John Benjamins.

Clark, E. V. (1983). Meanings and Concepts. In P. H. Mussen (Ed.), *Handbook of Child Psychology: vol III: Cognitive Development.* New York: Wiley.

Clarke, A. D. B. (1978). Predicting human development: Problems, evidence and implications. *Bulletin of the British Psychological Society*, *31*, 249–58.

Clarke, A. M., and Clarke, A. D. B. (1974). *Mental Deficiency: The Changing Outlook*. (3rd ed.) London: Methuen.

Clements, J. (1987). *Severe Learning Disability and Psychological Handicap*. Chichester: Wiley.

Cockroft, W. H. (1982). *Mathematics Counts: Report of the Committee of Inquiry into the Teaching of Mathematics in Schools*. London: HMSO.

Coles, G. S. (1978). The learning-disabilities test battery: Empirical and social issues. *Harvard Educational Review*, *48*, 313–40.

Conti-Ramsden, G., and Gunn, M. (1986). The development of conversational disability: A case study. *British Journal of Disorders of Communication*, *21*, 339–52.

Cromer, R. F. (1978). The basis of childhood dysphasia: A linguistic approach. In M. A. Wyke (Ed.), *Developmental Dysphasia*. London: Academic Press.

Cromer, R. F. (1983). Hierarchical planning disability in the drawings and constructions of a special group of severely dysphasic children. *Brain and Cognition*, *2*, 144–64.

Cromer, R. F. (1991). *Language and Thought in Normal and Handicapped Children*. Oxford: Blackwell.

Cromer, W. (1970). The difference model: A new explanation for some reading difficulties. *Journal of Educational Psychology*, *61*, 471–83.

Cronbach, L. J. (1984). *Essentials of Psychological Testing*. (4th ed.). New York: Harper and Row.

Crystal, D. (1985). *Introduction to Language Pathology*. London: Edward Arnold.

Curtis, M. E. (1980). Development of components of reading skill. *Journal of Educational Psychology*, *72*, 656–69.

Derry, S. J., Hawkes, L. W., and Tsai, C. J. (1987). A theory for remediating problem-solving skills of older children and adults. *Educational Psychologist*, *22*, 55–87.

Detterman, D. K. (1979). Memory in the mentally retarded. In N. R. Ellis (Ed.), *Handbook of Mental Deficiency, Psychological Theory and Research*. (2nd ed.). Hillsdale, NJ: Erlbaum.

Detterman, D. K., and Sternberg, R. J. (1982). *How and How Much Can Intelligence be Increased*. Norwood, NJ: Ablex Publishing Company.

Dockrell, J., and Campbell, R. (1986). Lexical acquisition strategies in the preschool child. In S. A. Kuczaj and M. D. Barrett (Eds), *The Development of Word Meaning*. New York: Springer–Verlag.

Dockrell, J. E., and Henry, C. (in press, due 1993). Assessment of the mentally handicapped. In J. R. Beech, L. M. Harding and D. Hilton-Jones (Eds), *Assessment in speech and language therapy*. London: Routledge.

Dockrell, J., and McShane, J. (1990). Young children's use of phrase-structure and inflectional information in form–class assignments of novel nouns and verbs. *First Language, 10*, 127–40.

Doris, J. (1986). Learning disabilities. In S. J. Ceci (Ed.), *Handbook of Cognitive, Social, and Neuropsychological Aspects of Learning Disabilities, vol. 1*. Hillsdale, NJ: Erlbaum.

Drillien, C. M., Jameson, S., and Wilkinson, E. M. (1966). Studies in mental handicap, Part 1: Prevalence and distribution by clinical type and severity of defect. *Archives of Disease in Childhood, 41*, 528–38.

Drucker, H., McBride, S., and Wilbur, C. (1987). Using a computer-based error analysis approach to improve basic subtraction skills in the third grade. *Journal of Educational Research, 80*, 363–5.

Dweck, C. S. (1975). The role of expectations and attributions in the alleviation of learned helplessness. *Journal of Personality and Social Psychology, 39*, 674–85.

Dweck, C. S., and Licht, B. G. (1980). Learned helplessness and intellectual achievement. In J. Garber and M. E. P. Seligman, (Eds), *Human Helplessness: Theory and Application*. New York: Academic Press.

Dykens, E. M., Hodapp, R. M., and Leckman, J. F. (1987). Strengths and weaknesses in the intellectual functioning of males with fragile x syndrome. *American Journal of Mental Deficiency, 92*, 234–6.

Eisenson, J. (1972). *Aphasia in Children*. New York: Harper and Row.

Ellis, A. W. (1985). The cognitive neuropsychology of developmental (and acquired) dyslexia: A critical survey. *Cognitive Neuropsychology, 2*, 169–205.

Ellis, N. C., and Cataldo, S. (in press). Spelling is integral to learning to read. In C. Sterling and C. Robson (Eds), *Psychology, Spelling and Education*. Avon: Multilingual Matters.

Ellis, N. C., and Miles, T. R. (1978). Visual information processing in dyslexic children. In M. M. Gruneberg, P. E. Morris, and R. N. Sykes (Eds), *Practical Aspects of Memory*. London: Academic Press.

Ellis, N. R. (1963). The stimulus trace and behavioral inadequacy. In N. R. Ellis (Ed.), *Handbook of Mental Deficiency*. New York: McGraw-Hill.

Ellis, N. R., and Cavalier, A. R. (1982). Research perspectives in mental retardation. In E. Zigler and D. Balla (Eds), *Mental Retardation: The Developmental-Difference Controversy*. Hillsdale, NJ: Erlbaum.

Endeby, A., and Davies, P. (1989). Communication disorders: planning a service to meet the needs. *British Journal of Disorders of Communication 24*, 301–32.

Engelmann, S. (1977). Sequencing cognitive and academic tasks. In R. D. Keedler and S. G. Tarver (Eds), *Changing Perspectives in Special Education*. Columbus, OH: Charles E. Merrill.

Engelmann, S., and Carnine, D. (1982). *Theory of Instruction: Principles and Applications*. New York: Irvington Publishers.

Engelmann, S., Haddox, P., and Bruner, E. (1983). *Teach Your Child to Read in 100 Easy Lessons*. New York: Simon and Schuster.

Englert, C. S., Raphael, T. E., Anderson, L. M., Anthony, H., and Stevens, D. D. (1991). Making strategies and self-talk visible: Writing instruction in regular and special education classrooms. *American Educational Research Journal, 28*, 337–72.

Epps, S., Ysseldyke, J. E., and Algozzine, B. (1983). Impact of different definitions of learning disabilities on the number of students identified. *Journal of Psychoeducational Assessment, 1*, 341–52.

Estes, B. W., and Combs, A. (1966). Perception of quantity. *Journal of Genetic Psychology, 108*, 333–6.

Eysenck, H. J. (1987). Speed of information processing, reaction time, and the theory of intelligence. In P. A. Vernon (Ed.), *Speed of Information Processing and Intelligence*. Norwood, NJ: Ablex.

Fagan, J. F. (1982). New evidence for the prediction of intelligence from infancy. *Infant Mental Health Journal, 3*, 219–28.

Fagan, J. F., Singer, L. T., Montie, J. E., and Sheperd, P. A. (1986). Selective screening device for the early detection of normal or delayed cognitive development in infants at risk for later mental retardation. *Pediatrics, 78*, 1021–6.

Fey, M. E., and Leonard, L. B. (1987). Pragmatic studies of children with specific language impairment. In T. Gallagher and C. Prutting (Eds), *Pragmatic Assessment and Intervention Issues in Language*. San Diego: College-Hill Press.

Fleisher, L. S., Jenkins, J. R., and Pany, D. (1979). Effects on poor readers' comprehension of training in rapid decoding. *Reading Research Quarterly, 15*, 30–48.

Fodor, J. (1983). *The Modularity of Mind*. Cambridge, MA: MIT Press.

Forness, S. R. (1988). The future of learning disabilities. In K. A. Kavale (Ed.), *Learning Disabilities: State of the Art and Practice*. San Diego: College-Hill Press.

Franklin, B. M. (1987). From brain injury to learning disability: Alfred Strauss, Heinz Werner and the historical development of the learning disabilities field. In B. M. Franklin (Ed.), *Learning Disability: Dissenting Essays*. London: Falmer Press.

Frith, U. (1985). Beneath the surface of developmental dyslexia. In K. E. Patterson, J. C. Marshall, and M. Coltheart (Eds), *Surface Dyslexia:*

Neuropsychological and Cognitive Studies of Phonological Reading. Hillsdale, NJ: Erlbaum.

Frith, U., and Snowling, M. (1983). Reading for meaning and reading for sound in autistic and dyslexic children. *British Journal of Developmental Psychology*, 1, 329–42.

Frostig, M., and Horne, D. (1964). *The Frostig Programme for the Development of Visual Perception*. Chicago: Folett.

Frumkin, B., and Rapin, I. (1980). Perception of vowels and consonant-vowels of varying duration in language-impaired children. *Neuropsychologia*, 18, 443–54.

Fryers, T. (1984). *The Epidemiology of Severe Intellectual Impairment: The Dynamics and Prevalence*. London: Academic Press.

Fundudis, T., Kolvin, I., and Garside, R. F. (1979). *Speech Retarded and Deaf Children: Their Psychological Development*. London: Academic Press.

Fuson, K. C. (1988). *Children's Counting and Concepts of Number*. New York: Springer–Verlag.

Gaddes, W. H. (1976). Prevalence estimates and the need for a definition of learning disabilities. In R. M. Knights and D. J. Bakker (Eds), *The Neuropsychology of Learning Disorders*. Baltimore: University Park Press.

Gagné, R. M., Mayer, J. R., Garstens, H. L., and Paradise, W. E. (1962). Factors in acquiring knowledge in a mathematics task. *Psychological Monographs*, 76, no. 7.

Galton, F. (1883). *Inquiries into Human Faculty and its Development*. London: Macmillan.

Garbarino, J. (1982). Sociocultural risk. In C. B. Kopp and J. B. Krakow (Eds), *The Child: Development in a Social Context*. Reading, MA: Addison–Wesley.

Gardner, E. G. (1962). Normative standardized scores. *Journal of Educational and Psychological Measurement*, 22, 7–14.

Garner, R. (1987). *Metacognition and Reading Comprehension*. Norwood, NJ: Ablex.

Garner, R., and Kraus, C. (1981–2). Good and poor comprehender differences in knowing and regulating reading behaviors. *Educational Research Quarterly*, 6, 5–12.

Garner, R., and Reis, R. (1981). Monitoring and resolving comprehension obstacles: An investigation of spontaneous text lookbacks among upper-grade good and poor comprehenders. *Reading Research Quarterly*, 16, 569–82.

Gathercole, S. E., and Baddeley, A. D. (1989). Evaluation of the role of phonological STM in the development of vocabulary in children: A longitudinal study. *Journal of Memory and Language*, 28, 200–13.

Gathercole, S. E., and Baddeley, A. D. (1990). Phonological memory deficits in language disordered children: Is there a causal connection? *Journal of Memory and Language*, 29, 336–60.

Geary, D. C. (1990). A componential analysis of early learning deficits in mathematics. *Journal of Experimental Child Psychology*, 49, 363–83.

Geary, D. C., Brown, S. C., and Samaranayake, V. A. (1991). Cognitive addition: A short longitudinal study of strategy choice and speed-of-processing differences in normal and mathematically disabled children. *Developmental Psychology*, 27, 787–97.

Geary, D. C., Widaman, K. F., Little, T. D., and Cormier, P. (1987). Cognitive addition: Comparison of learning disabled and academically normal elementary school children. *Cognitive Development*, 2, 249–69.

Gelzheiser, L. (1984). Generalization from categorical memory tasks to prose by learning disabled students. *Journal of Educational Psychology*, 67, 1128–38.

Gersten, R., and Carnine, D. (1986). Direct instruction in reading comprehension. *Educational Leadership*, 43, 70–7.

Gick, M. L., and Holyoak, K. J. (1987). The cognitive basis of knowledge transfer. In S. M. Cormier and J. D. Hagman (Eds), *Transfer of Learning: Contemporary Research and Applications*. San Diego: Academic Press.

Gillham, B. (1986). *Handicapping Conditions in Children*. London: Croom Helm.

Gillham, W. E. (1974). The British Intelligence Scale: A la recherche du temps perdu. *Bulletin of the British Psychological Society*, 27, 307–12.

Ginsburg, H. (1977). *Children's Arithmetic: The Learning Process*. New York: Van Nostrand.

Gipps, C., Steadman, S. D., Blackstone, T., and Stierer, B. (1983). *Testing Children: Standardized Testing in Local Education Authorities and Schools*. London: Heinemann Educational Books.

Gittelman, R., and Feingold, I. (1983). Children with reading disorders – I: Efficacy of reading remediation. *Journal of Child Psychology and Psychiatry*, 24, 167–92.

Gleitman, L. R., and Rozin, P. (1977). The structure and acquisition of reading 1: Relations between orthographies and the structure of language. In A. S. Reber and D. L. Scarborough (Eds), *Toward a Psychology of Reading*. Hillsdale, NJ: Erlbaum.

Glynn, T. (1980). Parent–child interaction in remedial reading at home. In M. M. Clark and T. Glynn (Eds), *Reading and Writing for the Child with Difficulties*. Educational Review, Occasional Publications Number Eight, University of Birmingham.

Goldman, S. R. (1989). Strategy instruction in mathematics. *Learning Disability Quarterly*, *12*, 43–55.

Goldman, S. R., Pellegrino, J. W., and Mertz, D. L. (1988). Extended practice of basic addition facts: Strategy changes in learning-disabled children. *Cognition and Instruction*, *5*, 223–65.

Goldstein, D. M. (1976). Cognitive–linguistic functioning and learning to read in preschoolers. *Journal of Educational Psychology*, *68*, 680–8.

Goldstein, H., Arkell, C., Ashcroft, S. C., Hurley, O. L., and Lilly, S. M. (1975). Schools. In N. Hobbs (Ed.), *Issues in the Classification of Children*. San Francisco: Jossey–Bass.

Goswami, U., and Bryant, P. (1990). *Phonological Skills and Learning to Read*. Hove: Erlbaum.

Greening, M., and Spenceley, J. (1987). Shared reading: Support for inexperienced readers. *Educational Psychology in Practice*, *3*, 31–7.

Gregory, R. P. (1980). Individual referrals: How naive are educational psychologists? *Bulletin of the British Psychological Society*, *33*, 381–4.

Groen, G. J., and Parkman, J. M. (1972). A chronometric analysis of simple addition. *Psychological Review*, *79*, 329–43.

Groen, G. J., and Resnick, L. B. (1977). Can pre-school children invent addition algorithms? *Journal of Educational Psychology*, *69*, 645–52.

Grossman, H. (Ed.), (1983). *Classification in Mental Retardation*. (3rd ed.). Washington DC: American Association of Mental Retardation.

Grunwell, P. (1985). *Phonological Assessment of Child Speech (PACS)*. Windsor: NFER–Nelson.

Guilford, J. P. (1967). *The Nature of Human Intelligence*. New York: McGraw–Hill.

Hall, P. K., and Tomblin, J. B. (1978). A follow-up study of children with articulation and language disorders. *Journal of Speech and Hearing Disorders*, *43*, 227–41.

Hallahan, D. P., and Bryan, T. H. (1981). Learning disabilities. In J. M. Kauffman and D. P. Hallahan (Eds), *Handbook of Special Education*. Englewood Cliffs, NJ: Prentice–Hall.

Hallahan, D. P., and Cruickshank, W. M. (1973). *Psychoeducational Foundations of Learning Disabilities*. Englewood Cliffs, NJ: Prentice–Hall.

Hallahan, D. P., and Kauffman, J. M. (1977). Labels, categories, behaviors: ED, LD, and EMR reconsidered. *Journal of Special Education*, *11*, 139–49.

Hamann, M. S., and Ashcraft, M. H. (1985). Simple and complex addition across development. *Journal of Experimental Child Psychology*, *40*, 49–72.

Hammill, D. D. (1972). Training visual perceptual processes. *Journal of Learning Disabilities*, 5, 35–46.

Hammill, D. D., and Larsen, S. C. (1974). The effectiveness of psycholinguistic training. *Exceptional Children*, 41, 5–15.

Hammill, D. D., Leigh, J. E., McNutt, G., and Larsen, S. C. (1981). A new definition of learning disabilities. *Learning Disability Quarterly*, 4, 336–42.

Harris, K. R. (1983). The use of estimated true scores, standard errors of measurement, and confidence intervals in reporting assessment data. *Diagnostique*, 8, 118–26.

Haynes, C., and Naidoo, S. (1991). *Children with Specific Speech and Language Impairment*. London: Mac Keith Press.

Henderson, L. (1982). *Orthography and Word Recognition in Reading*. London: Academic Press.

Heron, A., and Myers, M. (1983). *Intellectual Impairment: Battle Against Handicaps*. New York: Academic Press.

Heyns, B. (1978). *Summer Learning and Effects of Schooling*. New York: Academic Press.

Hindley, C., and Owen, C. (1978). The extent of individual changes in IQ for ages between 6 months and 17 years in a British longitudinal sample. *Journal of Child Psychology and Psychiatry*, 19, 329–50.

Hinshelwood, J. (1917). *Congenital Word Blindness*. London: H. K. Lewis.

Hodapp, R. M., and Burack, J. A. (1990). What mental retardation teaches us about typical development: The examples of sequences, rates, and cross-domain relations. *Development and Psychopathology*, 2, 213–26.

Hodapp, R. M., and Dykens, E. M. (in press). Toward an etiology-specific strategy of early intervention with handicapped children. In K. Marfo (Ed.), *Early Intervention in Transition: Current Perspectives on Programs for Handicapped Children*. New York: Praeger Publishers.

Hofmeister, A. (1975). Integrating criterion-referenced testing and instruction. In W. Hively and M. Reynolds (Eds), *Domain-Referenced Testing in Special Education*. Minneapolis: Leadership Training Institute/Special Education, University of Minnesota.

Holmes, D. R., and McKeever, W. F. (1979). Material specific serial memory deficit in adolescent dyslexics. *Cortex*, 15, 51–62.

Holzman, T. G., Pellegrino, J. W., and Glaser, R. (1982). Cognitive dimensions of numerical rule induction. *Journal of Educational Psychology*, 74, 360–73.

Holzman, T. G., Pellegrino, J. W., and Glaser, R. (1983). Cognitive variables in series completion. *Journal of Educational Psychology*, 75, 603–18.

Honzik, M. P., MacFarlane, J. W., and Allen, L. (1948). The stability of mental test performance between two and eighteen years. *Journal of Experimental Education*, 17, 309–24.

Honzik, M. P. (1983). Measuring mental abilities in infancy: The value and limitations. In M. Lewis (Ed.), *Origins of Intelligence: Infancy and Early Childhood*. New York: Plenum Press.

Hooper, S. R., and Willis, W. G. (1989). *Learning Disability Subtyping: Neuropsychological Foundations, Conceptual Models, and Issues in Clinical Differentiation*. New York: Springer-Verlag.

Horn, W., and Packard, T. (1985). Early identification of learning problems: A meta-analysis. *Journal of Educational Psychology*, 77 597–607.

Hornsby, B., and Miles, T. (1980). The effects of a dyslexia-centred teaching programme. *British Journal of Educational Psychology*, 50, 236–42.

Howe, M. J. (1988). Intelligence as an explanation. *British Journal of Psychology*, 79, 349–60.

Hudson, T. (1983). Correspondence and numerical differences between disjoint sets. *Child Development*, 54, 84–90.

Hughes, M. (1986). *Children and Number: Difficulties in Learning Mathematics*. Oxford: Blackwell.

Ingram, D. (1989). *Phonological Disability in Children*. (2nd ed.). London: Whurr Publishers.

Ingram, T. T. S. (1972). Classification of speech and language disorders in young children. In M. Rutter and J. A. M. Martin (Eds), *The Child with Delayed Speech*. London: Heinemann Medical Books.

Isakson, R. L., and Miller, J. W. (1976). Sensitivity to syntactic and semantic cues in good and poor comprehenders. *Journal of Educational Psychology*, 68, 787–92.

Johnston, J. C., and McClelland, J. L. (1980). Experimental tests of a hierarchical model of word identification. *Journal of Verbal Learning and Verbal Behavior*, 19, 503–25.

Jorm, A. F. (1983). Specific reading retardation and working memory: A review. *British Journal of Psychology*, 74, 311–42.

Kail, R. (1990). *The Development of Memory in Children*. (3rd ed.). New York: Freeman.

Kail, R., and Leonard, L. B. (1986). Sources of word-finding problems in language impaired children. In S. J. Ceci (Ed.), *Handbook of Cognitive, Social, and Neuropsychological Aspects of Learning Disabilities*. vol. 1. Hillsdale, NJ: Erlbaum.

Kamhi, A. G., Catts, H. W., Koenig, L. A., and Lewis, B. A. (1984). Hypothesis-testing and nonlinguistic symbolic abilities in language-impaired children. *Journal of Speech and Hearing Disorders*, 49, 169–76.

Kamhi, A. G., Nelson, L. K., Lee, R. F., and Gholson, B. (1985). The ability of language-disordered children to use and modify hypotheses in discrimination learning. *Applied Psycholinguistics*, 6, 435–52.

Kaufman, A. (1976). A new approach to the interpretation of test scatter on the WISC-R. *Journal of Learning Disabilities*. 9, 33–41.

Kavale, K. A. (1988). Status of the field: Trends and issues in learning disabilities. In K. A. Kavale (Ed.), *Learning Disabilities: State of the Art and Practice*. San Diego: College-Hill Press.

Kavale, K. A., and Nye, C. (1985–6). Parameters of learning disabilities in achievement linguistics, neuropsychological, and social/behavior domains. *The Journal of Special Education*, 19, 443–58.

Keeney, T. J., Canizzo, S. R., and Flavell, J. H. (1967). Spontaneous and induced verbal rehearsal in a recall task. *Child Development*, 38, 953–66.

Kellmer-Pringle, M., Butler, N. R., and Davie, R. (1966). *11,000 Seven-Year-Olds*. London: National Children's Bureau.

Kennedy, B. A., and Miller, D. J. (1976). Persistent use of verbal rehearsal as a function of information about its value. *Child Development*, 47, 566–9.

Kephart, N. C. (1960). *The Slow Learner in the Classroom*. Columbus, OH: Charles E. Merrill.

Kiernan, C. (1981). *Analysis of Programmes for Teaching*. Basingstoke: Globe Education.

King's Fund Centre (1980). *An Ordinary Life: Comprehensive Locally Based Residential Services for Mentally Handicapped People*. (Project Paper 24). London: King Edwards Hospital Fund for London.

Kintsch, W., and Greeno, J. G. (1985). Understanding and solving word arithmetic problems. *Psychological Review*, 92, 109–29.

Kirk, S., McCarthy, J., and Kirk, W. (1961). *Illinois Test of Psycholinguistic Abilities*. Urbana, ILL: University of Illinois Press.

Kirwan, B. (Ed.), (1992). *A Guide to Task Analysis*. London: Taylor and Francis.

Kistner, J. A., Osborne, M., and LeVerrier, L. (1988). Causal attributions of learning-disabled children: Developmental patterns and relation to academic progress. *Journal of Educational Psychology*, 80, 82–9.

Koegel, R. L., and Rincover, A. (1974). Treatment of psychotic children in a classroom environment: I. Learning in a large group. *Journal of Applied Behavior Analysis*, 7, 45–59.

Koorland, M. A. (1986). Applied behaviour analysis and the correction of learning disabilities. In J. K. Torgesen and B. Y. L. Wong (Eds), *Psychological and Educational Perspectives on Learning Disabilities*. New York: Academic Press.

Kopp, C. B., and McCall, R. B. (1982). Predicting later mental performance for normal, at risk, and handicapped infants. In P. B. Baltes and O. G. Brim (Eds), *Life Span Development and Behaviour, vol. 4*. New York: Academic Press.

Krupski, A. (1986). Attention problems in youngsters with learning handicaps. In J. K. Torgesen and B. Y. L. Wong (Eds), *Psychological and Educational Perspectives on Learning Difficulties*. New York: Academic Press.

Largo, R. H., Graf, S., Kundw, S., Hunziker, U., and Molinari, L. (1990). Predicting developmental outcome at school age from infant tests of normal, at-risk and retarded infants. *Developmental Medicine and Child Neurology, 32*, 40–5.

Lawson, M. J., and Fuelop, I. (1980). Understanding the purpose of strategy training. *British Journal of Educational Psychology, 50*, 175–80.

Leach, D. J., and Siddall, S. W. (1990). Parental involvement in the teaching of reading: A comparison of hearing reading, paired reading, pause, prompt, praise, and direct instruction methods. *British Journal of Educational Psychology, 60*, 349–55.

Lee, L. (1974). *Developmental Sentence Analysis*. Evanston, IL: Northwestern University Press.

Lees, J., and Urwin, S. (1991). *Children with Language Disorders*. London: Whurr Publishers.

Leifer, J., and Lewis, M. (1984). Acquisition of conversational and response skills by young Down Syndrome and non retarded young children. *American Journal of Mental Deficiency, 88*, 610–18.

Leonard, L. (1981). Facilitating linguistic skills in children with specific language impairment. *Applied Psycholinguistics, 2*, 89–148.

Leonard, L. (1989). Language learnability and specific language impairment in children. *Applied Psycholinguistics, 10*, 179–202.

Lezak, M. D. (1988). IQ: RIP. *Journal of Clinical and Experimental Neuropsychology, 10*, 3, 351–61.

Liberman, I. Y., Shankweiler, D., Fischer, F. W., and Carter, B. (1974). Explicit syllable and phoneme segmentation in the young child. *Journal of Experimental Child Psychology, 18*, 201–12.

Licht, B. G. (1983). Cognitive–motivational factors that contribute to the achievement of learning-disabled children. *Journal of Learning Disabilities, 16*, 483–90.

Licht, B. G., and Kistner, J. A. (1986). Motivational problems of learning disabled children: Individual differences and their implication for treatment. In J. K. Torgesen and B. Y. L. Wong (Eds), *Psychological and Educational Perspectives on Learning Disabilities*. New York: Academic Press.

REFERENCES

Lindsay, G. A., and Wedell, K. (1982). The early identification of educationally 'at risk' children revisited. *Journal of Learning Difficulties*, *15*, 4, 212–17.

Locke, A. (1978). The case against assessment. *Bulletin of the British Psychological Society*, *31*, 322–4.

Longhurst, T., and Grubb, S. (1974). A comparison of language samples collected in four situations. *Language, Speech and Hearing Services in the Schools*, *5*, 71–8.

Lovitt, T. C., and Fantasia, K. (1983). A precision teaching project with learning disabled children. *Journal of Precision Teching*, *3*, 85–91.

Lukose, S. (1987). Knowledge and behaviour relationships in the memory ability of retarded and nonretarded students. *Journal of Experimental Child Psychology*, *43*, 13–24.

Lundberg, I., Olofsson, A., and Wall, S. (1981). Reading and spelling skills in the first school years predicted from phonemic awareness skills in kindergarten. *Scandinavian Journal of Psychology*, *21*, 159–73.

Lynch, A., Vincent, C. M., Mitchell, C. B., and Trueman, M. (1982). How 'flat' are normal ability profiles in 4-year-olds? *Child Health Care and Development*, *8*, 39–49.

McBrien, J., and Foxen, T. (1981). *Training Staff in Behavioural Methods*. (Instructor's Handbook; Trainee Workbook). Manchester: Manchester University Press.

McEvoy, J., and McConkey, R. (1990). Correspondence errors in counting objects by children with a mental handicap. *Irish Journal of Psychology*, *11*, 249–60.

McFarland, C. E., and Weibe, D. (1987). Structure and utilization of knowledge among special children. In J. G. Borkowksi and J. D. Day (Eds), *Cognition in Special Children: Comparative Approaches to Retardation, Learning Disabilities, and Giftedness*. Norwood, NJ: Ablex.

McShane, J. (1980). *Learning to Talk*. Cambridge: Cambridge University Press.

McShane, J. (1991). *Cognitive Development: An Information Processing Approach*. Oxford: Blackwell.

McShane J., and Whittaker, S. (1988). The encoding of tense and aspect by three- to five-year-old children. *Journal of Experimental Child Psychology*, *45*, 52–70.

McShane, J., Whittaker, S., and Dockrell, J. (1986). Verbs and time. In S. A. Kuczaj and M. D. Barrett (Eds), *The Development of Word Meaning*. New York: Springer-Verlag.

Marsh, G., Friedman, M., Welch, V., and Desberg, P. (1981). A cognitive–developmental theory of reading acquisition. In G. E. Mackinnon and T. G. Waller (Eds), *Reading Research: Advances in Theory and Practice*. New York: Academic Press.

Mayer, R. E. (1979). Can advance organizers influence meaningful learning? *Review of Educational Research*, 49, 371–83.

Mehan, H., Meihls, S. L., Hertweck, A., and Crowdes, M. S. (1981). Identifying handicapped students. In S. B. Bacharach (Ed.), *Organizational Behaviour in Schools and School Districts*. New York: Praeger.

Meisels, S. J., and Wasik, B. A. (1989). Who should be served? Identifying children in need of intervention. In S. J. Meisels and J. P. Shonkoff (Eds), *Handbook of Early Childhood Intervention*. Cambridge: Cambridge University Press.

Menyuk, P. (1975). Children with language problems: What's the problem? In D. Dato (Ed.), *Georgetown University Roundtable on Language and Linguistics*. Washington DC: Georgetown University Press.

Menyuk, P., and Flood, J. (1981). Linguistic competence, reading, writing problems and remediation. *Bulletin of the Orton Society*, 31, 13–28.

Meyer, W. U., Bachmann, M., Bierman, U., Hempelmann, M., Ploger, F., and Spiller, H. (1979). The informational value of evaluative behaviour: Influences of praise and blame on perceptions of ability. *Journal of Educational Psychology*, 71, 259–68.

Michie, S. (1984a). Number understanding in preschool children. *British Journal of Educational Psychology*, 54, 245–53.

Michie, S. (1984b). Why preschoolers are reluctant to count spontaneously. *British Journal of Developmental Psychology*, 2, 347–58.

Miles, T. R. (1983). *Dyslexia: The Pattern of Difficulties*. London: Granada.

Miller, G. A. (1986). Dictionaries in the mind. *Language and Cognitive Processes*, 1, 171–85.

Miller, G. A., and Gildea, P. M. (1986). How children learn words. *Scientific American*, 257, (3), 94–9.

Mischel, W. (1977). On the future of personality measurement. *American Psychologist*, 32, 246–54.

Montague, M., and Bos, C. S. (1986). Verbal mathematical problem solving and learning disabilities: A review. *Focus on Learning Problems in Mathematics*, 8, 7–21.

Morgan, R., and Lyon, G. (1979). Paired reading: A preliminary report on a technique for parental tuition for reading with retarded readers. *Journal of Child Psychology and Psychiatry*, 20, 151–60.

Morley, M. E. (1972). *Development and Disorders of Speech in Childhood*. (3rd ed.). Edinburgh: Churchill Livingstone.

Muller, D., Munro, S. M., and Code, C. (1981). *Language Assessment for Remediation*. London: Croom Helm.

Neale, M. D. (1989). *The Neale Analysis of Reading Ability.* (Revised British Edition.) Windsor: NFER–Nelson.

Nelson, L. K., Kamhi, A. G., and Apel, K. (1987). Cognitive strengths and weaknesses in language impaired children: One more look. *Journal of Speech and Hearing Disorders,* 52, 36–43.

Nettelbeck, T., and Brewer, N. (1981). Studies of mild mental retardation and timed performance. In N. R. Ellis (Ed.), *International Review of Research in Mental Retardation, 10.* New York: Academic Press.

Newcomer, P., and Magee, P. (1977). The performance of learning (reading) disabled children on a test of spoken language. *The Reading Teacher,* 30, 896–900.

Nitko, A. J. (1980). Distinguishing the many varieties of criterion-referenced tests. *Review of Educational Research,* 50, 461–85.

O'Connor, N., and Hermelin, B. (1963). *Speech and Thought in Severe Subnormality.* London: Pergamon Press.

O'Hagan, F., and Swanson, I. (1983). Teachers' views regarding educational psychologists in schools. *Research in Education,* 29, 29–40.

O'Sullivan, J. T., and Pressley, M. (1984). Completeness of instruction and strategy transfer. *Journal of Experimental Child Psychology,* 38, 275–88.

Oakhill, J. V. (1984). Inferential and memory skills in children's comprehension of stories. *British Journal of Educational Psychology,* 54, 31–9.

Oakhill, J. V., and Garnham, A. (1988). *Becoming a Skilled Reader.* Oxford: Blackwell.

Oakhill, J. V., and Yuill, N. M. (1986). Pronoun resolution in skilled and less-skilled comprehenders: Effects of memory load and inferential complexity. *Language and Speech,* 29, 25–37.

Olofsson, A., and Lundberg, I. (1985). Evaluation of long term effects of phonemic awareness training in kindergarten. *Scandinavian Journal of Psychology,* 26, 21–34.

Olson, D. R. (1986). Intelligence and literacy: The relationship between intelligence and the technologies of representation and communication. In R. J. Sternberg and R. K. Wagner (Eds), *Practical Intelligence: Nature and Origins of Competence in the Everyday World.* Cambridge: Cambridge University Press.

Ornstein, P. A., Naus, M. J., and Liberty, C. (1975). Rehearsal and organizational processes in children's memory. *Child Development,* 46, 818–30.

Orton, S. T. (1937). *Reading, Writing and Speech Problems in Children.* New York: Norton.

Palincsar, A. S., and Brown, A. L. (1984). Reciprocal teaching of comprehension-fostering and comprehension-monitoring activities. *Cognition and Instruction*, *1*, 117-75.

Paris, S. G., Newman, R. S., and McKey, K. A. (1982). From tricks to strategies: Learning the functional significance of mnemonic actions. *Journal of Experimental Child Psychology*, *34*, 490-509.

Pennypacker, H. S., Koenig, C., and Lindsley, O. R. (1972). *Handbook of the Standard Behavior Chart*. Kansas City: Precision Media.

Perfetti, C. A. (1985). *Reading Ability*. Oxford: Oxford University Press.

Perfeti, C. A., and Lesgold, A. M. (1979). Coding and comprehension in skilled reading and implications for reading instruction. In L. B. Resnick and P. Weaver (Eds), *Theory and Practice of Early Reading, vol. 1*. Hillsdale, NJ: Erlbaum.

Pilliner, A. E. G. (1979). Norm-referenced and criterion referenced tests – an evaluation. In *Issues in Educational Assessment*. Scottish Education Department: HMSO.

Pinker, S. (1989). *Learnability and Cognition: The Acquisition of Argument Structure*. Cambridge, MA: MIT Press.

President's Committee on Mental Retardation. (1973). *MR-72: Islands of Excellence*. Washington, DC: Government Printing Office.

Pritchard, D. G. (1963). *Education of the Handicapped, 1760-1960*. London: Routledge & Kegan Paul.

Pumfrey, P. D., and Reason, R. (1991). *Specific Learning Difficulties (Dyslexia): Challenges and Responses*. Windsor: NFER.

Quicke, J. C. (1980). The cautious expert: An empirically grounded critique of the practice of Local Educational Authority Educational Psychologists. Unpublished doctoral dissertation. University of Sheffield.

Rapin, I., and Allen, D. A. (1983). Developmental language disorders: Nosological considerations. In U. Kirk (Ed.), *Neuropsychology of Language, Reading, and Spelling*. New York: Academic Press.

Reid, D. K., and Hresko, W. P. (1981). *A Cognitive Approach to Learning Disabilities*. New York: McGraw-Hill.

Reid, M. K., and Borkowski, J. G. (1987). Causal attributions of hyperactive children: Implications for teaching strategies and self-control. *Journal of Educational Psychology*, *79*, 296-307.

Resnick, L. B. (1983). A developmental theory of number understanding. In H. P. Ginsburg (Ed.), *The Development of Mathematical Thinking*. New York: Academic Press.

Resnick, L. B. (1986). The development of mathematical intuition. In M. Perlmutter (Ed.), *Minnesota Symposia on Child Psychology, vol. 19: Perspectives on Intellectual Development*. Hillsdale, NJ: Erlbaum.

Resnick, L. B., and Omanson, S. F. (1987). Learning to understand arithmetic. In R. Glaser (Ed.), *Advances in Instructional Psychology, vol. 3*. Hillsdale, NJ: Erlbaum.

Reynolds, C. R. (1984–5). Critical measurement issues in learning disabilities. *The Journal of Special Education, 18,* 451–75.

Rice, M., Buhr, S. C., and Nemeth, M. (1990). Fast-mapping word-learning abilities of language-delayed preschoolers. *Journal of Speech and Hearing Disorders, 55,* 33–42.

Riley, M. S., and Greeno, J. G. (1988). Developmental analysis of understanding language about quantities and solving problems. *Cognition and Instruction, 5,* 49–101.

Riley, M. S., Greeno, J. G., and Heller, J. I. (1983). Development of children's problem-solving ability in arithmetic. In H. P. Ginsburg (Ed.), *The Development of Mathematical Thinking*. New York: Academic Press.

Ringel, B. A., and Springer, C. J. (1980). On knowing how well one is remembering: The persistence of strategy use during transfer. *Journal of Experimental Child Psychology, 29,* 322–33.

Robson, D., Miller, A., and Bushell, R. (1984). The development of paired reading in High Peak and West Derbyshire. *Remedial Education, 19,* 177–83.

Rosch, E., Mervis, C., Gray, W., Johnson, D., and Boyes-Braem, P. (1976). Basic objects in natural categories. *Cognitive Psychology, 8,* 382–439.

Rutter, M., Cox, A., Tupling, C., and Yule, W. (1975a). Attainment and adjustment in two geographical areas: I. The prevalence of psychiatric disorder. *British Journal of Psychiatry, 126,* 493–509.

Rutter, M., Tizard, J., and Whitmore, K. (Eds), (1970). *Education, Health and Behaviour*. London: Longman.

Rutter, M., Yule, B., Quinton, D., Rowlands, O., Yule, W., and Berger, M. (1975b). Attainment and adjustment in two geographical areas: III. Some factors accounting for area differences. *British Journal of Psychiatry, 126,* 520–33.

Salvia, J., and Ysseldyke, J. (1985). *Assessment in Special and Remedial Education*. (3rd ed.). Boston: Houghton Mifflin.

Sattler, J. (1988). *Assessment of Children*. (3rd ed.). San Diego: W. B. Saunders.

Schunk, D. H. (1985). Self-efficacy and classroom learning. *Psychology in the Schools, 22,* 208–23.

Schunk, D. H., and Cox, P. D. (1986). Strategy training and attributional feedback with learning disabled students. *Journal of Educational Research, 78,* 201–9.

Seltzer, G. B. (1983). Systems of classification. In J. L. Matson and J. A. Mulrick (Eds), *Handbook of Mental Retardation*. Oxford: Pergamon Press.

Sexton, C. W. (1989). Effectiveness of the DISTAR Reading I program in developing first graders' language skills. *Journal of Educational Research, 82*, 289–93.

Seymour, P. H. K. (1986). *Cognitive Analysis of Dyslexia*. London: Routledge and Kegan Paul.

Seymour, P. H. K., and Elder, L. (1986). Beginning reading without phonology. *Cognitive Neuropsychology, 3*, 1–36.

Shepard, L. (1980). An evaluation of the regression discrepancy method for identifying children with learning difficulties. *Journal of Special Education, 14*, 79–91.

Shriberg, L., and Kwiatowski, J. (1980). *Natural Process Analysis (NPA): A Procedure for Phonological Analysis of Continuous Speech Samples*. New York: Wiley.

Siegel, L. (1979). Infant perceptual, cognitive and motor behaviours as predictors of subsequent cognitive and language development. *Canadian Journal of Psychology, 33*, 382–95.

Siegel, L., and Ryan, E. (1984). Reading disability as a language disorder. *Remedial and Special Education, 5*, 28–33.

Siegler, R. S., and Richards, D. (1982). The development of intelligence. In R. J. Sternberg (Ed.), *Handbook of Human Intelligence*. Cambridge: Cambridge University Press.

Siegler, R. S., and Robinson, M. (1982). The development of numerical understandings. In H. W. Reese and L. P. Lipsitt (Eds), *Advances in Child Development and Behavior, vol. 16*. New York: Academic Press.

Siegler, R. S., and Shrager, J. (1984). Strategy choices in addition: How do children know what to do? In C. Sophian (Ed.), *Origins of Cognitive Skills*. Hillsdale, NJ: Erlbaum.

Silva, P. A., Williams, S. M., and McGee, R. (1987). A longitudinal study of children with developmental language delay at age three: Later intelligence, reading and behaviour problems. *Developmental Medicine and Child Neurology, 29*, 630–40.

Simon, H. A. (1976). Identifying basic abilities underlying intelligent performance of complex tasks. In L. Resnick (Ed.), *The Nature of Intelligence*. Hillsdale, NJ: Erlbaum.

Skuse, D. (1984). Extreme deprivation in early childhood-II. Theoretical issues and a comparative review. *Journal of Child Psychology and Psychiatry, 25*, 543–72.

Smead, V. S., and Schwartz, N. H. (1987). Managing complexity: An informal procedure for achieving success with school failures. *Techniques: A Journal for Remedial Education and Counseling, 3*, 89–101.

Smiley, S., Oakley, D. D., Worthen, D., Campione, J. C., and Brown, A. L. (1977). Recall of thematically relevant material by adolescent good and poor readers as a function of written versus oral presentation. *Journal of Educational Psychology*, *69*, 381–7.

Smith, P. A., and Marx, W. (1972). Some cautions on the use of the Frostig test: A factory analytic study. *Journal of Learning Disabilities*, *5*, 110–14.

Sontag, L. W., Baker, C. T., and Nelson, V. L. (1958). Mental growth and personality development: A longitudinal study. *Monographs of the Society for Research in Child Development*, *23* (Whole no. 68).

Stackhouse, J., and Campbell, H. (1983). The unintelligible child: A problem for the health care team. *Child Care, Health and Development*, *9*, 327–37.

Stanley, G. (1978). Eye movements in dyslexic children. In G. Stanley and K. Walsh (Eds), *Brain Impairment: Proceedings of the 1977 Brain Impairment Workshop*. Victoria: Dominion Press.

Stanovich, K. E. (1986). Cognitive processes and reading problems of learning-disabled children: Evaluating the assumption of specificity. In J. K. Torgesen and B. Y. L. Yong (Eds), *Psychological and Educational Perspectives on Learning Disabilities*. New York: Academic Press.

Stanovich, K. E., Cunningham, A., and Freeman, D. (1984). Intelligence, cognitive skills, and early reading progress. *Reading Research Quarterly*, *19*, 278–303.

Stark, R. E., Mellits, E., and Tallal, P. (1983). Behavioral attributes of speech and language disorders. In C. L. Ludlow and J. A. Cooper (Eds), *Genetic Aspects of Speech and Language Disorders*. New York: Academic Press.

Stark, R. E., and Tallal, P. (1988). *Language, Speech, and Reading Disorders in Children*. Boston: Little Brown.

Starkey, P., and Cooper, R. G. (1980). Perception of numbers by human infants. *Science*, *210*, 1033–5.

Sternberg, R. J. (1978). Intelligence research at the interface between differential and cognitive psychology: Prospects and proposals. *Intelligence*, *2*, 195–222.

Sternberg, R. J. and Detterman, D. K. (Eds), (1986). *What is Intelligence?* Norwood, NJ: Ablex.

Stevenson, J. (1984). Predictive value of speech and language screening. *Developmental Medicine and Child Neurology*, *26*, 528–38.

Stokes, T. F., and Baer, D. M. (1976). Preschool peers as mutual generalization-facilitating agents. *Behavior Therapy*, *7*, 549–56.

Stokes, T. F., and Baer, D. M. (1977). An implicit technology of generalization. *Journal of Applied Behavior Analysis*, *10*, 349–67.

Sugden, D. A. (1989). Transfer skills across the National Curriculum: The role of cognitive strategies for children with learning difficulties. *International Journal of Disability and Education*, 46, 241–55.

Sugden, D. A., and Keogh, J. F. (1990). Problems in movement skill development. Unpublished manuscript. University of South Carolina.

Sugden, D. A., and Sugden, L. (1991). The assessment of movement skills problems in 7- and 9-year-old children. *British Journal of Educational Psychology*, 61, 329–45.

Summerell, S., and Brannegan, G. (1977). Comparison of reading programs for children with low levels of reading readiness. *Perceptual and Motor Skills*, 44, 743–6.

Svenson, O., and Broquist, S. (1975). Strategies for solving simple addition problems: A comparison of normal and subnormal children. *Scandinavian Journal of Psychology*, 16, 143–51.

Svenson, O., and Hedenborg, M. L. (1979). Strategies used by children when solving simple subtractions. *Acta Psychologica*, 43, 1–13.

Swanson, H. L. (1989). Strategy instruction: Overview of principles and procedures for effective use. *Learning Disability Quarterly*, 12, 3–14.

Szeszulski, P. A., and Manis, F. R. (1987). A comparison of word recognition processes in dyslexic and normal readers at two reading age levels. *Journal of Experimental Child Psychology*, 44, 364–76.

Tallal, P. (1976). Rapid auditory processing in normal and disordered language development. *Journal of Speech and Hearing Research*, 19, 561–71.

Tallal, P., and Piercy, M. (1978). Defects of auditory perception in children with developmental dysphasia. In M. Wyke (Ed.), *Developmental Dysphasia*. London: Academic Press.

Tallal, P., and Stark, R. E. (1981). Speech acoustic-cue discrimination abilities of normally developing and language-impaired children. *Journal of the Acoustical Society of America*, 69, 568–74.

Tansley, P., and Panckhurst, J. (1981). *Children with Specific Learning Difficulties*. Windsor: NFER–Nelson.

Thurlow, M. L., and Ysseldyke, J. E. (1979). Current assessment and decision making practices in model LD programs. *Learning Disability Quarterly*, 6, 172–83.

Tindal, G., and Marston, D. (1986). Approaches to assessment. In J. K. Torgesen and B. Y. L. Wong (Eds), *Psychological and Educational Perspectives on Learning Disabilities*. New York: Academic Press.

Tizard, J., Schofield, W. N., and Hewison, J. (1982). Collaboration between teachers and parents in assisting children's reading. *British Journal of Educational Psychology*, 52, 1–5.

Tomlinson, S. (1982). *A Sociology of Special Education*. London: Routledge & Kegan Paul.

Topping, K., and Wolfendale, S. (Eds), (1985). *Parental Involvement in Children's Reading*. London: Croom Helm.

Torgesen, J. K. (1977). The role of nonspecific factors in the task performance of learning disabled children: A theoretical assessment. *Journal of Learning Disabilities, 10*, 27–34.

Torgesen, J. K. (1979). What shall we do with psychological processes? *Journal of Learning Disabilities, 12*, 514–22.

Torgesen, J. K. (1989). Why IQ *is* relevant to the definition of learning disabilities. *Journal of Learning Disabilities, 22*, 484–6.

Torgesen, J. K., and Kail, R. V. (1980). Memory processes in exceptional children. In B. K. Keogh (Ed.), *Advances in Special Education, vol 1: Basic Constructs and Theoretical Orientations*. Norwood, NJ: Ablex.

Torgesen, J. K., Kistner, J., and Morgan, S. (1987). Component processes in working memory. In J. G. Borkowksi and J. D. Day (Eds), *Cognition in Special Children: Comparative Approaches to Retardation, Learning Disabilities, and Giftedness*. Norwood, NJ: Ablex.

Torgesen, J. K., and Licht, B. G. (1983). The learning disabled child as an inactive learner: Retrospects and prospects. In J. D. McKinney and L. Feagans (Eds), *Current Topics in Learning Disabilities, vol. 1*. Norwood, NJ: Ablex.

Torgesen, J. K., Rashotte, C., Greenstein, J., Houck, G., and Portes, P. (1988). Academic difficulties of learning disabled children who perform poorly on memory span tasks. In H. L. Swanson (Ed.), *Memory and Learning Disabilities*. Greenwich, CT: JAI Press.

Torrey, J. W. (1979). Reading that comes naturally: The early reader. In T. G. Waller and G. E. Mackinnon (Eds), *Reading Research: Advances in Theory and Practice, vol. 1*. New York: Academic Press.

Tuinman, J. J. (1973–4). Determining the passage-dependency of comprehension questions in five major tests. *Reading Research Quarterly, 9*, 206–23.

Tunmer, W. E., and Nesdale, A. R. (1985). Phonemic segmentation skill and beginning reading. *Journal of Educational Psychology, 77*, 417–27.

Van der Lely, H. (1990). Sentence comprehension processes in specifically language-impaired children. Unpublished doctoral dissertation. University of London.

VanDevender, E. M. (1986). Fingers are good for early learning. *Journal of Instructional Psychology, 13*, 182–7.

van Lieshout, E. C. D. M. (1986). Developing a computer-assisted strategy training procedure for children with learning deficiencies to solve addition and subtraction problems. Paper presented at the American

Educational Research Association annual meeting, San Francisco. Cited by Goldman (1989).

Vellutino, F. R. (1979). *Dyslexia: Theory and Research.* Cambridge, MA: MIT Press.

Vellutino, F. R. (1987). Dyslexia. *Scientific American, 256,* 3, 20–7.

Vellutino, F. R., Pruzek, R., Steger, J. A., and Meshoulam, A. (1973). Immediate visual recall in poor readers as a function of orthographic-linguistic familiarity. *Cortex, 9,* 368–84.

Vogel, S. (1974). Syntactic abilities in normal and dyslexic children. *Journal of Learning Disabilities, 7,* 103–9.

Wagner, R. K., and Torgesen, J. K. (1987). The nature of phonological processing and its causal role in the acquisition of reading skills. *Psychological Bulletin, 101,* 192–212.

Wagner, S., Ganiban, J. M., and Cicchetti, D. (1990). Attention, memory, and perception in infants with Down syndrome: A review and commentary. In D. Cicchetti and M. Beeghly (Eds), *Children with Down Syndrome: A Developmental Perspective.* New York: Cambridge University Press.

Warburton, F. W. (1970). The British Intelligence Scale. In W. B. Dockrell (Ed.), *On Intelligence.* London: Methuen.

Warnock, H. M. (1978). *Special Educational Needs: Report of the Comittee of Enquiry into the Education of Handicapped Children and Young People.* London: HMSO.

Webb, L. (1967). *Children with Special Needs in the Infants' School.* London: Colin Smythe.

Webster, A. (1986). *Deafness, Development and Literacy.* London: Methuen.

Weinberg, R. A. (1989). Intelligence and I.Q.: Landmark issues and great debates. *American Psychologist, 44,* 98–104.

Weiner, P. (1985). The value of follow-up studies. *Topics in Language Disorders, 5,* 78–92.

Weiss, B., Weisz, J., and Bromfield, R. (1986). Performance of retarded and non-retarded persons on information processing tasks: Further tests of the similar structure hypothesis. *Psychological Bulletin, 100,* 157–75.

Weisz, J. (1978). Transcontextual validity in developmental research. *Child Development, 49,* 1–12.

Weisz, J., and Yeates, K. O. (1981). Cognitive development in retarded and non-retarded persons: Piagetian test of the similar structure hypothesis. *Psychological Bulletin, 90,* 153–78.

Weisz, J., Yeates, K. O., and Zigler, E. (1982). Piagetian evidence and the developmental–difference controversy. In E. Zigler and D. Balla

(Eds), *Mental Retardation: The Developmental–Difference Controversy.*
Hillsdale, NJ: Erlbaum.

Weisz, J., and Zigler, E. (1979). Cognitive development in retarded and
nonretarded persons: Piagetian tests of the similar structure hypothesis. *Psychological Bulletin*, 86, 831–51.

Wheldall, K., Merret, F., and Colmar, S. (1987). Pause, prompt, and
praise for parents and peers: Effective tutoring of low progress
readers. *Support for Learning*, 2, 5–12.

White, O. R. (1986). Precision teaching–precision learning. *Exceptional
Children*, 52, 522–34.

White, M., and East, K. (1983). *The Wessex Revised Portage Language
Checklist.* Windsor: NFER–NELSON.

White, O. R., and Haring, N. G. (1980). *Exceptional Teaching.* (2nd ed.).
Columbus, OH: Charles E. Merrill.

Wiig, E., Semel, E., and Nystrom, L. (1982). Comparison of rapid
naming abilities in language-learning-disabled and academically
achieving eight-year-olds. *Language, Speech, and Hearing Services in
Schools*, 13, 11–23.

Willson, V. L. (1989). Cognitive and developmental effects on item
performance in intelligence and achievement tests for young children.
Journal of Educational Measurement, 26, 103–19.

Wolfendale, S. (1987). *Special Needs in Ordinary Schools.* London:
Cassell.

Woods, S. S., Resnick, L. B., and Groen, G. J. (1975). An experimental
test of five process models for subtraction. *Journal of Educational
Psychology*, 67, 17–21.

Young, R. M., and O'Shea, T. (1981). Errors in children's subtraction.
Cognitive Science, 5, 153–77.

Ysseldyke, J. E. (1987). Do tests help in teaching? *Journal of Child
Psychiatry and Psychology*, 28, 21–4.

Ysseldyke, J. E., and Algozzine, B. (1983). LD or not LD: That's not the
question! *Journal of Learning Disabilities*, 16, 29–31.

Ysseldyke, J., Algozzine, B., and Epps, S. (1983). A logical and empirical
analysis of classifying students as handicapped. *Exceptional Children*,
50, 160–6.

Ysseldyke, J., and Thurlow, M. L. (1984). Assessment practices in
special education: Adequacy and appropriateness. *Educational Psychologist*, 9, 123–36.

Yuill, N., and Oakhill, J. (1988). Understanding of anaphoric relations
in skilled and less skilled comprehenders. *British Journal of Psychology*,
79, 173–86.

Yuill, N., Oakhill, J., and Parkin, A. (1989). Working memory, comprehension ability and the resolution of text anomaly comprehenders. *British Journal of Psychology*, *80*, 351–61.

Yule, W., and Rutter, M. (1976). Epidemiology and social implications of specific reading retardation. In R. M. Knights and D. J. Bakker (Eds), *The Neuropsychology of Learning Disorders*. Baltimore: University Park Press.

Yule, W., and Rutter, M. (1985). Reading and other learning difficulties. In M. Rutter and L. Hersov (Eds), *Child and Adolescent Psychiatry: Modern Approaches*. (2nd ed.). Oxford: Blackwell Scientific.

Zeaman, D., and House, B. J. (1963). The role of attention and retardate discriminate learning. In N. R. Ellis (Ed.), *Handbook of Mental Deficiency*. New York: McGraw–Hill.

Zeaman, D., and House, B. J. (1979). A review of attention theory. In N. R. Ellis (Ed.), *Handbook of Mental Deficiency, Psychological Theory and Research*. Hillsdale, NJ: Erlbaum.

Zigler, E. (1969). Developmental *versus* difference theories of mental retardation and the problem of motivation. *American Journal of Mental Deficiency*, *73*, 536–56.

Zigler, E., and Balla, D. (1982). Motivational and personality factors in the performance of the retarded. In D. Balla and E. Zigler (Eds), *Mental Retardation. The Developmental–Difference Controversy*. Hillsdale, NJ: Erlbaum.

Zigler, E., Balla, D., and Hodapp, R. M. (1984). On the definition and classification of mental retardation. *American Journal of Mental Deficiency*, *89*, 215–30.

Zigler, E., and Hodapp, R. M. (1986). *Understanding Mental Retardation*. New York: Cambridge University Press.

Index of Authors

Index of Subjects